POLITICAL SCIENCE AND HISTORY

How Capitalism and the Liberal Market-System Fostered Organized Crime, Corruption and Ecocide

Why Social Democracy Will Stand for Post-Capitalism

POLITICAL SCIENCE AND HISTORY

Additional books and e-books in this series can be found on Nova's website under the Series tab.

POLITICAL SCIENCE AND HISTORY

HOW CAPITALISM AND THE LIBERAL MARKET-SYSTEM FOSTERED ORGANIZED CRIME, CORRUPTION AND ECOCIDE

WHY SOCIAL DEMOCRACY WILL STAND FOR POST-CAPITALISM

RODOLFO APREDA, PHD

Copyright © 2020 by Nova Science Publishers, Inc.

All rights reserved. No part of this book may be reproduced, stored in a retrieval system or transmitted in any form or by any means: electronic, electrostatic, magnetic, tape, mechanical photocopying, recording or otherwise without the written permission of the Publisher.

We have partnered with Copyright Clearance Center to make it easy for you to obtain permissions to reuse content from this publication. Simply navigate to this publication's page on Nova's website and locate the "Get Permission" button below the title description. This button is linked directly to the title's permission page on copyright.com. Alternatively, you can visit copyright.com and search by title, ISBN, or ISSN.

For further questions about using the service on copyright.com, please contact:
Copyright Clearance Center
Phone: +1-(978) 750-8400   Fax: +1-(978) 750-4470   E-mail: info@copyright.com.

NOTICE TO THE READER

The Publisher has taken reasonable care in the preparation of this book, but makes no expressed or implied warranty of any kind and assumes no responsibility for any errors or omissions. No liability is assumed for incidental or consequential damages in connection with or arising out of information contained in this book. The Publisher shall not be liable for any special, consequential, or exemplary damages resulting, in whole or in part, from the readers' use of, or reliance upon, this material. Any parts of this book based on government reports are so indicated and copyright is claimed for those parts to the extent applicable to compilations of such works.

Independent verification should be sought for any data, advice or recommendations contained in this book. In addition, no responsibility is assumed by the Publisher for any injury and/or damage to persons or property arising from any methods, products, instructions, ideas or otherwise contained in this publication.

This publication is designed to provide accurate and authoritative information with regard to the subject matter covered herein. It is sold with the clear understanding that the Publisher is not engaged in rendering legal or any other professional services. If legal or any other expert assistance is required, the services of a competent person should be sought. FROM A DECLARATION OF PARTICIPANTS JOINTLY ADOPTED BY A COMMITTEE OF THE AMERICAN BAR ASSOCIATION AND A COMMITTEE OF PUBLISHERS.

Additional color graphics may be available in the e-book version of this book.

Library of Congress Cataloging-in-Publication Data

Names: Apreda, Rodolfo, author.
Title: How capitalism and the liberal market-system fostered organized
   crime, corruption and ecocide : why social democracy will stand for
   post-capitalism / Rodolfo Apreda.
Description: Hauppauge : Nova Science Publishers, 2020. | Series: Political
   science and history | Includes bibliographical references and index. |
Identifiers: LCCN 2020010704 (print) | LCCN 2020010705 (ebook) | ISBN
   9781536176544 (hardcover) | ISBN 9781536176551 (adobe pdf)
Subjects: LCSH: Capitalism. | Social responsibility of business. |
   Organized crime. | Corruption. | Nature--Effect of human beings on.
Classification: LCC HB501 .A6567 2020 (print) | LCC HB501 (ebook) | DDC
   330.12/2--dc23
LC record available at https://lccn.loc.gov/2020010704
LC ebook record available at https://lccn.loc.gov/2020010705

Published by Nova Science Publishers, Inc. † New York

To Dominga Amarfil, my wife, best friend, and colleague

Contents

Preface		ix
Acknowledgments		xiii
Chapter 1	Governance and Politics	1
Chapter 2	How Accountability and Transparency Become Social Learning Processes	27
Chapter 3	Political Conflict-Systems, the Clinical Approach to Conflicts of Interest, and Dual Governance	61
Chapter 4	Dysfunctional Governance, the Capture of the State, and Corruption	103
Chapter 5	The Governance and Politics of Organized Crime and Ecocide	135
Chapter 6	The Day of Reckoning for Capitalism and the Liberal Market-System	167
Chapter 7	Social Democracy, Social Markets, and the Welfare State Will Stand for Post Capitalism	197
References		235

Copyright Credits	**245**
About the Author	**247**
Index	**249**

Preface

For all intents and purposes, the world is going toward post capitalism. Social democracies on the one hand, and authoritarian or non-democratic regimes on the other, are already competing and standing for capitalism, a political and economic system which have failed so deeply as to be burnt out by its own contradictions. Even worse, the wealth distribution problem and the shameless lack of concern for social issues are steadfastly bringing forward the curtain call for such long-standing historical experience.

Our Line of Argument

It is our contention that two pervading developments have been utterly consequential in the debasement of the old capitalist system: to wit, the increasing decomposition of social capital and trust all over the world, as well as the overwhelming influence of organized crime, corruption and ecocide. Those processes became ubiquitous, traversing not only representative democracies but also opposite partners in non-democratic countries, hence damaging institutions on either side of the political archway.

This book advocates and spells out that capitalism and the liberal market-system provided the tools and architecture that allowed the triad comprising organized crime, corruption and ecocide to grow beyond national boundaries and political arrangements with the criminal connivance of businessmen, lawyers, accountants, banks, economists, and transnational companies; indeed, all of them have been profiting from off-shore locations and globalization, complicit governments and politicians, lack of transparency and shameful contempt of law.

THE ROADMAP FOR THIS BOOK

Let us put forward a roadmap for this work. In chapter 1 we will lay the grounds to a comprehensive treatment of governance and politics, which must be assessed as complementary attempts in pursuit of the common good[1]. Furthermore, political networks and their governance will be brought to the shore since they are changing the way politics is being crafted at the end of the day.

Chapter 2 will focus on the basic tenets of sound governance and politics: firstly, accountability (as the interplay of both commitments and responsibilities), secondly, transparency. Against the mainstream approach, it will be ascertained that both features must be regarded as social learning processes. Finally, it will highlight the governance and politics of secrecy.

It is for chapter 3 to deal with political conflict systems, claiming for a clinical approach to conflicts of interest, also introducing the notion and scope of dual governance that proves essential whenever we address the subject of state-owned firms.

Chapter 4 will enlarge upon dysfunctional and opaque styles of governances, moving on to the capture of the state by groups of interest and spreading corruption. Due heed will be given to regulation, gatekeepers and connivance.

---

[1] The reader will find, at the beginning of each chapter, an abstract as well as an introduction to their main contents.

Chapter 5 is devoted to the governance and politics of organized crime and ecocide, what amounts to a new approach to criminal organizations that sheds light to their partnership with bad governance and worse politics.

Chapter 6 points out to the comprehensive failure of both capitalism and the so-called liberal market-system. Markets in the flesh will be described further, whereas several misunderstandings involved in the predicated coalescence between capitalism and democracy will be debunked eventually. Afterwards, the hideous consequences of the military industrial complex in the most powerful countries, as well as the shock doctrine advocated by most graduates from the so-called Chicago School economists (joining forces with followers of the Washington Consensus) will be related together so as to connect the dots that lead to the crumbling of capitalism.

The last chapter will describe why, in the context of representative political systems, both social democracies and social markets will likely stand for post capitalism. Last but not least, a statute of governance will show how social democracies could steer clear of organized crime, corruption and ecocide.

TOWARDS SOCIAL DEMOCRACY

We realize that this book entails an innovative although non politically correct approach to our current affairs. Be that as it may, we regard our proposal timely and worthy of being discussed. The world is at crossroads between two contending viewpoints. On the one side, authoritarian or populist systems; on the other, we find representative political systems, not only capitalist ones pervaded by neo liberal strands, but also those that advocate social democracies. In my opinion, we should get rid of old mindscapes that prevent us from taking the path of social democracy, a healthy political course of action that vouchsafes survival, welfare, equity, freedom, decency, human rights, participation and the rule of law.

ACKNOWLEDGMENTS

Last but not least, two heartfelt acknowledgments are well deserved. One for Nadya Gotsiridze-Columbus, President of Nova Publishers, Inc., Alexandra Columbus and Nova staff: they gave not only positive encouragement to the book project, but unremittingly provided this author with advice and patience. The other goes to my wife, Dominga Amarfil, who has been a staunch supporter of my book from beginning to end.

Chapter 1

GOVERNANCE AND POLITICS

ABSTRACT

Along the present chapter, we intend to provide strong connections between governance and politics. The roadmap will be the following: firstly, we set forth a functional meaning of governance and politics, bringing into focus the contrast among government, governance and the ability to govern, as well as the nature of representative democracies; secondly, we will give heed to cognitive clusters that bind governance with politics together, like the process of responsiveness and the role of fiduciary duties; lastly, we will enlarge upon social, political and trust networks, which have come into view as a timely topic, because networks are changing the way of doing politics worldwide.

INTRODUCTION

At the beginning of this book we want to raise a query: which are the relationships that link up governance with politics? It is my contention that shedding light on this issue seems of the essence if we wish to improve the way governments should be run in the flesh.

We intend to work out the query by turning over in our minds the wide-ranging notion of *common good* which, broadly speaking, could be described as follows:

> By common good is meant the time-honored pool of collective resources and values that are sought, needed, expected, owned, recognized, or claimed by all members of organizations and communities[2] for the sake of their survival, growth, fairness and culture.

Needless to say, it is for the State to meet the expectations, rights and responsibilities involved in the prior connotations of the expression "common good"[3].

The starting point of our argument will consist in contrasting government, governance and the ability to govern[4]; another polarity that will be needed is the one between political person and corporate actors. Afterwards, due care will be given to political systems and representative democracies.

Governance and politics are not separated notions. On the contrary, they are conjoined like the faces of a compact whose basic purpose is the common good. That's why our line of argument deals with the main connectors of that compact: responsiveness of governments to citizen's preferences as well as fiduciaries duties and agency relationships.

Last of all, we couldn't help including in this chapter a considered account of networks, either the technological, social, political or trust ones, closing with an appraisal of their governance.

---

[2] In chapter 7, section 7.1, we are going to search into the relationship between social capital and the common good, taking advantage of the latest approach put forward by Robert Reich (2018) which has consequential insights for political analysis.
[3] If certain government relinquishes the goal of attaining the common good, bad governance and worse politics will ensue; more on this will be found in chapter 4.
[4] This is sometimes denoted by the expression "governability".

1.1. Let's Start with an Intuitive Notion of Governance

How could you explain the meaning of this word, which etymologically derives from the art of steering a ship, that is to say, of controlling its direction so as to reach destination? Well, this seems a good baseline, because it conveys the idea of management. Hence, governors have to carefully steer a course in pursuit of the objectives that ultimately benefit the crew.

As long as we keep thinking about this topic, we realize that people spend their lives in many social groupings that need to last; they are denoted *organizations,* from the most basic ones like families or kinships, till government offices, corporations, non-government associations, tour operators and airlines, retail stores, hospitals, schools, theatres, farms, media networks, legislatures, hotel chains, newspapers, and the like. All of these social arrangements share two features: they are purpose-built systems unfolding through time, and they ought to be handled by proficient sailors or governors. *Therefore, the underlying intuition of governance leads us to organizations or systems that must be steered so as to hold them over their better course.*

Another standpoint to deal with the meaning of "governance" consists in looking it up in a good dictionary. Let us take the Cambridge Advanced Learner's Dictionary to find out a quite austere insight:

> The way organizations or countries are managed at the highest level, and the systems for doing this[5].

Such statement uncovers two important hallmarks of governance: it has to do with any sort of organizations and governments; besides, it deals with structures of social action to manage those organizations. Nonetheless, we realize that a more exacting approach would be welcome if we wanted to

---

[5] See Cambridge Advance Learner's Dictionary, Fourth Edition, Cambridge University Press, 2015.

establish a field of learning and practice at the juncture of political science, government studies, sociology, administration of organizations, history, even social psychology.

1.2. LOOKING FOR A MORE ENCOMPASSING DEFINITION

Governance is a point in question to which many scholars in social sciences and also practitioners (including law-makers and judges) have been giving their best effort and proficiency for many decades up to now. In the corporate realm, for instance, reliable research dates back only to sixty years, whereas a systematic study in global governance has evolved along an even shorter span of time. By the same token, public governance has been topical for centuries, although its expansion in a sort of independent branch of knowledge is not long past[6]. Such variety of nurturing sources had led to an endless debate when seeking consensus on a definition. For this reason, a further clarification will be helpful in regard to the notions of "definition" and "field of learning and practice".

On Definitions

Definitions should be deemed as semantic vehicles on behalf of any considered reader who may ask himself: which is the meaning the author attaches to such and such expression? However, the word itself turns social scientists rather uneasy and triggers off adversarial reactions, as the history of ideas has witnessed so frequently. Therefore, instead of using the label "definition", we have chosen the expression "statement of meaning", which points out to its conventional nature. There is nothing wrong with the word "definition", apart from its fuzziness and ideological abuse; in point of fact, the reader will sparsely meet such word throughout the text as synonym of 'statement of meaning'.

---

[6] Corporate, public, and global governance are developed in Apreda (2006, 2007, 2012)

We will keep a standard format in these statements of meaning: they will consist of a set of assertions (or sub-statements) chosen to make the concept operational (in other words, time-scalable, usable, and modifiable); each assertion will convey either a purpose, a task to be pursued, a linking feature, an assumption, or a characteristic attribute to be claimed.

On Fields of Learning and Practice

In my opinion, both governance and politics entail a dual nature. On the one hand they are activities and tasks, that is to say, pragmatic behavior dealing with down-to-earth issues and problems that can be comprised in a field of practice. On the other hand, we refer to governance or politics as systematic efforts to understand, explain, and anticipate processes, trends or events in the midst of political systems; that is to say, they become fields of learning.

Profiting from the foregoing methodological guidelines, we now put forth the meaning behind the word "governance"[7].

Statement of Meaning 1 – Governance

By Governance we are to understand a field of learning and practice whose main tasks are

- *the search of principles, procedures and practices that allow organizations or countries to be run within the constraints of evolving institutions, changing regulations, and the pool of resources provided by social capital[8];*
- *to design, implement and follow-up functional structures of social action for participation, representation, conformity, dissent, voting*

---

[7] There will be offered a statement of meaning for politics in section 1.3.
[8] The expression 'social capital' will be interpreted in section 7.1, chapter 7.

and countervailing monitoring, by means of inducements, learning, and standards of performance;
- *the fostering of accountability, transparency and fiduciary duties[9], as well as the management of conflicts of interest among natural persons, corporate, and political actors.*

Poring over these assertions, three consequences spring up: the first one shows that the search of principles, procedures and practices is constrained by social context and its institutions; the second one depicts governance as a blueprint, even an architecture for desirable social behavior; the third one stresses the role of commitments, responsibilities, transparency as well as the management of conflicts of interest. To put it shortly, governance is context dependent, setting up systems on design so as to handle both social action and shifting conflicts of interest.

1.3. POLITICS

Let us start with an intuitive approach, as we did before with governance. If we looked it up in *The Concise Oxford English Dictionary* (2009), we would find out that politics comprises

- *the activities associated with the governance of a country or area;*
- *the principles relating to or inherent in a sphere of activity, especially when concerned with power and status.*

It is a very fruitful definition, firstly because it establishes an overlapping linkage between politics and governance; secondly, it envelops activities and also principles that take for granted contexts of learning and practice. Nonetheless, we still need a more elaborated framework to explain how those principles and activities should be sorted out together.

---

[9] Fiduciary duties will be enlarged in section 1.4, whereas accountability and transparency will be treated together in chapter 2, and conflicts of interest in chapter 3.

Before putting forward an appropriate statement of meaning, let us remind ourselves what the expression 'political system' could amount to, by means of the classical submission given by Robert Dahl (1963) as those systems of dynamic human relationships that involve the employment of power, control, authority and influence[10].

Statement of Meaning 2 – Politics

By Politics is meant a field of learning and practice whose main tasks are:

- *the exercise of activities that take place through the workings of organizations and countries; that is to say, within political systems;*
- *the design and implementation of mechanisms by which those activities might convey the purposes of the underlying governance of each political system;*
- *setting agendas, competing, negotiating and being responsive [11] to the needs, demands and values of the civil society, in pursuit of the common good.*

For the sake of analysis, it's worth bringing to light some operational notions closely linked to our subject, namely: the distinction among government, governance and the ability to govern; the relationship between political and corporate actors; the tenets of representative democracies; and the cluster of meanings stemming from polyarchies, participation and contest.

---

[10] Chapter 3 will enlarge this viewpoint by thoroughly addressing political conflict-systems.
[11] Responsiveness is a key factor in the process of government and we are going to elaborate on this point further in section 1.4.

Government, Governance, and the Ability to Govern

At this stage of the current section, we intend to make a contrast among three words that, although having a common root, deliver connotations at variance with each other.

In the past, social gatherings faced the trial of coordinating human and material resources in order to survive; such a process couldn't move forwards unless a group of people engaged themselves in handling persistent, daily and purposeful patterns of behavior. This development gave rise to a new professional assignment, the "governor", who was endowed with power and skills to subsequently steer the tribe, community, village, city, kingdom, empire, and much more later, the nation-state that followed from the Peace of Westphalia in 1648.

To accomplish their jobs, governors required staff, offices, and commissions, also territorial expanses. In other words, they built up organizations to run the State (broadly speaking, the seat of coercive power, legitimacy, authority and territoriality). Beyond such intuitive rendering, we could narrow down the meaning this way: *government consists in persistent structures of human behavior that put up, as time passes by, a network of distinctive offices to discharge organizational jobs, meet expected goals, listening to people's demands, and keep up the existence of the State; it is managed by governors with the help of their officers.*

Hence, between government and governance can be ascertained a deep linkage: the latter turns out to be the considered design of systems of social action that enables the decision-making of the former.

If we looked upon the expression "the ability to govern" (*governability*), it usually points to an environment in which the government may carry out his goals successfully (take into account the phrase govern-ability). When a government loses ground, for instance through an impending crisis, policy failures, fierce opposition or people revolt, it is said that the ability to govern is threatened, even to the extent that the incumbent government could be overthrown.

From this viewpoint, *the ability to govern can be assessed like a recursive process between the governance structure and the extent to which the government shows responsiveness to the demands of society.* In other words, governability is contingent on politics.

Corporate Actors

It was the sociologist James Coleman (1974) who distinguished between natural (or physical) persons and corporate actors (or "juristic persons"). Among the latter, we may pick out corporations, limited liability companies, foundations, cooperatives, trade unions, professional associations, churches, restaurants, universities, social clubs, partnerships, political parties, state-owned enterprises, even government agencies (for instance, the Internal Revenue Service), and the like. Corporate actors share the following attributes: from the mere fact of their existence, it doesn't follow that they are profit-seeking entities (cooperatives and foundations come to our mind); on the other hand, they have many of the legal rights enjoyed by natural persons: ownership, transacting with third parties, the ability to act under their own will, establishing and breaking off relationships, also being held accountable for their actions; as a result, they turn out to be self-governing entities.

Whenever a person relates to any corporate actor, a new kind of exchange emerges that is quite different from informal person-to-person interrelationships as they happen in everyday life. Coleman states that any relation engaging persons and corporate actors gives rise to a consequential mismatch between the particular interests of a person and those stemming from the interests such person ought to comply with on behalf of the organization for which she works. However, the alignment between them is not a foregone conclusion:

> its strength depending on how tightly the corporate actor has tied its agent's personal goals to the corporate goals. (p. 93)

We shouldn't forget that a deep transformation of society has taken place since the nineteenth century by which any natural person, argues

Coleman, is no longer a mere component of certain organization; instead, he has to become conversant with overlapping structures of relations between natural persons and corporate actors.

Example

Let us consider the connection between the government, through its Internal Revenue Service, and any organization. The government turns out to be a stakeholder[12] of the organization, claiming the payment of taxes. In this kind of transaction, parties are corporate actors, regardless of the fact that both may resort to single human beings under the guise of agents or employees who bring the task into completion, or through the interface provided by the web page of the tax collector.

Representative Democracies

Democracy stands out as a disputable concept, since an all-purpose definition has been almost impossible to be framed for ages. Early in this long-standing debate, a natural split ensued between two styles of democracy: direct and indirect. The former entails that all citizens participate in decision-making processes related to their search for the common good, whereas the latter requests a selected group of representatives or mediators to reach consensus on the most important issues that affect the government and welfare of the commonwealth. As different peoples and their cultures evolved over time, the role of governments as caretakers of their civil society hinged upon variegated assortments that can be called democratic systems.

Be that as it may, size and scope have been increasingly constraining the efficacy of direct democracy alternatives. The smaller the community, the more suitable becomes direct democracy. But as long as social groupings

---

[12] The concept of 'stakeholder' is consequential in governance and politics, and it clusters around a set of cognate expressions like claimants, discontents, claimers; we are going to elaborate on this subject later in chapter 3, section 3.1.

have been growing in complexity and sheer numbers, some sort of delegation was ultimately required to handle the government duties. This development led to political systems relying on representation.

According to Bernard Manin (1997) the expression *representative democracies* come down to a misnomer:

> What today we call representative democracy has its origins in a system of institutions (established in the wake of the English, American, and French revolutions) that was in no way initially perceived as a form of democracy or of government by the people. (p. 1)

In ancient times, there were variegated styles of indirect democracy, in which deputies, delegates, or representatives came elected by majorities, and they were expected to make decisions and carry out the roles of government. Nowadays, in comparison with the past, we can witness how representative democracies are widespread in the world, mainly after the demise of the Soviet Union, to the extent that almost every country can claim its membership to political systems based in general elections for the appointment of government officials and law-makers.

It goes without saying that there are many examples of representative democracies. Thus, it's worth noticing here what Manin underlines as common attributes of them:

> *Four principles have invariably been observed in representative regimes, ever since this form of government was invented:*
>
> 1. *Those who govern are appointed by election at regular intervals.*
> 2. *he decision-making of those who govern retains a degree of independence from the wishes of the electorate.*
> 3. *Those who are governed may give expression to their opinions and political wishes without these being subject to the control of those who govern.*
> 4. *Public decisions undergo the trial of debate. (p. 6)*

Polyarchies, Participation and Contest

Looking for an alternative step in the search of a key characteristic of any representative democracy, Robert Dahl (1971) argued in favor of a continuing responsiveness to the preferences or demands[13] posed by its citizens, which amounts to three conditions to be fulfilled:

- citizens have a right to make known their preferences;
- also, they are able to disclose their preferences to government and other political actors by means of individual or collective action;
- they expect from the government a receptive and fair understanding of their preferences.

Those systems that meet the foregoing constraints, evincing levels in which participation and opposition reach the highest degree of development, are named *Polyarchies*[14].

When dealing with representative democracies we shouldn't disregard the fact that any process of democratization involves two overlapping and persistent activities, namely the *right to participate,* and *the exercise of public contestation.* The latter measures up how open-minded or competitive the political system becomes, by enabling citizens to make their preferences be known. The former signals the extent of inclusiveness we can find out in that political system; in other words, how many of its citizens are allowed to participate in full view, mainly through the empowerment of the voting franchise; shortly, participation means that citizens actually take part in politics.

Governance deals with conflict-systems that are complex and purposeful, as we are going to enlarge later in chapter 3. Among the many mechanisms that foster their dynamics, we single out three patterns of

---

[13] Preferences and demands stem not only from everyday needs and choices, but also from the social capital, that pool of resources which includes culture, values, beliefs, history, as it will be analyzed in chapter 7, section 7.1. Responsiveness will be dealt with in next section.

[14] Robert Dahl (1971). *Polyarchy.* Yale University Press.

behavior that shed light along the usual paths for participation and contest: *loyalty, voice and exit.* Although the distinctive semantics for these words was firstly coined and expanded on by Hirschman in his already classic book (1977), he gave only scant heed to the public sector in that work. However, Hirschman later faced this topic in a perceptive paper[15] published in *World Politics* in 1978. We believe that his perspective will help understand the logic of how governance links up with politics.

Political agents or groups can shape up *loyalty* by means of *mechanisms of support*. We usually say that actor A supports actor B when either A acts on behalf of B, or A agrees and endorses B´s goals or actions. Accordingly, support ranges from broad cooperation levels to advocacy and involvement[16].

Taking the opposite standpoint, what can be stated when disagreement, lurking conflicts of interests, widespread discontent, even fits of rage, turmoil and crisis spring up to surface? In those circumstances, political agents in representative democracies get access to a couple of behavioral responses: *voice and exit*. Either we can voice our claims within the current governance to get the grievances redressed, or we can exit by rejecting the governance in disagreement with its tenets or the way political affairs are carried out eventually.

1.4. GOVERNANCE AND POLITICS

In keeping with the aims of this book, we have chosen two features that join politics to governance: firstly, responsiveness of governments to citizens' preferences; secondly, fiduciary duties and agency relationships.

---

[15] *Exit, Voice and the State*, World Politics, volume 31, number 1, pp. 90-107.
[16] There is a deep similarity between support and the fiduciary principle; on the other hand, differences arise eventually, as it will be seen below in next section.

Responsiveness

Let us suppose that we are interested in what the government does or intends to do, *public policies*, and what any government is able to do, *capabilities*. There is always a wedge between the former and the latter, which measures the extent of *responsiveness* showed up by the government towards political demands and needs. It is for politics listening to people's demands so as to redress those wrongs that may bring about cleavages among political groups, inequalities, broken promises, and pervading unfairness in the cultural texture of the civil society[17].

In other words, *responsiveness measures the extent by which public policies and capabilities come closer and meet each other in pursuit of the public good*. To accomplish such political goal, there is an internal governance device that oversees and provides with feedback to the whole system. By all means, we are speaking about checks and balances, although in a much broader sense than the usual one. Let us slow down and take stock: firstly, the notion will be upgraded and, secondly, its main connotations will follow.

By Checks and Balances, we understand a system of countervailing monitoring by which some group of political actors in the government or civil society can restrain other groups from becoming too powerful or influential, by setting up standards of agreement about what kind of actions or decisions abide by the law, the constitution and the underlying governance of the system.

The conventional debate about checks and balances focused on how the three main branches of government managed to constrain each one to fulfill its expected functions, not allowing any other to intrude in their defining tasks. It is a mechanism that wards off Executive, Legislative and Judiciary conflicts of interest. However, the subject matter of countervailing actions

---

[17] Przeworsky, Stokes and Manin (1999) is a helpful reference on this matter, conveying subtle insights and serious scholarship.

that grant the balance of adversarial groups of interest goes further the classical government division of labor.

- We know for certain that branches in a system of separate powers are subject to political discipline through mechanisms of apportionment and budget allocation, as well as discharge procedures, legislative overruling and constitutional review. Nevertheless, it should be noticed the operational contrast between the principle of separation of powers and the notion of checks and balances. The former spells out three branches of government that behave independently from each other: executive, legislative, and the judiciary. The latter conveys the idea of any branch looking over the tasks expected from the others and preventing entrenchment towards their own activities.
- By all means, checks and balances should not be regarded as processes that only take place in the government realm. There are two wide-ranging contexts of application where this tool of governance fits political analysis: organizations on the one hand; journalism and gatekeepers on the other.
- In a variegated spate of private or public organizations, we always find two powers that countervail each other: the supervisory board, and the management. After so many scandals and failures in the last decades, we must admit that such role has fallen into staggering disrepute and that's why in this book we are going to advocate the enforcement of a compliance function and a statute of governance for each organization.
- Within representative democracies, journalism performs the role of a watchdog. Among their quests, journalists must disclose skeletons in the cupboards; cut through conspiracies of silence and veils of denial; engaging themselves in muckraking the dirtiest facts in political life, those which could bring about the most detrimental consequences for the common good; they must report the public about organized crime, corruption and ecocide.

- Lastly, there are several political actors who work together in granting responsiveness to people's demands, namely: non-governmental organizations; scholars who do research and publish their results; minorities and opposition parties; churches and trade unions; and social networks so efficacious nowadays.

Fiduciary Duties and Agency Relationships

Is there any yardstick that makes reasonable or acceptable the claims and counterclaims between organizations and stakeholders in their many-sided relationships? Fiduciary duties and agency relationships provide a convenient answer to such issue.

Statement of Meaning 3 – Fiduciary Duties

It is said that a single person, corporate actor, or a social grouping owes fiduciary duties to a counterpart when two things happen:

- *the former commits good faith, loyalty, and care to carry out some purposeful tasks or services on behalf of the counterpart;*
- *the relationship between the former and the latter rests on a binding agreement that stems either from cooperation, mutuality of interest, or the rule of law.*

Remark

The political actor who complies with his fiduciary duties is called the *fiduciary*, whereas the counterpart is usually termed the *beneficiary*.
Broadly speaking, by *good faith* is meant that parties harbor legitimate hopes based on good will and trust, whereby it is expected from the fiduciary

agent to be honest and helpful towards the beneficiary. On the other hand, the duty of *loyalty* hinges upon the idea of support and fair dealing in the relationship, which underlies the fact that the fiduciary actor must work on behalf of some stated interests of the beneficiary, mainly by refraining from self-dealing practices. Lastly, the duty of *care* entails paying attention and becoming diligent in decision-making processes, devoting a reasonable span of time and effort to perform the promised undertakings that one part owes to the other.

The request of a binding agreement seems of the essence. On one extreme of a notional continuum, we can find very loose and informal agreements (we take a taxi expecting not to be mugged or kidnapped, but safely carried to our destination instead). On the other extreme, we can notice enforceable settlements with intricate legal constraints (for instance, when buying a house by means of a bank loan). In between we can locate numberless examples and daily political circumstances revolving around such agreements.

Last, but not least, assertion 2 in the statement of meaning above marks the right of the beneficiary to hold accountable the fiduciary when bad faith, disloyalty, or negligence spoil their relationship, bringing material consequences against the former. As we are going to press home in next chapter, there is a lasting and conflicting dynamics between commitments and responsibilities, both of which define what the expression 'accountability' stands for. In other words, fiduciary duties (as well as agency relationships) place accountability at the core of the subject.

Example

Let us assume that John wins the municipal election in our town, being swept to the Mayor's office by a landslide victory. He will become accountable for his performance, what amounts to making commitments and to be held responsible for how well or badly he complies with them. Looking into the commitments of an elected officer, there is a prominent one that consists in his compliance with the fiduciary duties towards the whole community. Besides, he must follow promises and values of his political party, as well as the regulatory background to mayoral tasks. Moving on to responsibilities, they refer to how commitments are supposedly delivered. The negative of the fiduciary duties are bad faith (opposite to good faith), disloyalty (against loyalty), and negligence (neglect of diligence). For these misdeeds, he can be prosecuted, discharged, and sent to jail. Conversely, John can be rewarded if he succeeds in his mayoral performance, that is to say, he could get another term of tenure, or being promoted to higher political appointments.

Agency Relationships

In every organization, agency relationships[18] provide clear prototypes of fiduciary roles and duties stemming from contracts or binding undertakings agreed between the parties. The common feature behind this kind of relationship entails that the agent willingly behaves on behalf of his counterpart, the principal, who grants some sort of compensation on account of good faith, loyalty and care. By and large, such momentous notion deserves further precision.

Statement of Meaning 4 – Agency Relationship

We say that between actors A and P (either single or corporate actors) there is an agency relationship when the parties bring to completion the following agreement:

- *Firstly, actor A, known as the agent, commits care, good faith and loyalty on behalf of P.*
- *Secondly, actor P, who is known as the principal, commits in good faith compensation or incentives to the agent; reciprocally, he*

---

[18] They are also called principal-agent relationships.

bestows decision rights on the latter, and holds back preemptive control rights over his performance.
- *Lastly, explicitly or implicitly, the relationship binds agent and principal to their mutual advantage but also to be held responsible to each other.*

Clearly, the first assertion embeds this kind of relationship into the context of fiduciary duties. On the other hand, compensation packages do not stand for monetary rewards only, since members of boards in foundations or cooperatives, for instance, frequently seek public credits like reputation, or the feeling of being an involved citizen.

Bear in mind the third assertion: agent and principal are to be held responsible to each other. In point of fact, the principal-agent relationship is a dual concept. From one standpoint, it is a linking path from the principal to the agent; but from another standpoint, the converse may hold true, with a reversal of both roles. This duality leads to deeper connections between multiple relationships and mutuality of interests, a topic that will be enlarged in chapter 2, section 2.2.

Example

Whenever investors put their savings into financial portfolios[19], they become principals of the investment fund, an organization that in fact manages resources that belong to others and, therefore, must carry out a reliable and proficient behavior toward their principals. If things went badly, investors could claim in courts, alleging bad faith, negligence or disloyalty in the way the agent fulfilled his fiduciary duties. Madoff's disgraceful story is a case study that bears witness to the detrimental consequences of flouting the agency relationship and the rule of law[20].

---

[19] Examples of non-financial portfolios are numerous: for instance, a portfolio of commodities (cereals, metals, livestock); also, one comprising real estate (land, farms, condominiums).
[20] Investigative reporter Ewin Arvedlund (2009) thoroughly brought to light Madoff wheeling and dealing.

Dispelling a Misconception about Fiduciary Duties and Principal-Agent Relationships

There is a widespread misconception around the notions of fiduciary duties and the principal-agent relationship, as if they were examples of hierarchical arrangements only. Although we can find lots of examples in which vertical assortments convey the features of subordination, we still find many other cases that do not match such scanty picture. Let us give more heed to this subject.

Vertical Assortments
It is within military, corporate, religious, and government organizations that we find how the fiduciary stands in a lower position than the beneficiary, who commands or rules the former; in other words, the principal behaves like a "boss" towards his subordinate or agent.

Multiple Fiduciary Roles and Agency Relationships
As from the 1980s, with the increasing power and spread of means of communication, the old-fashioned picture conveyed by hierarchical duties and relationships gave rise to a broader meaning, which included multiple fiduciaries roles as well as multiple agency relationships. The common features of this standpoint can be portrayed by the following example: a beneficiary can become fiduciary of his own fiduciary because the relationship affords such ordering reversal. For instance, let us imagine a mayor elected to rule certain town to which his own clinician belongs; the latter is beneficiary from the mayor who is the fiduciary towards his town polity, which includes the clinician; but the clinician is the fiduciary of the mayor who carries on his role of principal as patient.

Summing up this Section

Going after meaningful connections between governance and politics, we laid down a distinctive weight on responsiveness, which measures the success or failure of public policies and capabilities. Afterwards, some issues of the utmost importance were highlighted, namely fiduciary duties and agency relationships claims for accountability, transparency, good faith, loyalty and diligence; in other words, those features that are ingrained in the governance of the social fabric.

1.5. POLITICAL NETWORKS

Since the dawn of human settlements, networks have been growing hand in hand with social arrangements. Primitive societies raised lots of them among cities and ports by means of natural grids like rivers, lakes, valleys and islands. As long as these societies fostered trading roads among farther places, they got used to social lattices involving trusting procedures for exchanging goods and services. As time passed by, commercial partnerships aroused, which were endorsed by governors under the purview of armies, religious orders, alliances among local warlords, and incipient leagues of traders, artisans, and technicians. As from the sixth century BC onwards, Greeks, Romans, Chinese, and Middle-Eastern peoples, expanded the coherence and complexity of social networks, mainly through the Silk Roads which became the melting pot of commercial, cultural, scientific, philosophical, and religious developments [Frankopan (2016) latest book discloses not only the impressive history but also the present-day relevance of the so-called Silk Roads].

The Concept

Looking for common ground, we can say that a network consists in a system comprising nodes (the participants or components), as well as relationships that come from and go to nodes, building up in that way lattices whereby nodes share among them multiple associations and many-sided objectives.

From Technological to Social Networks

There are time-honored illustrations to be noticed: rivers and roads connecting cities and villages; railroads, electricity grids and the mail system; the Web; the structure linking airports with airlines all around the world; the lattice stemming from federal and local government offices as they work together, and the like. In most of these networks there is human agency: they stem from technological inventions and improvements. It was from the middle of the nineteenth century however, that some of the foregoing networks started to frame a social dimension as they never had before, to the extent that Internet has lately pushed forward the linking of human beings beyond any seemingly constraint.

Social Networks

In social networks, the nodes are single persons or human groups, corporate actors or political parties, syndicated hospitals around the country, credit-card holders and their issuing banks, tourist and travel dealers (including travel agencies, hotel chains, airlines, tour operators, car-hiring companies), religious communities, and the like. Relationships that spring out of each node in their looking for and finding of counterparts at the receiving end are variegated: from informal to formal, spontaneous to purposeful, spurious to reliable, illegal to legal, from onshore to offshore locations, from human beings to machines.

We can ask to ourselves: what are the contents and defining features of such relationships? Firstly, they exchange information, skills, knowledge, goods and services. Secondly, they flow through ubiquitous locations towards anywhere else. Thirdly, each node tries to reach only those exhibiting relevant contents of interest and keeps away from the remaining ones. Fourthly, it follows that many relationships are fortuitous, short-termed, and noncommittal. Last of all, each node can participate in one or more distinguishable networks, entering into a complex structure of relationships with several destination components.

Political Networks

As long as computers, mobile phones, and the Internet have empowered so many people to manage their own communication agendas, political actors took advantage of a pool of resources circulating over social networks, which could be invested in electoral campaigns and mass participation through online assemblies, and focus groups. Through social networks, people started to demand from government the redress of inequalities and the deliverance of public goods. They got used to Internet capabilities, voicing their grievances and pointing out to broken promises.

In other words, by political networks is meant the active participation of social networks in the cut and thrust of political life either in villages, towns, cities, communities, nations, markets and groups of interest.

Trust Networks

Social arrangements along history show how networks stretched from very simple structures like families or kinships to huge systems of interconnections. As this increasingly complexity evolved, a consequential feature settled down: what if human beings entered in networks to protect themselves and their families, villages, towns, organizations and groups of friends? And such was for certain what they did, to prevent being harmed from hazards pervading the external world: foreigners, rivals, enemies, and wild animals, famines, plagues, or climate change. Each person or corporate actor – that is to say, every node in the network – intended to join other nodes if and only they could expect cooperation, loyalty, safety, and the faithful persistence of their exchanges.

At first, trust networks allowed social groupings to go over and above their daily transactions. Afterwards, they were functional to politics, because they committed the participants to reliable, steady, accountable, transparent and responsive patterns of behavior. In other words, political and trust networks stand for how multiple fiduciary duties and agency relationships take place and hold nowadays.

It's worth quoting what Charles Tilly (2005) depicted as being the quintessence of trust networks:

> Trust consists of placing valued outcomes at risk to others' malfeasance, mistakes, or failures. Trust relationships include those in which people regularly take such risks. Although some trust relationships remain purely dyadic, for the most part they operate within larger networks of similar relationships. Trust networks, then, consist of ramified interpersonal connections, consisting mainly of strong ties, within which people set valued, consequential, long-term resources and enterprises at risk to the malfeasance, mistakes, or failures of others. (page 12)

Governance of Networks

In the last decades, criticism has sprung up from some quarters arguing about the apparent lack of governance in networks. Their viewpoints can be briefed this way:

a) networks do not depend on underlying organizations; in particular, they lack of physical locations;
b) governance means management of a system, so critics complain that such feature is missing in networks;
c) it is unlikely that single persons or corporate actors performing like nodes in their defining networks could comply with the main categories of governance, from the founding charter and the supervisory body, till accountancy, transparency, and good practices.

With regard to the first and second type of criticism, it all goes down to the meaning we attach to the word "organization". If we meant a grouping of human beings within a factory or an office building, then some critics would have their point. But organizations stand for broader assortments of people, at least from the twentieth century. Let us recall what we said in section 1.1:

People spend their lives through many social groupings that need to last and be steered. [...] All of these social arrangements share two features: they are purpose-built systems unfolding through time, and they are to be handled by proficient sailors or governors.

Human beings and corporate actors engage themselves in networks as components of a system, establish interrelations and exchanges, and bring to completion manifold purposes, from mere chatting and being entertained, to buying books, food, and medicines, and also paying their bills.

In spite of an apparent lack of management, networks make a manager of each and every participant. And there are certain nodes more prominent than others, which are denoted "concentrated nodes"; they stand for hubs or coordinating centers that can handle manifold tasks, requests, and deliverance from numberless fellow nodes (if in doubt, look at Amazon, the Federal Postal Service, or the Internal Revenue Service).

As for the last type of criticism, if we looked at the statement of meaning 1, in section 1.2, pertaining governance, we would find that social networks, and political ones in particular, match the first and second assertions almost as a matter of course. It is with regard to the third one[21] where critics seem to gain some points in the ongoing debate. For example, Internet is an ubiquitous ocean of information that can be sorted out into two broad categories: on the one hand, lies, manipulations, corruption, slandering, abuse, libeling, fraud, blame avoidance, fake news, spinning; on the other hand, academic information sharing, highly reliable technical reports, safe home banking, trading of goods or services, first rate investigative journalism, and the like. To grant that principles and practices of governance may stem from the granular behavior of participants in the World Wide Web seems easier said than done. However, and this makes rather difficult for the critics' objection to stand firm, it is for the concentrated nodes to nurture accountability, transparency and fiduciary duties which spread over their

---

[21] We quote: "*the fostering of accountability, transparency and fiduciary duties, as well as the management of conflicts of interest among natural persons or corporate and political actors.*"

stakeholders in the end, as we can uphold when dealing online with a bank, a hospital, or any government agency.

Conclusion

This chapter brought forth the intimate linkage between governance and politics; in point of fact, both of them nurture a close partnership in the task of managing the government, and empowering the State to care for the common good.

In contrast with the conventional approach that confines itself to merely defining governance and politics following the template "X is Y", we have preferred to design "statements of meaning" whereby governance and politics come down as fields of learning and practice that must meet certain tasks, expectations and features, hence stressing functionality and simplicity.

Furthermore, this viewpoint allowed us to handle in quite a natural approach the cognitive cluster that merges the issues of government, governance and the ability to govern, on the one hand, with representative democracies on the other.

Afterwards, we enlarged on two enablers of governance and politics: responsiveness and fiduciary duties. As regards the former, we expanded on the extent of how far checks and balances improve the governance not only of government branches, but also of organizations and watchdogs. On the side of fiduciary duties, we added agency relationships because they actually permeate organizations in real life.

Last but not least, this chapter featured how social, political and trust networks are nowadays embedded into both governance and politics.

Chapter 2

HOW ACCOUNTABILITY AND TRANSPARENCY BECOME SOCIAL LEARNING PROCESSES

ABSTRACT

This chapter sets forth a new approach to accountability and transparency based on a compact which comprises commitments, expectations, responsibilities, compliance risks and public information, all of them embedded into a dynamic structure that performs as a coaching manager and leads to a social learning process. An application closes the chapter, giving heed to secret organizations and their governance.

INTRODUCTION

In earlier publications of mine[22], I have pointed out that accountability should not be regarded as consisting in responsibilities only, since such a

---

[22] Apreda (2014, 2012). It should be noticed that Apreda (2014) was the first paper that developed the idea of accountability and transparency as social learning processes, and it has influenced the framework of this chapter.

constricting standpoint would leave out the role of commitments in any accountability process. By the same token, I have pressed home that there has been a longstanding neglect in the academic literature addressing transparency as if this were a topic scarcely unrelated to accountability[23].

Things as they are, I advocate a new approach that will be called the Accountability Compact which consists of the following features:

- commitments and responsibilities are the main building blocks of the compact;
- it is a dynamic system, that is to say, a well-defined structure that evolves and changes along time, by taking into account expectations, new information and feedback;
- the compact includes a compliance function that deals with compliance risks, and also coaching mechanisms that lay the grounds for transparency and responsiveness;
- last of all, the compact grows into a social learning process.

As an application of the new approach, the chapter closes with a disreputable subject matter: the governance of secrecy.

2.1. THE CONVENTIONAL MEANING OF ACCOUNTABILITY

Let us start with the meaning portrayed by the Black's Law Dictionary (1999), which has only one entry under the label of "accountable" as the quality of "being responsible or answerable"; astonishingly, it has no entry for "accountability"; neither has one for "transparency". More encouraging seems the wide-ranging Concise Oxford English Dictionary (2009) that defines "accountable" as what seems "required or expected to justify actions or decisions" and also adds the meaning of "explicable or understandable".

---

[23] An heterodox approach to accountability and transparency can be found in Hood (2011) and Apreda (2007b, 2012, 2014).

For more than a century, there has been a suspiciously biased attitude holding the view that accountability can only be achieved if we merely comply with current regulations. Even though this behavior usually brings about windfall earnings for complicit law and auditing firms, it turns out to be self-defeating because of two troublesome developments.

On the one hand, it seems unlikely that any organization, in the long term and persistently, could refuse to comply with the law or regulations; otherwise they would face material consequences[24] that could even threaten their own survival. However, and since the dawn of the twentieth century, there has been an increasing shift of investments, operations, branching and logistics towards offshore locations that provide with secrecy and opaque governance, hence making a mockery of accountability and transparency[25].

On the other hand, even if companies remained working onshore they would gain access to a wide spate of mechanisms that prevent information from reaching their stakeholders by means of powerful blame avoidance tools: for example by hiring expert advise from public relations agencies; business and marketing coaching; political counselors, pollsters, and the so-called spin doctors. On this point, we deem that books by Stauber and Rampton (1995), or Hood (2011) should be a must-read assignment for students and teachers in Business Schools[26].

2.2. ACCOUNTABILITY FROM A BROADER VIEWPOINT

Only commitments lend meaning to responsibilities. Otherwise, on what grounds should anybody be held accountable to a counterpart if we took commitments out of the picture? Being responsible for failures, non-

---

[24] This statement assumes representative democracies that abide by the law and order. It goes without saying that it doesn't apply to countries where crony capitalism, populism, corruption or antidemocratic practices have become a way of life.

[25] An example of wrongdoing was the Northern Rock Bank in the last financial crisis that started in 2007; it has been researched by Shin (2009). Opaque governance is tracked down in Apreda (2012) and we will expand on it in chapter 4. On offshore locations the best reference seems Palan (2006).

[26] We are going to delve into this issue in chapter 5, dedicated to organized crime.

compliance, even achievements, it would become an abstract endeavor if we did not attempt to make a distinction between what one actor has promised to deliver, and how well or badly he actually matched his objectives at the end of the day. Let us expand on this further.

Firstly, by *"commitments"* we mean *a kind of voluntary behavior that binds counterparts to keep limits on their activities, targets and discretion*[27]. Secondly, accountability should be thought like an interactive structure of behavior among single or collective agents and their reciprocal linkages. Thirdly, we are going to highlight such structure by disclosing a pair of concurring characteristics: multiple accountabilities and mutuality of interests.

Multiple Accountabilities

It should be borne in mind that commitments do not pertain only to one actor (the one who promises compliance). In point of fact, there is a give-and-take exchange between the party who demands the commitment (*the holder*) and the counterpart that will be held responsible for carrying out the commitment (*the holdee*). Although this relationship singles out the main actors, in many cases the whole process requires a double-tiered frame of analysis: the one based in the holder-holdee direction, whereas the other tier leaves room from a reversal of roles, by which the holdee also behaves as a holder towards his counterpart.

Recently, the study of accountability in teams has expanded the customary analysis: there can be one or several holders (in a Board of Directors each member carries out the role of holder towards the Chief Executive Officer), as well as one or several holdees (in the President's cabinet, each minister; in a football team, each player). This sort of development will be called *"multiple accountabilities"*.

---

[27] We take into account the Concise Oxford English Dictionary entry for commitment: *an engagement or obligation that restricts freedom of action*. In the text above, we had in mind a shade of meaning that fits in much better with governance analysis.

We use the expression "actor" here as any meaningful collective that comprises, among other participants, individuals, corporate divisions, government offices, regulatory bodies, social and political networks, church communities, the bank where you have taken a loan, gatekeepers, the media and the like[28]. It is in the context of politics that commitments and responsibilities link organizations with stakeholders[29], the government with the opposition, political parties with citizens, one government with other governments in the world.

Mutuality of Interests

We assert that holders and holdees enter upon their bond by acknowledging their "mutuality of interests", a structure that comes defined by three features:

- although the binding between holders and holdees can be predicated on a covenant, contract, specific law, or a mere convention, their lasting association also derives from reciprocal interests;
- holders and holdees often realize that their linkage allows them the pursuit of other kind of targets, some of them shared with their stakeholders;
- as long as the holder-holdee partnership unfolds, both direct and indirect interests end up eventually in success, blame, failure or recognition bestowed to counterparts.

Despite the fact that such relationship usually conveys payments on behalf of the holdee, we find several settings in which this is not the case: membership in the board of directors in foundations related to scientific research, charities, clubs, youth organizations (for instance, boy- or girl-scouts), schools (also colleges and universities), boards of trustees to

---

[28] On social and political networks we refer the reader to section 1.6 in chapter 1.
[29] The scope and function of stakeholders is to be enlarged in chapter 3, section 3.1.

museums and performing arts centers, churches, public libraries, juries in courts of law, professional bodies, parents and teachers associations. In most of these examples, holdees are unlikely to receive cash payments but reputational goods instead.

Another Semantics for Accountability

Availing ourselves of the foregoing analysis, we can put forward a distinctive definition of accountability stemming from regular patterns of behavior in organizations.

Statement of Meaning 1 – Accountability

By accountability is meant a compact of adaptable behavior in organizations and the government that links a holder with a holdee to a process that entails the following attributes:

- *the relationship takes place through an agreed or plausible span of time within the rule of law and regulatory habitats;*
- *the holdee engages himself to a set of commitments on behalf of the holder and stand responsible for their fulfillment;*
- *the holder will likely claim upon the set of responsibilities arising from the commitments pledged by the holdee;*
- *multiple accountabilities and mutuality of interests evolve from the production and exchange of material information and reciprocal expectations[30];*
- *there are mechanisms to cope with discrepancies between what has been promised and what has been accomplished eventually.*

---

[30] Although "material" is a catchword, there is at least a meaning that has proved useful for governance analysis. In accordance with the Black's Law Dictionary, "material" is understood as *something of such nature that knowledge of the item would affect a person's decision-making process.*

Within the context of each organization, holders and holdees stand for individuals, groups, corporate actors, or government agencies and officials. Any distinctive holder-holdee relationship comprises the production and exchange of material information and reciprocal expectations as it is stressed in the fourth statement in the definition above; in other words, transparency comes to be an enabling condition for accountability[31]. At this stage of our analysis, the topic of fiduciary duties comes to our mind[32]: in point of fact, both the fiduciary duties and agency-relationships themselves can only be brought to completion when they are linked with accountability assumptions.

Remarks

Does this frame of analysis exclude accountability among family members, patient-physician, or student-tutor relationships? By no means, since they are samples of civil groupings that perform as molecular and rather informal arrangements.

We should mark here that the first assertion in the statement of meaning above stresses the fact that accountability amounts to a behavior that abide by the law and regulations. For the time being, opaque and criminal governances are kept aside of the analysis; we are going to expand on this major issue further in section 2.9 as well as chapters 4 and 5.

2.3. THE INNER STRUCTURE OF THE ACCOUNTABILITY COMPACT

Let us denote the accountability compact as *C(date)*, to stress the fact that both its components and their connections are time-dependent. So as to

---

[31] We are going to survey this assertion in section 2.4.
[32] See chapter 1, section 1.5

become operational, the compact defined in the statement of meaning 1 would require the following inner structure:

a) Commitments and responsibilities are the building blocks of the compact.
b) Basically, it must contain feasible and attainable rules of behavior tying up the counterparts, as well as goals, strategies, expected outcomes and relevant information for holders and their holdees.
c) Furthermore, it comes furnished with mechanisms to work out disputes, conflicts of interests, rewards and penalties, as well as arbitration procedures.
d) As time passes by, *C(date)* includes a considered choice of measures that gauge how prior commitments have been performed.
e) Moreover, *C(date)* is dynamic, it evolves and changes during an agreed period of analysis, whereby counterparties nurture and gain access to new information which will be processed, employed, shared and stored in the compact[33]; in other words, there is a learning mechanism.
f) Lastly, *C(date)* also conveys the description of basic features pertaining the mutuality of interests that makes their multiple relationships meaningful for both parties and their stakeholders.

Offshore locations provide with a well-known example of an opaque compact of commitments and responsibilities widely used by organizations that choose to flout regulations, by taking advantage of blame-avoidance contrivances.

---

[33] Needless to say, items a) and d) show that transparency is an essential component of this compact. More on this topic can be found in section 2.4, this chapter.

Example: The Underlying Compact of Offshore Locations

Introduction

The global economy comprises not only onshore locations, but offshore ones as well; the latter behave at odds with the former and grow as shadowy hideouts for tax evasion, organized crime, and corruption[34]. Against the background of corporate scandals, financial crises, outrageous misrepresentation of information, and the channeling of money out of criminal activities towards offshore conduits, academics and practitioners have recently increased their grasp of what is happening down-to-earth in such places. As money invested in offshore locations can't remain idle, there are secret arrangements whereby banks make use of the money to grant loans to their onshore customers, distributing open-handed fees and rewards to offshore government officials and intermediaries (mainly investment banks and funds, as well as law and accountancy practitioners).

The Context

I believe that the best way to understand the obnoxious covenant between an offshore location (in the role of a holdee) and corporate actors or individuals (playing like holders), consists in spelling out what the expression "*offshore location*" stands for[35].

By offshore centers (or locations) we mean sovereign places[36] around the world that are able to frame and enforce their own laws with the purpose of providing economic actors from other nations with the following services:

- *Separating real from legal locations;*

---

[34] Chapter 5 will be devoted to the governance and politics of organizations that play in most cases a criminal game against accountability, transparency, regulations, and the rule of law.
[35] For a thorough expansion of this issue, see Apreda (2012).
[36] From nation-states like Switzerland, to protectorates like Cayman Islands, also including city-states like Singapore, internal states like Nevada, Vermont and Delaware in the USA, or special chartered places like the City of London [Serious research on offshore locations can be found in Palan (2006), Shakson (2011) and Naylor (2004)].

- *incorporating organizations or opening personal accounts on behalf of non-resident individuals and corporate actors with ease of procedures and very low costs;*
- *offering zero, or near zero, taxation levels;*
- *bestowing secrecy jurisdictions beyond the reach of other countries or regulators and, by the same token, strong protection from creditors;*
- *making available a stable and friendly political background;*
- *giving access to virtual bookkeeping and lenient disclosure duties.*

Underlying Commitments

Among the instruments and tailor-made organizations that offshore centers make affordable in their commitments towards customers, we can list the following: offshore banking licenses, hidden current and saving deposit accounts, captive insurance companies, offshore corporations, special-purpose vehicles, segregated account companies, use of tax havens for individuals, hedge funds for non-residents, preferential tax regimes, export processing zones, e-commerce, and flags of convenience.

Mutuality of Interests

Although some interested quarters could remind us about the legal foundations of these locations, they will likely fail to point out that those places actually become purchasers and sellers of sovereignty, granting secrecy, setting up shell companies and hedge funds in the shadows, catering for corporate actors and single investors that seek more pliable outlets for their transactions. Even worse, they also supply their services to big players in drug dealing, terrorism, political corruption, tax evasion, gambling, and weaponry brokerage.

Responsibilities

Sidestepping central banks, security exchange commissions, internal revenue services, gatekeepers and stakeholders, they promise concealment and impunity, and they deliver both, with the connivance of financial advisers, lawyers and accountants[37].

2.4. MAKING OF TRANSPARENCY A CONSEQUENTIAL NOTION

Transparency seems a ubiquitous concept that calls for an operational definition. So far, a suitable description of transparency seems the one drafted by the Bank of International Settlements (1998), which states that information becomes transparent when *it is timely, relevant, reliable, checkable, and changeable.*

It is my belief that something is missing in this well-known test that ascertains whether any kind of information could be reckoned as transparent or not. *I argue that unless the duty of disclosing public information became embedded into the notion of transparency, we wouldn't be able to go beyond mere political rhetoric or window dressing.* It's worth noticing that we have broadened the conventional analysis since the public consists of those stakeholders that have a say, or can lay claims to the organization. To all intents and purposes, stakeholders appear to be the real characters in the narrative of accountability and transparency.

If relevant information were not available, how could stakeholders assess the running and efficacy of the organization? This is the perverse logic behind blame avoidance, which is the subject of next section. To give an outrageous example of such logic, we can point to the information contained in the web-pages of so many corporations where it is not possible

---

[37] Professor Palan´s book is a must on this subject. Apreda (2012) offers an inclusive study of opaque governance, whereas section 5.2, chapter 5 in this book embraces the topic in length.

to find the names, track record and contact addresses of their Directors, senior managers or, still worse, their compliance officer.

Keeping an embracing perspective in the context of governance, the expression *"public information"* must be understood as *that sort of information whose concealment entails material consequences*[38] *for any of the stakeholders involved with a particular organization.* Bearing this in mind we move on to an alternative concept regarding transparency.

Statement of Meaning 2 – Transparency

By transparency is meant management of information[39], meeting the following conditions:

- the information must be reliable, timely, relevant, and the sources as well as the procedures put into use have to be disclosed[40];
- there must be a corporate actor, in the organization or the government, who is held responsible for the delivery of such information;
- the information must be made public: that is to say, available to internal and external stakeholders;
- it involves a process by which counterparts agree, follow up, disagree, update, and request changes upon the quantity or quality of the information, so as to grant compliance not only with standing regulations but also with ongoing commitments and responsibilities, which the organization or government ought to pledge towards its stakeholders.

---

[38] The meaning of material consequences can be found in footnote 9, this chapter.
[39] Management of information, in the context of this book, embraces purposeful activities like research, production, sorting out, releasing, saving, retrieving, deleting, and updating information.
[40] We acknowledge in this assertion that the Basel Bank approach to transparency is a good starting point towards a broader statement of meaning like the one given above.

Remark

The statement of meaning sheds light on how deeply transparency is joined to the accountability compact; to wit, read again the second and fourth assertions.

We should not assess transparency as merely the production of information without additional qualifications because, more often than not, any organization can provide stakeholders with misleading information, by hiring Public Relations (PRs) firms that grow so proud of writing and releasing blatant lies or preposterous fictions on behalf of their clients.

Let us pick up from the food industry an illustration of deceitful transparency, a subject to be further developed in chapter 5, devoted to the governance of organized crime and ecocide.

Example – The Food Industry

Since the dawn of the Industrial Revolution, an onslaught of complaints started to being heaped against faulty and unreliable practices in the food industry. In most countries, for instance, the packaging of foodstuff includes the list of ingredients used for any product, a practice that triggers off many-sided doubts and criticism.

How could we feel safe about the list of contents, either in the naming of components or their proportions as stated in the labels? On the one hand, the consumer cannot undertake any verification; on the other, it is conspicuous how regulators fail in their duties of controlling information. Moreover, there are so many items in the market that transaction costs would become higher than the budget allocated to regulatory agencies.

Norms also prescribe that chemicals used to stretch out the shelf life of the product must be attached to the list of contents. This is good news, but it does not help consumer to increase their understanding with technical abbreviations; still more worrying, in many non-developed countries such shortening of jargon expressions actually conceals the adding of toxic chemicals.

This predicament extends to the whole industry that caters for and distribute foodstuff, mainly to restaurants, coffee stores, bakeries, food and beverages warehouses, hotels and supermarkets. How often have you read in newspapers that outrageous lack of hygienic and sanitary conditions have hurt, crippled and even killed customers who happened to eat at those venues, or bought takeaway food to be consumed at their homes? Apparently, labels cannot warrant customers that producers had really complied with non-polluting practices pertaining crops, fruits, cattle, poultry, and most of the processed stuff.

When consumers cry out their dissatisfaction with this state of affairs, there seems that nobody can take the complaint at the receiving end, as we are to learn in next section about the blame avoidance game. Is there a way out of this riddle? Broadly speaking, there are at least five mechanisms that contribute to improve transparency standards:

- to understand, once and for all, that transparency and accountability are social learning processes, as we will expand on section 2.8;
- to require from any corporate actor in the industry the enactment of their own Statute of Governance[41];
- to legislate and enforce a federal law protecting consumers so as to prevent and punish guileful mishandling of commitments and responsibilities;
- to install a "name and shame" campaign in the media by showing the gap between what the product or service promised and what it really delivered;
- to set up a code of good practices, that is to say, procedures and regulations by which organizations should comply with; otherwise, they must explain their refusal to have such a code.

---

[41] Further details and applications about the statute of governance can be followed in chapter 3, section 3.8.

2.5. BLAME AVOIDANCE

Imagine that we can map something good, praiseworthy or reliable onto certain single person or corporate actor. In other words, we give credit to him, or he can take credit for having delivered the goods, as a matter of course. Politicians, legislators, judges, public-office holders, are very keen on being recognized for their performance; it is rewarding, enhances their reputation, and helps them towards a likely promotion. Looking deeper into this topic, we find out that in political action there are commitments and responsibilities that warrant success.

Now, let us go into reverse by assuming that we can map something bad, reprehensible, or unreliable onto some individual person or corporate actor. That is to say, we blame him. Will he take the blame? Most of the time, political actors are encouraged in favor of denying their responsibilities, blunders, or mischievous deeds. Even worse, evidence is being gathered about the increasing habit in politics of playing the game of blame avoidance, by which *the political actor concurs in denying any blame or designing courses of action to deflect the blame on others or in circumstances foreign to him.*

The subject has recently come topical on account of worthy contributions by several scholars, practitioners and institutions, on behalf of better governance for organizations and countries. Among outstanding experts, we could point to Christopher Hood (2011), who noticed, firstly, the components of blame processes:

- the perceived avoidable harm or loss;
- the perceived responsibility or agency;

and secondly, the players of this game:

- the blame makers, who do the blaming;
- the blame takers, who are on the receiving end.

But we would be misguided if we thought that blame avoidance is something that links with certain pathology of accountability and nothing else; on the contrary, it is a many-sided behavior that overlaps with other daily-life concerns. Sadly to be recognized, but we are living in a world where corporate and political actors whitewash their misdeeds and hire experts that steer them clear of any public embarrassment or expensive trials in courts. The following examples will lay bare the core of this issue.

Outsourcing Staff and Services

The consumer wants to make a complaint but there is no official in the company or government agency to deal with it, because "it is a fault to be attributed to outsourced staff", which amounts to finding a scapegoat. An alternative answer could be "the service you are requesting is a responsibility of the provider"; needless to say, the provider has run out of business or, if that were not the case, he would counterclaim that the company is not telling the truth.

Codes of Good Practices

The customer tries to claim about wrongdoings that are in blatant denial of the code of good practices that is supported by the website of the company. People from headquarters, never identifying themselves, tell the annoyed client they are updating the code and that is why the new draft has not been uploaded yet, hence spinning their way out of trouble. Even worse, when the complainer insists on his demand and gathers further information, he realizes that the denoted *"code"* is not such thing, but a catalogue of current operations and services offered to the customer base. In some countries, bank clients are given a printout of a pretended code that merely describes what current or time-deposit accounts are like, or extols the wide-ranging supply of investment services the financial institution "graciously" provides their investors with.

Computerized Switchboards and Online Services

Very often, when a client intends to channel his request to the company by phone, the first thing he comes across consists in music excerpts (Vivaldi seems favored), and the second is a message that promises the customer a quick answer to his query. Next, they keep the complainant listening to Vivaldi and the ludicrous message ever. An alternative course of action consists in inviting the customer to submit his e-mail to the company's representatives, whose identities are not provided. The mechanism ultimately proves to be unreliable: firstly, they are seldom replied; secondly, if they are replied at all, the customer is told by a ghost that the complaint should be addressed to an outsourced provider, like in the foregoing tale of outsourced staff and services.

Corporate Social Responsibility

Again and again, these statements are so fictional that cannot be verified or followed up by any considered customer. For instance, let assume that the company boast about its commitments to a safer and healthy environment, while condemning children's work at sweatshops in the shadows. Sooner or later, however, an investigative journalist reports that one of its foreign branches exploits children outrageously whereas another branch has been polluting the nearby river where the factory is located to such levels that inhabitants drink unhealthy water in their homes. If the reader is in doubt, he is referred to the book *Toxic sludge is good for you: lies, damn lies, and the Public Relations Industry,* by Stauber and Rampton (1995).

Blame Avoidance in Politics and Governance

In chapter 5, devoted to the study of organized crime, we are going to delve into blame avoidance carried out with the connivance of political and professional actors.

2.6. COMPLIANCE RISKS

Once we have acquainted ourselves with the foremost conceptual tenets of accountability and transparency, a legitimate question might arise from practitioners and regulators alike: in actual practice, to what extent both processes could be followed up? A sound discussion of this issue leads us to a managerial device that has become instrumental all around the world: the compliance function, which attempts to cope with compliance risks.

In April 2005, the Bank for International Settlements at Basel (BIS) issued a paper under the title of *Compliance and the Compliance Function in Banks*[42]. To start with, *compliance risk* comes defined as

> the risk of legal or regulatory sanctions, material financial loss, or loss to reputation a bank may suffer as a result of its failure to comply with laws, regulations, rules, related self-regulatory organization standards, and codes of conduct applicable to its banking activities. (page 1)

Afterwards, it explains that the *compliance function* [43] amounts to *staff carrying out compliance responsibilities*. Although both notions are distinctive and relevant in governance analysis, two queries comes to our mind:

> Are the tools of compliance risk and the compliance function to be used only for the improvement of banks' governance, or could we also profit from them when dealing with governance issues that concern to any other sort of organization[44]?
> How would it be possible to lay foundations whereby independence from internal auditing, even from management in private or state-owned companies, might be granted in practice?

---
[42] There was a preliminary draft issued in 2003 under the title of *The Compliance Function in Banks*, which was intended as a consultative document.
[43] In the preliminary draft issued in 2003, the compliance function came defined as "*An independent function that identifies, assesses, advises on, monitors and reports on the the bank´s compliance risk.*"
[44] Apreda (2007a) proved that the extension is not only feasible, but also consequential.

The remainder of this section will address the first question whereas the second will be dealt with in section 2.7.

Moving upon the private or public fields, where non-financial organizations meet together in their transactional environments, and are subject to complex networks of stakeholders, we must ask ourselves whether compliance risk bears for them any distinctive relevance eventually. To positively dispel such concerns, let us set forth a broader definition, in keeping with our purposes:

> The expression 'compliance risks' means the risks of sanctions, or material loss of any kind, that any organization may go through if it fails to comply with the manifold constraints of its institutional environment.

It seems noteworthy that laws, regulations, rules, related self-regulatory organization standards for each industry, as well as patterns of behavior, all of them actually pertain to institutional habitats within which any organization strives towards the fulfillment of its goals. But such constraints are much more variegated when we deal with non-financial enterprises, including features like logistics current practices, international trade regimes, gatekeepers monitoring and punishing, as well as commercially time-honored arrangements. Hence, it becomes apparent that compliance risks do actually matter in governance, whatever the kind of organization we intend to deal with.

2.7. THE COMPLIANCE FUNCTION

> The expression "compliance function" stands for a managerial function whose task consists in independently handling the compliance risks that spring up in any sort of organization. In other words, there is always a likely forward discrepancy between what is forecast and what happens afterwards (that is what risk entails, by all means); the worthiness of compliance lies in how it contributes to bridge the gap defined by a risky context of decision-making arising from internal practices of organizations.

Whereas the compliance function seems to be an innovative managerial function, it raises at least two daunting issues revolving around the topic of independence.

To what extent does the compliance function keep itself independent from the auditing function?

Even for organizations that already have an internal auditor, framing up their compliance functions does not seem out of place. However, costs and regulations might prevent the function from being carried out, and in such setting the internal auditor ought to undertake the compliance function in full[45].

To whom is the Compliance Function Office accountable?

"Independence" denotes not to be under the control of any other internal body in the staff of private or public organizations. That is to say, overlapping with accountability lines would make impossible for the compliance function to become the governance superintendent of the whole organization.

But independence also stands for the capacity to perform expected tasks in a self-contained way. Following this course of analysis, we are going to stress three key factors that would turn out the compliance function independent:

- at staff level, it should be held accountable only to the CEO´s office; however, the head of the Compliance Function Office (also called the compliance officer) ought to be granted a statutory exception

---

[45] For financial institutions, the Bank for International Settlements issued guidelines on the role of the Internal Audit department. (BIS, 2002).

from reporting the CEO´s Office so that it could directly complain to the Board of Directors[46] or its Auditing Committee instead;
- the Compliance Function Office must get unlimited access to any information regarded as relevant to meet its duties, from any other department in the company;
- the Board of Directors is to request and review a Performance Annual Report from the head of the Compliance Function Office.

The Statute of Compliance Risks

Taking advantage of the prior discussion, it's time for dealing with a minimal set of governance principles and practices that may contribute to the exercise of an internal compliance function not only in financial but also in non-financial organizations. It will be denoted *Statute of Compliance Risks*. For the sake of illustration, we provide the reader with a model[47].

Principle 1 – On Compliance Risk

Compliance risk is about assessing and preventing the risk of sanctions, or material loss of any kind that an organization may suffer as a result of its failure to comply with the manifold constraints of its institutional environment.

Practice 1 The Board of Directors will request from the Senior Management, or a qualified external source, to draw up the company's Compliance Risk Statute as well as mechanisms to make it enforceable.

---

[46] In the case of state-owned companies it would be more meaningful to refer instead to the Supervisory Body, but conventional usage has increasingly been enlarged to comprise the latter into the expression "Board of Directors". By the same token, instead of speaking about the Chief Official in those companies, usage has preferred the expression "Chief Executive Officer".

[47] Besides, in section 3.6, chapter 3, we will introduce the "statute of governance" in general, which is a compact of principles and good practices that give account of how the organization commits its governance to internal and external stakeholders.

Practice 2   It is for the Chief Executive Office to be held accountable to the Board of Directors for the fulfillment of the Statute.

Principle 2 – On the Compliance Function

In order that the Statute of Compliance Risks be enacted, run and enforced, the Chief Executive Office must set up the compliance managerial function.

Practice 1   The CEO designs and brings into motion a Department of Compliance Risks, in accordance with the Board of Directors.

Practice 2   The CEO will make provision for staffing the Department of Compliance Risks.

Practice 3   The appointment of a qualified Manager within the company, or an external expert with a qualifying track record, for the Department of Compliance Risks is to be handled by the Auditing Committee, according to a procedural mechanism established by the Board of Directors.

Principle 3 – About the Compliance Function Independence

The Board of Directors must enact and shield an independent Compliance Function

Practice 1   At staff level, it is held accountable only to the CEO's office.

Practice 2   The compliance officer is granted a statutory exemption from reporting to the CEO's office so that it could directly inform the Board of Directors or its Auditing Committee about extremely sensitive matters regarding malpractice or malfeasance.

Practice 3   The Department of Compliance Risks is provided with unlimited access to any information deemed relevant to meet its duties, from any other operational center or division in the company.

Practice 4   The Board of Director will request and review a Performance Annual Report from the Head of the Department of Compliance Risks.

2.8. HOW ACCOUNTABILITY AND TRANSPARENCY BECOME SOCIAL LEARNING PROCESSES

In actual practice, accountability and transparency are interactive processes among political actors that evolve out of commitments, purposeful activities, responsibilities, public disclosure of information, expectations about future actions and exchanges, even strategies to be achieved as time passes by. Nonetheless, if we wanted to assess how well or badly the accountability compact brought forth in section 2.3 unfolds eventually, we would bump into difficulties. Firstly, assessments usually hang on subjective and debatable assumptions, because intuitions and subconscious activities usually convey lies, cheating, cover-ups, rationalistic delusion, the design of safeguards to avoid loss of reputation (Haidt, 2013). Secondly, the whole process is fraught with forward events and contingencies over which we have no control. Notwithstanding these sort of stumbling blocks, and trying to cope with them, innovative viewpoints and techniques have arisen in social sciences giving rise to influential contributions from scholars and practitioners in the fields[48] of Economic Sociology (Swedberg, 2003), Behavioral Economics (Kahneman, 2011), Cognitive Analysis (Lakoff, 2009 and Mc Gilchrist, 2010), Sociology (Zerubavel, 2006, 1997) and Psychology (Haidt, 2013).

---

[48] We bring up here only introductory books that come with appropriate references for further study.

In my opinion, the current literature on accountability and transparency has been oblivious so far of what I regard the kernel of the matter: *that both activities amount to concurrent learning processes*. This is an alternative viewpoint that I intend to describe next by means of articulated stages.

Relating Information and Knowledge to Learning Processes

What does the "social learning" mean in the context of this book? By learning we mean acquisition and application of knowledge (either explicit or tacit), that is to say, the mastering of a cluster of activities and information we acquire through practicing and studying, availing ourselves not only of feedback mechanisms but also essential advantages we might draw from social capital[49]. Shortly, learning stems from social processes.

The Role of the Compact C(Date) in Learning: Adjustment, Feedback and Responsiveness

Let us assume that we analyze, at a certain date t, the accountability compact $C(t)$ within which a distinctive set of performance measures or yardsticks $P(t)$ is drawn up to gauge how well or badly commitments agree with responsibilities. Furthermore, as time moves on, $C(t)$ undergoes changes and raises new questions[50] by means of adjustments, feedback and responsiveness.

---

[49] More on social capital in chapter 7, section 7.2.
[50] The decision-making horizon or interval can be denoted by $H = [t; T]$ whereas t stands for the starting date, T the maturity date, and any in-between moment will be denoted by $t + \Delta t$.

Questions on Adjustments

Are we able to uncover, at date "$t + \Delta t$", any traceable and purposeful action that may hinder or spoil the accountability process, namely blame avoidance techniques, opacity in the information, outright breach of commitments, rent-seeking behavior, malfeasance, tunneling[51], and soft-budget constraints[52]?

Is it advisable to alter the course of the process? If so, which are the covenants at date t in $C(t)$ that enable both stakeholders and actors to introduce changes? Do we need to revise any covenant or substitute a new one for the older? Do we have to rectify the set of performance measures $P(t)$, taking advantage of new information gathered up to date "$t + \Delta t$"? What if we must add other kind of measures, or delete older ones?

Questions on Feedback

What sort of experiences, reactions or new information may be included in the compact as a consequence of exchanging or transacting within or outside the organization?

Can stakeholders find out whether the organization distorts or misconstrues $C(t)$?

Who is to benefit from such deviant behavior?

Questions on Responsiveness

Can the compact draw positive and swift response to any disturbance arising from commitments and responsibilities?

---

[51] Tunneling will be treated in chapter 4.
[52] Courses of action leading to mishandling are dealt with in chapter 4 devoted to dysfunctional governances, and chapter 5 that takes care of organized crime. The reader is also referred to Apreda (2012, 2007a).

Can we explain the gap between what is committed and what is delivered? Who will be held responsible for the gap? How can the compliance function cope with this gap?

To what extent do holdees provide holders with transparency? And not less relevant, what about the other way around?

Mutuality of Interests and Trust Building

Accountability and transparency shed light, respectively, on political action and information requirements that are vital not only to holders and holdees, but also to all stakeholders that might play a role in the mutuality of interests that affect each other. When referring to stakeholders, they are customarily qualified as single actors, unconnected and self-sufficient. Contrariwise, they should be regarded like interacting and learning actors, taking part in trust networks. Hence, the process that underlies the exercise of accountability not only improves compliance, but also builds up trust between holders and holdees[53].

Embedding the Compliance Function into the Learning Process

The compliance function plays a substantial role in the accountability process: it keeps all political actors within the boundaries of compliance with both law and regulations. On the one hand, internal stakeholders (Boards, senior Management, departments and workers in the organization) have to interact among themselves, setting into motion adjustment processes to learn from each other, improving their reciprocal compliance standards. On the other hand, external stakeholders also profit from the compliance function of the organization and exert pressure in their bid for transparency. Ultimately, they will take heed of their own compliance functions. *Such*

---

[53] We are going to delve into the connection among trust, cooperation, and social capital in chapter 7, section 7.1.

sequence shows why the compliance function grows like a cooperative mechanism of learning in pursuit of better governance.

Learning Processes are Staples of Sound Governance

As far as we follow the threads that run through the connections between accountability and transparency, the introduction of learning as the organizer of such connections seems beneficial on the following grounds:

- accountability and transparency involve not only holders and holdees, but also stakeholders;
- participants engage themselves in the social interactive process that leads to streamlining the accountability compact.

2.9. SECRECY AND GOVERNANCE

If we look up the word *secret* in a well-known referential dictionary, we will find something like this[54]:

noun	*a piece of information that is only known by one person or a few people and should not be told to others.*
adjective	*if something is secret, other people are not allowed to know about it.*

Profiting from this conventional meaning, we can retool it on behalf of our line of argument, by splitting the connotations of the word *secret* into two separate components:

- as an agreed behavior of counterparts to hide something from the reach of somebody or something else;

---

[54] Cambridge Advanced Learner's Dictionary, Fourth Edition, 2015, CUP, London.

- as an explicit or implicit object or purpose of such hiding.

To all intents and purposes, secrecy clouds the actual workings of any organization. When secrecy grows as a way of life in companies or government offices, the gates are open to disregard accountability and transparency, paving the way to the rise of organized crime.

Keeping an agnostic mind over this subject, let us notice four different organizational environments that deploy cultures of secrecy, starting with those that could be labeled "tools of the trade" to the ones involved with criminal organizations. In particular, we are going to delve into the following settings:

- conventionally "tools of the trade" secrets;
- secret services and intelligence agencies;
- secret societies and religious sects;
- criminal organizations.

To uncover how each of them affects their underlying governances, we are going to handle the first three cases in this section and leave criminal organizations for a detailed expansion in chapter 5.

Secrets as "Tools of the Trade"

Common knowledge spells out that secrets in private, state-owned firms, or government branches and agencies can be deemed effective and operational devices in the pursuit of day-to-day tasks and purposes; that is to say, tools of the trade. Supporters of this point of view highlight multiple contexts of application in which secrets should be marked as noticeable.

To begin with, keeping Chinese walls among departments and divisions of the organization prevent people from being sidetracked in their own working places and duties; hence, it would be desirable that communication and disclosure of information could flow from the authorized channels upwards to senior levels.

Afterwards, Human Resources shouldn't lay bare information on salaries, remunerations to managers and Directors, incentive plans, track records of employees, because the consequences could trigger off debate, criticism, discontent and upsetting questions; it is perfunctorily said, rather cynically, that all these factors would be "detrimental to the personnel morale".

Next, administrative procedures, technical methods, research and development protocols or innovative courses of action, information technology, encryption procedures and computerized databases, could bring damage to any organization if disclosed to stakeholders, mainly their suppliers and competitors.

Lastly, conventional wisdom supports the idea that as long as the organization complies with the law and regulations, this way of handling secrecy does not pose any threat to the attainment of good accountability and transparency.

Broadly speaking, however, this amounts to a double-edged sword. On the one side it fosters a culture of expediency; on the other, it unlocks a mindset that rewards an informal culture of multiple standards. If the "tools of the trade" approach became ingrained in the organization, where should we to draw the line beyond which we would enter into the domain of dysfunctional governance? Let us add further details to this topic.

Firstly, if an organization keeps secrets in a systematic way from the reach of stakeholders and such behavior has material consequences, the meaning of governance as it was put forward in chapter 1 breaks down because there is neither accountability nor transparency. We must bear in mind that among the stakeholders we gather the Internal Revenue Service, regulators and the Courts, shareholders and lenders, suppliers, customers and communities. It seems that organizations shrouded in secrecy could not claim reliability of any sort.

Secondly, secretive organizations entail at least dysfunctional governances, and when there is a resolute attempt to carry out their daily operations in concealment, although pretending that nothing had happened with the old one, we will speak about opaque governance (chapter 4). From bad to worse, the lack of accountability and transparency to enable deviant purposes easily translates into criminal governance (chapter 5). Summing up: dysfunctional, opaque and criminal governances play in another league quite distant from those that pledge playing on the "good governance" side, that was shaped in section 1.2, chapter 1.

Finally, there still remains a connotation that lends credence to the widespread belief that in non-deviant organizations and government branches, we should make provisions for a behavioral sense of secrecy that might become beneficial and helpful. On this regard, we should ask to ourselves: are there alternative paths along which we can strengthen the governance of these organizations? Let us point out two pieces of advice:

- Embed in the statute of governance, within the section devoted to accountability and transparency, an assortment of principles and practices isolating those secrets that might be regarded as "tools of trade".
- Interpolate in the statute of compliance risks a whole depiction of what would be a behavior of secrecy that would not convey material consequences for the organization.

The Secret Services and Intelligence Agencies

Secret is of the essence in these organizations, not as a tool of their trade as we noticed in the former example but as their livelihood; in all the most important ways, it is the quintessence of service agencies and intelligence units.

The public knows almost nothing about their governance or their track record. There is not a hint about the identity of their members, salaries, working places, fringe benefits, taxes or social security; for sure, those features are shrouded in secrecy. Spies are held responsible only to the Congress, which deals with them through special commissions under the veil of secrecy too. In short, citizens in the country are not allowed to inquiry about the deeds and errands of the service.

We face here a type of governance at odds with the framework set forth in chapter 1; indeed it comes down as a dreadful deviance, almost similar to the one found in criminal organizations, barring two distinctive factors: in almost all countries there is a Law ruling secret services; also, they don't pursue profits as it happens in criminal organizations.

The key support for such underhanded governance is "reason of state", surveillance and homeland security. Neither intelligence units nor their members can be prosecuted and are free from punishment while performing their duties, unless they infringe their enabling law and regulations. It goes without saying that is very little what can be done to streamline the governance of this kind of organization in relation to external stakeholders, although internal accountability and transparency might likely be improved.

Secret Societies and Sects

There are lots of organizations that make of secret their sole affair. If we recall the two-tier structure shaped from the meaning of the word "secret", at the beginning of this section, we can single out their distinctive features.

At the outset of these sects, a group of persons agree to systematically hide their activities, even their identities and the places of their meetings, from the reach of the community or the country where they live in; that is to say, they isolate themselves from society, as if they were ghosts. Entrance protocols are hard and exacting; the candidates are tested and screened out and, when accepted, are sworn to secrecy; their meetings are held in concealment as well as the tasks performed to match their goals.

As for their purposes, this kind of social arrangement shows a variety of samples that can be briefed this way: they intend to detach bodies and souls from their native community by following a leader who could be religious or political; or fight against the people outside, who are regarded infidels, heretics, enemies; also keeping themselves to themselves in ascetic surroundings or monastic orders.

If we tried to assess their governance, we would find it tightly designed and efficiently employed in their internal structure of accountability, transparency and fiduciary duties. In contrast, we find out that the external structure grows as an utter failure, because secret societies cloak themselves from the world outside. Among the most conspicuous examples, we can choose the following ones: churches and other religious sects on the one hand, terrorism on the other. We are going to focus on churches in this chapter, leaving terrorist networks for chapter 4 when we will link terrorism with the so-called sociopath frame of mind.

Churches and Other Religious Sects

These organizations intend to enroll adepts, converters, or good souls eager to obey some canon of behavior presumably put down by remarkable founders. They also exhibit a will to help their members in good and bad times, and non-members alike (by means of schools, parishes, dispensaries, hospitals, which also care for enrollment and evangelizing). From this viewpoint, churches and religious sects have conveyed social concerns and moral messages. But, on the other side, their governance is rather peculiar. Let us give heed to the Catholic Church, because it shows well-defined features to be discussed.

It is a global organization with a chief executive officer, the Pope, who lives in Rome, the headquarters' location. The College of Cardinals regularly convenes following the way boards of directors are used to, and they even elect a new Pope. Although the church abides by the law in every country, it also follows its own legal framework in matters regarding faith, membership, finance, proselytizing, and the internal trappings of the whole organization. Accountability and transparency are notoriously foreign to stakeholders, who have no clues about what happens inside the church.

Secrecy is so entrenched in the church that the underlying social grouping grows shrouded in concealment and blame avoidance; the senior managers (mainly bishops and cardinals) mimic the behavior of their peers in big corporations and some government plutocracies when we look the way they live, the goods and chattel they relish, the places they inhabit and their plush surroundings, the cars they use, the attendants they hire, the fringe benefits they enjoy, among which we can notice high salaries along their tenure in office, and a hospitable retirement scheme for the remaining of their lives.

For ages, they have stashed away their activities and masked their behavior. In our own century, a shameful and obnoxious string of misconduct have been brought to light: firstly, widespread crimes by pedophile clergy men; then an astonishingly number of children born out of wedlock and fathered by priests; afterwards, financial and real state outrageous scandals. Unfortunately for the many true believers and honest clerics in the rank and file of the organization, evidence on these crimes is overwhelming and has become topical for investigative journalists and the courts of law. Facing the universal outcry claiming punishment and deep changes in the church, responsiveness has been unconvincing so far, regretfully conniving with the culprits by means of conspiracies of silence, to say the least. On this topic, Zerubavel's book, *The Elephant in the Room: Silence and Denial in Everyday Life* (2006), is a must-read.

CONCLUSION

We have broadened not only the conventional meaning of accountability and transparency, but their scope and functionality as well.

Firstly, we set up the accountability compact, which allow internal and external stakeholders to follow up how the organization or government manages their accountability and transparency engagements; such compact performs like a coaching manager. Secondly, the blame avoidance game was brought to light in order to track down how both organizations and governments purchase impunity and connivance to public relations companies, spin doctors, law and accountancy firms, so as to steer clear of responsibilities and punishment. Thirdly, the chapter provided a tool to cope with compliance risks: the so-called compliance function that carries out a superintendent role over the organization. Fourthly, we put forward how accountability and transparency grow into social learning processes. Lastly, the contents displayed along the chapter were applied to the thorny issue of secrecy in organizations and governments, and how this impinges on their deviant governances.

Chapter 3

POLITICAL CONFLICT-SYSTEMS, THE CLINICAL APPROACH TO CONFLICTS OF INTEREST, AND DUAL GOVERNANCE

ABSTRACT

After introducing the main characters in the life of organizations and governments, that is to say claimants, stakeholders, complainers and discontents, we will distinguish between cooperative and adversarial conflicts of interest. Next, organizations will be featured as political conflict-systems, giving heed to the extremely engaging subject of dual governance, which seems truly consequential for social democracies. Last of all, a clinical approach will be enlarged upon, including two complementary devices: the clinical report on conflicts of interest and the design of the statute of governance. In the technical appendix, this approach will be applied to the dual governance of a state-owned bank.

INTRODUCTION

This chapter sets about a heterodox framework for the analysis of governance, regarding any organization as a political conflict-system. We take a step further and assert that politics can be viewed, among other things, as a purposeful set of activities that attempt to make the best, or the worst, out of conflicts of interest.

Firstly, the main actors will be brought to light, namely claimants, stakeholders, complainers and discontents, as well as their transactional environment, within which a distinction arises between information and regulatory habitats.

Afterwards, it will be underlined that conflicts of interest can be either cooperative or adversarial, a line of argument that leads to coalitions, agenda building and factions; next, we advocate the employment of a clinical approach to governance which provides two devices to accomplish such target: the clinical report on conflicts of interest and the statute of governance.

Next, we will address the notion and implications of dual governance when viewed from the fertile ground of political conflict-systems; this subject matter permeates the nature of those organizations featured by a two-tiered structure, one related to private and the other to public governance, as it is the case of state-owned firms. The latter part of the chapter will focus on state-owned banks, and in the technical appendix, samples will be provided to illustrate their statute of governance, and how to draft a clinical report on their conflicts of interest.

3.1. STAKEHOLDERS

Even though the notion of stakeholder seems rooted to that of a claimant, it is when we deal with organizations that such usage turns out to be rather slippery. Hence, we need to ascertain what the expression "stakeholder" stands for in the context of this book.

To begin with, *claimants* are those who regard themselves to be entitled to certain rights. This broad meaning also encompasses making claims on single transactions. For instance, how many times in your life did you ask for lost baggage at the proper office in an airport? Seldom actually, since it is an example of a rare event. Instead, when using the term *stakeholder*, we are aware of the fact that, although it refers to a claimant, its semantic range narrows down when dealing with organizations and their governances:

- for one thing, we place emphasis on the relationship linking the stakeholder to the organization; far from being based on a standalone basis, we rate it like a persistent bond that remains steady along a relevant span of time;
- for another, we have to add a connotation which predicates that, in this kind of relationship, not only the success of the organization but also its failures bear upon the interests of any stakeholder.

Statement of Meaning 1 – Stakeholders

By stakeholders of certain organization, we mean single or collective actors submitting claims that match two constraints:

- *they arise out of persistent and enduring relationships;*
- *claimants affect and are affected both by the success or failure of the organization.*

Borderlines between being a claimant or a stakeholder clearly stem from the definition. For instance, if we do our shopping in a store near our holiday place, we are merely transient customers, likely claimants by right, but not stakeholders in the sense conveyed by the foregoing notion. Contrariwise, its regular suppliers and customers can be deemed stakeholders of that store, as well as creditors, employees, managers, and the Internal Revenue Service. All of them benefit from the store's success, while they all stand to lose in quality, price, conveniences, tax collection, and debt repayments if the business fails, suffers financial distress or goes bust.

In spite of textbooks, business schools and the media that portray an optimistic outlook of stakeholders keeping a friendly, even blissful association with organizations, it is in real life that the picture we watch tells another story: stakeholders carry out their partnership in a ceaseless state of conflicts of interest, some of which are cooperative, but most of them grow adversarial in the end.

Let us now stress two types of claimants within political systems who oppose wrongdoings or unfairness of organizations: we are speaking of complainers and discontents.

Complainers

It will be needful to raise a distinction between claimant and complainer, the latter being a claimant who is dissatisfied with the performance of corporate or political actors on the following fundamentals:

- there would have been cutting corners, blame avoidance, broken promises and flouting of regulations, negligence, or criminal action on the side of organizations or government branches;
- there would be groups of claimants ready to contest the political behavior of the government or some of its agencies; seldom do their complaints take place in persistent and systematic ways, albeit they might convey momentous consequences.

Consequently, a complainer can be viewed as a claimant that tries to put right a wrong or be requited for a wrong done. In contrast, a claimant goes beyond the dark sides of commitments and also acknowledges the bright ones, conveyed by entitled rights or demands of fairness that stem from a covenant, a contract, or even the Constitution.

Discontents

This turns out to be a sensitive topic because of its political connotations. There have been discontents since primeval social arrangements along the history of humankind. But it was since the dawn of modern age, by the sixteenth century, that discontents have been getting little by little, and at a slow pace, their social awareness. The whole process changed gears as from the end of the eighteenth century and grew stronger mainly through triggering events as electoral franchises, the independence of the United States, the French Revolution, the fight for better labor conditions, the American Civil War, the widespread influence of socialists and Marxists, and the enlargement of the trade-union membership base.

In our own day and age, the road traveled by discontents has been paved with outrageous failures in capitalist countries, as well as ubiquitous suffering and swelling poverty in the majority of the remaining ones. To cap it all, there might surely be a mistake to underrate or dismiss what amounts to the core of their social claims: inequality, unfairness, lacking of opportunities, hunger and abuse, health ravages and environmental wreckage. Certainly, it is the want of government responsiveness that keeps claimants bearing their grudges, feeling that their grievances and unfair circumstances call for disruptive political action (as when people took to the streets in the aftermath of the financial crisis that broke out in 2007).

Furthermore, dissatisfied claimants can organize themselves around their beliefs and expectations so as to fight for their rights. One course opened for them in representative democracies consists in building up a new political movement or, more formally, a dissenting political party from which they can make a bid for power so as to redress the wrongs. Tackling another course, discontents can resort to authoritarian, even fanatical or violent types of social movements among which two varieties are conspicuous nowadays: religious fundamentalism (the sort of Al Queda or Isis activists) or populism[55].

3.2. TRANSACTIONAL ENVIRONMENTS

Irrespective of the kind of organization we choose to deal with, either in the civil society or government, they stage themselves as dynamic systems

---

[55] On terrorist networks as vehicles of social and political discontent see section 5.2 in chapter 5. On populism, the reader is referred to chapter 4, section 4.4.

in which numberless exchanges come to the fore from their inside or outside. The ultimate units of any exchange, as Oliver Williamson (1996) has pointed out in his book on the mechanisms of governance, are to be called *transactions*[56]. In my opinion, this standpoint should be broadened so as to include political systems and government branches, by comprising transactions that stem from policies, capabilities, responsiveness, elections, law-making, opposition discourses, commitments, responsibilities, transparency, and the like.

It has to be noticed the fact that although organizations are the main participants in this narrative, no detriment is meant to transactions carried out among individuals: they can be regarded as molecular organizations on their own, as it happens in social and political networks through Internet.

Statement of Meaning 2 – Transactional Environments

By transactional environments we mean:

- *institutional arrangements by which organizations manage their internal and external transactions;*
- *a variegated set of interfaces that allow organizations to bring transactions into completion.*

The notion of interface is akin to governance. A political example can be found in the electoral process, which is the interface between the citizens and the political parties running for elections. More subtle illustrations are the following: accountancy procedures and judiciary protocols. As for the former example, transactions involve a shift or transfer of something from one organization to another one; accountants provide with bookkeeping and documentation, both processes making for the interface in support of the

---

[56] In other words, any exchange can be broken down into separate components, some of which cannot be split further without losing meaning or function; they are called transactions. We buy a TV set, a CD recorder, and a computer printer; the exchange comprises the three items and each of them is a complete transaction. If we irreversibly damaged the printer by crushing it into two chunks, we would not have a full transaction on their own.

exchange. On the other hand, when a criminal is arrested, prosecuted and put into jail, there is a chain of protocols, regulations, numberless documents and judiciary instruments that stand for the transferences and relocations of the culprit, a true system of interfaces ranging from the police station to the prison premises. Let us give heed to well-known habitats where regular transactions are enacted: economic and political markets.

Economic Markets

Merchandises and services markets, where the company trades its own outputs, purchases its own inputs, including reputation assets and liabilities; or internally manages its own throughputs[57].

Labor markets, those settings from which manpower, technicians, professionals, and managerial talent are usually tapped into organizations, or outsourced eventually.

Financial markets, where the company seeks out monetary resources to finance its investment decisions or working capital shortages, acquire financial assets issued by governments or companies alike, through the agency of capital markets, banks and investment funds.

Political Markets

In representative democracies we have political parties, stakeholders, legislatures, the judiciary, gatekeepers, which meet on different political grounds and exchange their commitments, responsibilities, purposes, demands, negotiations, agendas, proposals and the like.

---

[57] This is a concept increasingly used in business, economics, and organization theory. By throughput is meant *"the amount of work done, or people, materials, etc. that are dealt with in a particular amount of time"*. (Cambridge Business English Dictionary, 2011)

Information and Regulatory Habitats

For transactions to be accomplished in a lasting way, rules of the game and behavior constraints must be enforced, what amounts to say that institutional arrangements ultimately shape any kind of social interchange. Be that as it may, this picture has undergone major adjustments since the 1980s in the last century when two processes evolved to an extent that had not been witnessed before: the globalization of markets and the ripening of successful information-based cultures. Such unprecedented events brought about distinctive transactions whose features could not be figured out in the realm of much simpler markets; we are speaking about new habitats that entail, respectively, information and regulatory frameworks.

Information Habitats

The basic transaction in this scenario consists of information, either as input, throughput or output of organizations; it usually appears as a commodity because it can be exchanged, priced and bargained as well. However, only to a certain extent should we predicate that information is a sort of commodity. As a matter of fact, the word 'information' connotes facts about situations, persons, or events. Actually, information hardly meets the requirement of becoming standardized: otherwise, asymmetric information would not become an essential issue. The main outgrowth of this development consists in *the brokerage of asymmetric information and the trade of reputation assets.*

a) The Brokerage of Asymmetric Information[58]

Wherever demand for, and supply of goods and services enter into contestable transactions, we must cope with asymmetric information: one of the parties could have an advantage if they gained access to information not available to their counterpart. At this stage, one of them seeks the advice of

---

[58] Prior research on this kind of brokerage can be found in Apreda (2007).

a broker who can enlarge such asymmetry with her own endowment of valuable information on behalf of her client; it is likely that the counterpart also may look for a broker on his own.

Intermediaries are the outgrowth of technological innovation, division of labor, professional credentials and regulatory constraints; above all, asymmetric information has become the most pervasive feature in modern markets, as Scitovsky (1990) argued so forcefully. In his opinion, sellers and intermediaries carry out their jobs in markets whose structure is asserted upon monopolies, chiefly through logos and brands[59]; therefore, they must also engage themselves in non-price competition, nurturing buyers' markets by means of ancillary conveniences ultimately bundled in the products and services purchased by customers.

b) The Trade of Reputation Assets

Organizations are reputation-seekers, partly due to the fact that reputation seems a good thing to compete for in market (as it has been the case for centuries), but mostly because it is certainly an asset that places a premium over and above other goods and services. In order to cope with the issue of asymmetric information, organizations resort to intermediaries in reputation, whose job consists in making any organization more reliable to their stakeholders. Unfortunately, this picture can be muddled by divergent behaviors like concealment and secrecy or, to make matters worse, organized crime. In the case of deviant behavior, instead of intermediaries that grant reputation, organizations resort to some notorious specialists in connivance and blame avoidance, like accountancy and law firms, public-relations agencies, lobbyists, investment banks and hedge funds, as we are going to see in chapters 4 and 5.

---

[59] Scitovsky is a good starting point to this relevant matter, whereas the book *No Logo* by Naomi Klein (2000) sets forth a demolishing argument against the obnoxious usage of logos and brands.

Regulatory Habitats

Looking back to the last century, we can't help noticing how deeply governments and their regulatory agencies involved themselves in the economy and politics of their countries as well as the running of their organizations. Sometimes, regulators redress wrongs, but in other circumstances they dare to spoil and downgrade the workings of markets, their scope for innovation, even the mechanisms of value formation. Let us draw up a short list of key issues on which watchdogs have a last say in governance:

- they prescribe how we can set up organizations either for-profit or non-profit ones, in the private or government field of action; in other words, they state how many different organizational arrangements will be allowed and which will be forbidden;
- they establish a pecking order related to processes by which some stakeholders would become more prominent than others; furthermore, they rule about ownership structure; voting, control and decision rights; the supervisory-body composition, managerial functions, and the like;
- they make their voice heard about entry or exit of organizations in political or economic markets, providing with compulsory habitats for conflict mediation or resolution.

3.3. CONFLICTS OF INTEREST

For better or worse, conflicts are naturally embedded in the life of organizations and political actors. At first sight, this may be regarded as a nasty output of social settlements, but on a more careful approach to the topic, conflicts of interests may be placed along a continuous arch comprising, on the one side, the state of being "the salt of social life"; on the other side, "a road to hell". It's worth taking this matter further, since it helps us to realize how organizations can last through enduring social arrays, albeit being prone to come down with illnesses, even risking survival or going under. The alignment of personal goals with those endorsed by their organizations has brought about a fertile subject of debate for the last fifty years. I argued elsewhere that we have to get used to unrelenting clashes of interest among different stakeholders in the civil society and government[60] as a matter of course.

Now, let us avail ourselves of an operational concept to translate the expression 'conflicts of interest' within the compass of this book, by assuming two parties, *A* and *B*, which interact between them in a persistent way over certain spread of time; they could be human beings, or corporate actors, including groups (departments within organizations, even institutions in the government, foreign countries, markets, and the like).

Statement of Meaning 3 – Conflicts of Interest

By a conflict of interest between A and B is meant the following process alongside a particular span of time:

- *the set of A's preferences, either in wants, needs, purposes, or courses of action grow in opposition to those in B's own set in the sense that they cannot be mutually met or fulfilled;*
- *both actors' preferences turns out to be at odds with available resources.*

The expression "set of preferences" entails a wide-ranging semantics. If we took into account agent A, for instance, her set would contain the following building blocks:

---

[60] Apreda enlarged this approach in two books published by Nova, New York, (2007, 2012) whose foremost consequences are included in this section.

- a distinctive information set, which includes her database, as well as her knowledge (learning from information) and skills (practical procedures to deal with information);
- her goals, perceptions, opinions, beliefs and assumptions about how the world functions; this comprises her subconscious drivers and self-deception mechanisms[61];
- her proficiency in assessing and choosing issues pertaining transactions settled down with her counterpart.

It was in chapter 1 where we dealt with the topic of multiple agency relationships and mutuality of interests. By the same token, we could now speak about multiple conflicts of interest, anytime we face conflicts that involve not only two counterparts but also a collection of participants. Put it differently, instead of speaking about actors A and B, we could shift gears to multiple participants as $A_1, A_2, \ldots, A_N$; such will be the case later on when dealing with issues like agenda building, agenda setting, coalitions and factions. As regards as *mutuality of interests*, the expression points to a group of participants that share a pool of assorted interests, and willingly promote them ahead, albeit being in conflict or not with other counterparts.

Hence, *the foregoing notion conveys a flexible format, to the degree that we can use it even when a single actor bears himself a conflict of interest between two activities or personal choices.* For example, Mr. X could play a role, R_1, in performing like the company's CEO and, at the same time, following another role, R_2, in acting as member of the Environmentalist Group, a non-profit that fights pollution stemming from companies like his own one.

We must keep in mind that social actors show themselves as forward-looking and end-seeker creatures. In pursuing this logic, therefore, both A and B are likely to disagree over their preferences, any time they are not able to attain them simultaneously. Choices depend not only upon objective

---

[61] Goleman (2005) has made a remarkable contribution to the knowledge of what he called the psychology of self-deception.

preferences but also subjective ones, like tastes, opinions, values, and even skills assessment.

Cooperative and Adversarial Conflicts of Interest

When *A* and *B* find out that they are involved in a conflict of interest, such state of affairs may be tracked down onto the sources of their basic discords by looking for sensible answers to the following questions:

- which are the desirable goals and affordable means;
- where is the starting point as from which *A* and *B* can negotiate;
- to what extent are their preferences compatible between them;
- who is to decide about the scarce resources at hand and how each party is entitled to their ultimate allocation?

A considered analysis of these issues will require, firstly, to make a clear distinction between cooperative and adversarial conflicts of interest; secondly, to deal with the far-reaching notion of conflict systems.

Cooperative Conflicts of Interest

By *cooperative conflicts of interest,* we are going to understand those coming up in well-defined playing fields, with enforceable rules that take place in competitive surroundings, allowing clear mechanisms for settling disputes, and whereby the counterparts realize there are superior goals that stand higher than their own. Several examples spring to our mind: sports, suppliers' biddings, the workings of real markets, sensible discrepancies in the life of organizations, marketing and institutional campaigns, entrance tests to universities, electoral contests in representative democracies.

Adversarial Conflicts of Interest

In contradistinction to cooperative ones, we say that conflicts of interest become *adversarial* when they unfold through the following pattern:

- *A* and *B* fathom out that there is a conflict of interest between them;
- one party grows aware that certain events or courses of action would benefit her to the detriment of her counterpart;
- the time comes when one of the actors makes up their mind to not follow the rules of the game, hence laboring on her own personal agenda in disregard of her counterpart's claims, benefits, or entitlements.

One way or another, by *adversarial conflicts of interest* we are going to mean those arising out of purposeful or subconscious attempts from any or both counterparts to flout some features of cooperative conflicts of interest. Therefore, we should beware of how adversarial conflicts of interests evolve and become material, an issue that rests at the root of many shortcomings in the field of governance, namely the failure to hold up healthy internal political coalitions, the inherent frailty of business or political relationships, and the hazardous bargain between short- and long-term plans for any sustainable process of growth.

Taking advantage of the prior discussion, we move on to examine conflicts involving multiple players, such as agenda building and the problem of factions.

Agenda Building and Agenda Setting

Let us imagine that certain political agent *G* faces a finite set of alternative courses of action[62] from which he will pick out one of them over the others. Relevant to our analysis, several contingencies should be noticed:

---

[62] Actually, human beings only face finite sets of alternative courses of action, albeit some so-called experts and books predicate sets of infinite alternatives for the sake of mathematical needs, regardless of empirical facts and common sense.

- Are there feasible courses of action independently assessed, and implemented by G?
- Might they be attainable when available resources grow scarce?
- Would they be conditional upon the prior agenda of another decision-maker?

The first question depicts a highly implausible state of the world: the political agent is not so free to choose as neoclassical and neo liberal textbooks intend us to believe; in fact, he will trade off feasibility and achievement against prior availability of resources and bounded rationality. The second question has a positive answer, although it needs an additional qualification since agendas do not hang merely on resources but on adversarial moves from other political agents as well. Although the third question refers to current hindrances, it amounts to a hard issue to cope with: decisions frequently are contingent not only on resources, but also on whom has chosen the list of paths of action before G could start doing his own business.

Statement of Meaning 4 – Agenda Building

By agenda building in organizations is meant a decision-making process that involves one or more groups of stakeholders and which consists of the following overlapping features:

- *stakeholders put forth a set of items that translates their preferences, interests and concerns to be discussed;*
- *each group of stakeholders seeks that most of their cherished issues be included in the list that might be lastly regarded as the definitive agenda;*
- *the negotiation of counterparts over such issues follow governance rules of the game, namely:*
  i. they must be held on behalf of the organization;

ii. in the final draft of the agenda, topics and preferences are constrained by regulatory habitats.

Different endowments of information (a context that entails asymmetric information) make some actors more powerful than others, and the problem is compounded by opportunistic behavior from all sides. On the other hand, transaction costs usually prevent weak actors with fewer resources from contesting and prevailing over stronger ones. Such circumstances point to the difference between *agenda building* (a matter of good will, choice, freedom and cooperation) and *agenda setting* (a matter of power, influence, opportunistic behavior, and confrontation); that is to say, the former endeavor maps onto cooperative, while the latter onto adversarial conflicts of interest.

Agenda building evolves out of negotiations among different groups of stakeholders, a process that broaches the following query: *What is the extent of influence for any stakeholder to decide the options that must be included and the ones that should be ruled out?*

Conversely, agenda setting unveils an adversarial political contest within any organization. For the sake of example, in most open companies with highly dispersed ownership structure, it is for senior management to draw up the agenda. However, we can watch a strikingly different picture in closely held family-owned organizations, where few people own and manage their company; in this case, the fact remains that agenda-setting would coalesce with agenda building in the end.

The Problem of Factions

Which would be the underlying causes that make the process of agenda building to be opposed to the one of agenda setting? Well, in the first place, negotiations might have gone sour. On the other hand, a dominant stakeholder might have substituted agenda setting for agenda building. Sooner or later, if such background became persistent as time passes by, it s likely that *factions* might have developed.

Any organization can be viewed like a two-tiered structure: one consisting of the whole set of political actors that work for the organization, the other as a collection of challenging subgroups of political actors (infighting over the yearly budget in any company or government branch is a case in point). The best test to know whether we should be worried or not with conflicts of interest consists in answering the question: are the subgroups in conflict keeping themselves within the boundaries of common knowledge, values and objectives held up by the organization? If one subgroup in certain organization pursues its own roadmap to the extent of damaging the organizations' agenda, then it might become relentlessly confrontational. As far as this pattern of behavior turns out to be robust, the process of agenda setting goes from bad to worse, and factions enter to play a conclusive part in the game. Let us frame this notion in detail.

Statement of Meaning 5 – Factions

We will understand by faction any subgroup within an organization that sets up a pattern of behavior whose distinctive features are the following:

- *they stick to a persistent and long-lasting bid for power against other subgroups or the whole organization;*
- *conflicts of interests become adversarial, and the challenger sets up an agenda that clashes with the one backed up by their opponents;*
- *they substitute contest and power-seeking for cooperation and common goals;*
- *their opportunistic behavior with guile may unleash a threat against the company's long-term strategies and its structure of governance.*

Frequently, the topic of factions is introduced in dark undertones. Although it is true that factions convey, more often than not, a threat to the governance of the organization, what if a group of good fellows play a beneficial role attempting to oust the bad fellows sitting on the Board or the senior management? If such were the case, it eventually becomes a coalition that changes the former governance for the better.

3.4. ORGANIZATIONS AS POLITICAL CONFLICT SYSTEMS

Let us move on further in search of the concept of purpose-built systems and delve into the political nature of conflict-systems.

Purpose-Built Systems

The mainstream definition of a purpose-built system predicates that it consists of a set of components linked by explicit relationships in pursuit of one or more purposes. Political and social actors (groups or individuals) stand for the elementary components of this construct. Interactions among components make sense within the context of transactional environments, internal or external to the organization. Finally, purposes stem from objectives, agreements, tasks and regulatory habitats for the components playing out their ongoing relationships.

Conflict-Systems

In an insightful paper, James March (1962) introduced the idea of conflict-systems, which helped him shape a perspective from which organizations in the private sector could be looked upon as evolving political coalitions whose goals are attained by persistent negotiations. It was not surprising that this work came out in *The Journal of Politics*[63] since the whole approach intended to become consequential for political analysis as well. While keeping up with the grist of his viewpoint, we are going to

---

[63] James March (1962), *The Business Firm as a Political Coalition*, The Journal of Politics, volume 24, number 4, pp. 662-678.

engineer a concept of conflict-system that may come in handy to organizations and branches of any government as well.

Statement of Meaning 6 – Political Conflict-Systems

By a political conflict-system is meant any structure with the following attributes:

- *it is a purpose-built system;*
- *conflicts of interest arise from the fact that preferred states of the system are not attainable at the same time to the mutual agreement of most components;*
- *assumptions, agendas, relationships, goals, and means, are contestable;*
- *groups of stakeholders may build up cooperative agendas or set up defiant ones, turning out into factions eventually.*

On Conflict-Systems and Political Action

As from the dawn of our century, political analysts have been nurturing mixing feelings about how the world is getting on. For one thing, the downfall of the Soviet Union and the shift of most countries towards varieties of market economies and representative democracies by the end of last century, allowed for a judicious optimism in international affairs. For the other, there were pervading developments of populism and fundamentalism, sharing a common assertion in their social and political discourse: "those who are with us are friends, and the remaining people are our foes".

It shouldn't be forgotten that the intermission between the two World Wars in the first half of last century, gave rise to a dramatic intercourse of adversarial conflicts of interest. Some scholars of that time tried to set forth countervailing governances, to the extent that one of them, Carl Schmitt

(1932), attempted to lay the foundations for the political as the inexorable struggle between friends and enemies. If we delve into the discourse of populists and fundamentalists, we will have to take into account this sort of argument by one controversial (and for many people, despicable) author who was, at the same time, a devout catholic, a virulent anti-Semite, and zealous member of the Nazi party[64]. Be that as it may, whole nations and their global, public and private governances have been fiercely vilified by the friend-enemy banner polluting their organizations with bigoted and war-like perceptions of human affairs.

3.5. THE CLINICAL APPROACH TO GOVERNANCE

Human beings usually visit a medical clinician prompted by three alternative intents:

- *Either seeking guidelines to overcome some illness, by means of treatment or surgery;*
- *or to know how the illness will unfold so as to gain time in dealing with personal and family matters before meeting their Maker;*
- *or to undergo a check-up so as to prevent ailments and, at least, put them off.*

This kind of setting furnishes a suitable metaphor to be mapped onto organizations. Actually, governance consultants, senior management, owners and directors, journalists, investment bankers, political consultants, lawyers and auditors, market analysts and regulators, usually perform a sort of clinician role, to prevent organizations from growing ill or, ultimately, to treat the ailing ones[65]. Such was the starting point of Selznick (1943) and

---

[64] He was later suspected a traitor to that movement, by which his influence waned up in the Germany political habitat during the Second World War. An available edition of *The Concept of the Political* is the one published by the University of Chicago Press, with translation, introduction, biography and notes by George Schwab, and a critical assessment by Leo Strauss on Schmitt's essay.

[65] Our own contributions to this approach can be found in Apreda (2012).

Pranger (1965), who campaigned on behalf of the so-called 'clinical approach to organizations' whereby the consultant could become an observer who provides advice for the healing and redress of unhealthy developments.

We should bear in mind that the clinical approach consists in linking facts with values. It goes without saying that companies and government branches, as well as the clinician herself, inherit values from the underlying culture and institutional habitats that shape their behavior and fashion their preferences, for better or worse. How could we take advantage of this holistic technique? The answer leads to the clinical report on conflicts of interest, and the statute of governance.

The Clinical Report on Conflicts of Interest

It consists in drawing up a report conveying, firstly, a diagnosis of the main conflicts of interest ailing the organization and, secondly, setting up a therapy to improve the governance of that organization. For the sake of illustration, in the technical appendix at the end of this chapter we provide an example to be used with a state-owned bank.

The Statute of Governance

This kind of statute embodies a compact of principles of governance and good political practices to run organizations in the flesh. It will be introduced in next section, whereas a practical expansion of this covenant to state-owned banks can be found in the already referred technical appendix.

3.6. THE STATUTE OF GOVERNANCE

For the last decades, dysfunctional governances have been a matter of the deepest concern due to pervasive waves of wheeling and dealing among corporate actors. How should we cope with this sort of illness spreading around the world? The statute of governance is one of the instruments that come in handy when using the clinical approach to organizations.

On Principles of Governance and Codes of Good Practices

At this point, three methodological provisions are worthy of being noticed:

- Principles should be enabling.
- The fewer, the better.
- Principles must not be mixed with good practices.

As for principles to be enabling, this means that they might give organizations latitude to do things without hindering its inner workings or stated goals.

Contention about the number of principles has to do with pragmatism, but also with the desirable fact that principles set forth guidelines for prudential decision-making. It should not be forgotten that the Founding Fathers needed only seven articles to set up the Constitution that still rules the United States.

Most of the time, the third concern turns out to be a thorny one. For each good practice we should be able to find its matching governance's principle. The latter involves a precept that the former translates into a real course of action. Let us deal with principles firstly, and good practices later.

Statement of Meaning 7 – Principles of Governance

By principles of governance we mean precepts, that is to say, mandatory statements about which would be the features of governance each organization will commit to follow and hold true.

When drawing up the principles, designers must avoid the kind of mistake that securities and exchange commissions in some countries made in the past when advising listed companies to implement codes of good practices: they mixed principles with good practices. For instance, by stating that the Board of Directors should have majority of independent members (which is a principle) and, at the same time, that they ought to be appointed following a staggering arrangement; also requiring a tenure of two years with only one reelection, and asking them to meet once a month to deal with the Board agenda (all of which are practices).

Precepts are a necessary step to build up well-grounded governances, but they are not sufficient; by far, they are commandments to do some things regarded as basic, almost to be accepted without opposition on behalf of the organization's interests and values. However, principles usually lack of functionality. They tell us "what we must do", but remain silent about how they should come down to earth. It will be for the so-called "good practices" to cope with this problem, placing any governance structure into the pragmatics of political action[66].

Statement of Meaning 8 – Codes of Good Practices

By a code of good practices is meant a list of political activities which meets the following requirements:

- *each of them derives from a specific principle of governance;*
- *their intended purpose consists in giving contexts of application to principles;*
- *they abide by the law and the regulatory framework within which the organization runs its daily businesses;*
- *they are operational, that is to say, they are employable, observable, time-scalable, contestable, and upgradeable.*

---

[66] See Apreda (2009, 2007) for details and examples.

It is to be noticed that codes of good practices are not compulsory but discretionary. Broadly speaking, in most countries they are not regulated, except for their financial institutions; in this regard, a comparative study can be found in Lopez Iturriaga (2009). On the other hand, the third assertion in the definition stresses that any code must abide by the law and current regulations. We should call to mind that several social groupings display codes of practices that might be regarded efficient although being utterly illegal: namely, those widely used by mafia-like or drug-dealing organizations.

As time passes by, an increasing number of regulatory bodies are getting used to adopting a practice denoted as "comply or explain" or, alternatively, "if-not, why-not". What these expressions stand for can be briefly stated in the following way: if certain company does not want to design a code of good practices, it has the right of not having one; but in such case it must absolutely explain why it would rather have none.

Whereas codes of good practices have become customary around the world, they apply almost exclusively to listed companies, either financial or non-financial, which publicly trade their shares and bonds either in stocks or over-the-counter exchanges. Therefore, the codes are naturally constricted only to a slim batch of companies, most of them doing businesses in countries displaying the Anglo-Saxon style of governance. In the realm of private governance, however, most companies do not issue securities to be placed through public offers, and their ownership structure hinges upon the so-called "closed and family-owned companies"[67]. It is our viewpoint that we ought to give heed to any sort of organization worldwide (either closed or open companies); furthermore, it does not seem sensible to limit the universe of organizations only to profit-seekers; hence, we must also allow for local and regional cooperatives, state-owned companies, venture capital and private equity investment funds, government agencies[68], and the like.

---

[67] On private placements and closed companies, see Carey et al. (1993).
[68] Hansmann (2000) even assimilates a corporation to a cooperative of creditors. For key remarks on such topic, see section 7.1. b), chapter 7.

The Statute of Governance

In keeping with our line of argument, we strongly advocate that a specific statute of governance should be designed for each type of organization. Such statute will be contingent upon the agreement of the board of directors and should be passed as a by-law through an ordinary meeting of the relevant owners or stakeholders. It goes without saying that if the organization were not a corporation, instead of a board we would point out to the supervisory body that fits best with its purpose.

Statement of Meaning 9 – The Statute of Governance

By Statute of Governance we mean a construct consisting of two interrelated components:

- *the principles chosen by the organization as the foundation of its governance;*
- *the operational practices that stem from each principle.*

The statute of governance cannot be regarded only as a list of principles and good practices that stand apart from each other, because there must be a focal correspondence between them: for each principle the organization formally adopts some practices linked with such principle. It is for the supervisory body and the governors to make the statute not only binding but also performing. Moreover, it is for the statute to highlight those precepts from which the governance of the organization can be explained, while good practices entail the pragmatic instances whereby those principles can walk in real life.

Relationships between the Statute, the Foundational Charter and the Law

What are the linkages among the foundational charter, regulations and the statute of governance? The charter and the compact of regulations pertaining to any organization are separate vehicles of governance that convey relevant features to take into account when drawing up the statute (on this point, see chapter 4, section 4.3). Neither the charter nor regulations should be embedded in the statute, albeit some features from each of them can connect the dots; that is to say there will be overlapping among some issues, as well as cross-references relating principles and good practices to provide coherence in some particulars only.

The Statute of Governance and Politics

To believe that the statute of governance is a miraculous medicine for any kind of dysfunctional governance would be an unwarranted assumption. It is my contention that the statute fosters better organizations from the institutional standpoint, although we can't assume it entails the end of the illness, but rather a treatment and a heedful course of action. Beyond certain point, the ailments of governance remit their case to the political conflict-system underpinning any organization.

Be that as it may, outdated categories of thought, both in political and economic viewpoints only make for precarious and slippery decision-making, preventing many organizations and agencies of government from dealing with current issues employing the right frame of mind. As the neuroscientist Lakoff (2009) asserted in his book *The Political Mind*, human beings at the dawn of the twenty first century are still slaving themselves with mindscapes that belong to the eighteenth and nineteenth centuries.

3.7. THE POLITICS OF DUAL GOVERNANCE

There are blurring boundaries between organizations in the private and public realms. Nothing illustrates better this situation that the fuzzy nature of state-owned firms. On the one hand, they behave as private entities; on the other hand, they are state-owned, which means a kind of public inner structure. Should we study their governance through their separate components? Overwhelming evidence points to the fact that in doing so, we would lose meaningful features that arise out of the synergy of both governances, since each of them cannot do without the other. Hence, we should learn to handle these arrangements by means of a more embracing perspective that we denote *dual governance*. We will move on to an organization that makes use of dual governance: any state-owned bank.

Dual Governance

In many countries around the world, there are state-owned airlines. In that fashion, they perform their job contesting with private companies for the same customer base. From outer appearances, both types of organizations seem similar. But they are not.

Firstly, private airlines entail a type of corporate governance whereby owners mostly seek earnings, market share and profits. These companies compete – fiercely, I would add – among them; besides, in the last decades several well-known enterprises, denoted "low-cost", have been trying to persuade a wide spate of travelers to fly in their planes without frills whatsoever so as to pay less for their tickets.

Secondly, a state-owned airline exhibits a sort of hybrid governance. On the one hand, it behaves like a private company, as if it were also a commercial carrier. On the other hand, the state is the owner of the airline, and profit is not the most important purpose, being substituted by sovereignty, national interest, social commitments, fiduciary duties, and geopolitical grounds.

Thirdly, the interplay of both roles, acting as a commercial and a state firm, do not make things easier to state-firms in comparison with their counterparts in the private realm. To begin with, destinations, crews, maintenance, local and foreign branches, all mean quite different issues, cost structures and strategic concerns. But to the detriment of private carriers, most of the time state-owned airlines resort to exemptions and monopolies, being the tax-system foremost among them.

As we reach this point, we wonder: which is the most suitable governance to favor state-owned airlines? Should we focus on the private or the public alternative? This may be regarded as a puzzle; it is not. There is no denying that to understand this kind of hybrid organization a different standpoint will be required, revolving around what I call dual governance[69]:

Statement of Meaning 10 – Dual Governance

By dual governance we are to mean a system whose main components are

- *a setting that stems from public governance;*
- *another one that is peculiar to private governance;*
- *albeit their interconnections arise from a higher structure consisting of functional relationships which come defined by political design in pursuit of the common good.*

The foregoing statement highlights two important characteristics of dual governance: it is a system with only two components comprising different governances, one pertaining to the private realm, the other to the public one; on the other hand, the political conflict-system that arises out of this compact stands in a higher level of complexity that the ones stemming from each of their single governances.

---

[69] An extensive development this issue can be followed in our book devoted to Public Governance (Apreda, 2007), where another type of dual governance is also addressed: the one regarding global organizations.

A Proposal of Dual Governance for a State-Owned Bank

We are going to set forth a new kind of governance for a state-owned bank, intended to cope with the manifold conflicts of interest that also come out in other state-firms. To put it differently, real life circumstances point to the pressing need of overhauling the whole structure of state-owned firms so widely tainted with opaque governances conniving with political clientelism and corruption. For the sake of illustration, let us firstly delve into the conventional governance running in state-owned banks nowadays.

The Conventional Governance of a State-Owned Bank

To start with, this peculiar organization performs as a commercial bank, like its siblings in the financial system of any country in the world: it has depositors and borrowers; it also entice investors to put their savings into trust funds that were set up by the bank; it carries out foreign exchange transactions for particulars and companies; it handles several ancillary services, from credit and debit cards to factoring and treasury management for any kind of firms; it hires out safe-deposit boxes, and engages itself in international trade on behalf of its customers. Last of all, it reports to the Central Bank, in compliance with the regulatory framework every bank in the field is expected to follow.

On the other hand, this organization is a state-owned firm, which amounts not only to being owned by the state, but also to discharging its operations in quest for one or more social purposes. As regards the ownership feature, it has one notional stockholder, the civil society; hence, the state must meet a pervading and ultimate fiduciary role toward society through the government agency.

The social issue is one of paramount relevance. Firstly, the bank is a non-profit organization. Thereafter, its foundational charter usually states an impressive social agenda: fostering regional economies; catering for low-income groups in need of borrowing money at lenient terms and maturities; playing a decisive role in helping small- and medium-sized companies that more often than not are neglected by private for-profit banks; managing the collection and payment of social security transfers; carrying out the role of financial representative of municipal, provincial, or federal agencies of the government; administering financial transactions that arise from judiciary commitments and social assistance to unemployed people; becoming the receiving end of tax collection; and the like.

In fact, social commitments entail advantages and disadvantages, like a two-edged sword. On the side of advantages, there are many tasks that the bank can accomplish whereas the private counterpart keeps it away from doing them; for instance, the latter does not open an office located in isolated or poverty-ridden areas, but the former meets this mission sooner or later. The latter gives a loan on account of credit-risk and profit-seeking standards, whereas the former takes other strands of analysis when granting a loan mainly on social concerns, and following the lines of the economic policy enacted by the government. On the side of disadvantages, there are deviances of behavior like political clientelism, rent-seeking, soft-budget constraints, or outright corruption which, unfortunately, become part and parcel of these organizations.

A New Governance for a State-Owned Bank[70]

Looking for more accountability and transparency, we put forward a new blueprint for the governance of any state-owned bank; in doing so, we hope to strengthen the upsides and curb the downsides of the streamlined governance reviewed in prior paragraphs.

The state-owned bank should consist of a commercial bank, as well as an internal branch with the mission of handling what I call the *subsidizing portfolio,* an expression that stands for all the tasks involved in discharging the social mission of the bank. The governor of the bank would direct both the commercial component and the subsidizing branch, each under the

---

[70] An earlier rendering of the proposal can be found in Apreda (2007).

management of separate vice-governors. We could speak, alternatively, about the CEO and his vice-presidents.

The state-owned bank will have a Board of Directors including the governor and the vice-governors in the role of executive directors but neither of them can be appointed as Chair of the Board. To fill the remaining places in the Board, only independent directors can be appointed from a list of candidates submitted by the government to the Senate.

Furthermore, there will be two non-overlapping Auditing Committees sitting in the Board, one for the commercial bank, the other for the subsidizing branch. No executive director could be appointed member of any of those committees. If an independent director belongs to one Auditing Committee, this fact prevents him from sitting in the other.

A modern approach to organizations deems that they consist of two interlocking portfolios, one containing its assets, the other its liabilities and equity; furthermore, they should be handled so that the rate of return on the former might be higher that the one on the latter. In other words, the whole organization can be regarded as a portfolio of portfolios.

When we give heed to the context of a state-owned bank, we find a more complex setting because it comprises two parallel systems of portfolios:

a) as a commercial bank, it will administer the conventional combo of assets, liabilities and equity, so as to attend the business side of its activities;
b) the subsidizing branch, consisting of one portfolio that handles the apportionment of subsidies, and another to record not only the sources of funding but also the equity structure.

For dual governance to hold in full, it must comply with the *Separation Principle*, which establishes that the composite portfolio of the commercial bank (assets, liabilities, and equity) is totally separated from the one of the subsidizing branch; a fact that also entails the separation of their financial statements, compliance risks reports, even their statements on the sources and applications of their cash flows.

The Funding of the Subsidizing Branch

As for the funding of the subsidizing branch, we have to give heed to its regular incoming and outgoing cash flows.

- *Incoming cash flows*: they will come out of provisions in the Annual Budget of the federal government, enforced by the Congress, and handled either by the Ministry of Economy, the Treasury, or the Central Bank.
- *Outgoing cash flows*: they will be allocated for subsidizing projects and related operations, only under approval of the Board of Directors and after the considered opinion of the pertinent Auditing Committee.

Some Remarks Regarding the Subsidizing Branch

An alternative approach to the foregoing proposal would consist in constraining the state-owned bank to perform as a commercial unit, whereas setting up another state-owned bank to fulfill social commitments. Nonetheless, there are at least three objections to this approach.

In most countries, experience shows state-owned banks handling both roles; there is no telling evidence against the suitability of this sort of arrangement, albeit many criticisms could be raised on the quality of their governance.

Notwithstanding the fact that the sort of dual governance brought forward above cannot prevent conflicts of interest from arising, chances are that a state-owned bank only devoted to social purposes could compound many times conflicts of interest and become a vehicle co-opted for clientelism and all-pervasive corruption.

While some companies or single political actors, as well as municipalities, provinces and state-owned firms avail themselves of the subsidizing branch, it is frequent that they also become time-honored customers of the commercial counterpart, in operations and transactions that do not involve the subsidizing portfolio (for instance, working-capital loans, current accounts, short-term deposits, credit and debit cards, and the like); this context stresses how functional dual governance can become in the end.

TECHNICAL APPENDIX

The Clinical Report Pertaining to a State-Owned Bank

Before drawing up the clinical report, we are going to single out the bank's most frequent sources of conflicts: infringements to the Fiduciary Role, accountability and transparency failures, rent-seeking and soft-budget constraints.

Infringements to the Fiduciary Role

Overwhelming evidence points to the fact that the Board of Directors carries out a fiduciary role on behalf of the State only on the surface owed to their connivance with the incumbent government and political groups of interest. Apparently, the Board of Directors acts as the principal towards senior management, but the latter becomes most of the time an unfriendly contestant of the agency relationship, because as the saying goes "directors come and go, whereas the professional staff remains and thrives".

Accountability and Transparency Failures

It has been an outrageous and long-standing tradition of state-owned banks in Latin American, African and Asian countries as from the twentieth century and thereafter, to openly flout the law, disregarding constitutional tenets, and trespassing any standard of good accountability and transparency. It could not come as a surprise that state-owned banks had become lenient partners in setting a pattern of misbehavior, reinforced by their autarchy that amounts to budgetary independence and its inbuilt no-bankruptcy covenant.

Opportunistic Behavior with Guile through Rent-Seeking and Soft-Budget Constraints

The state-owned bank performs as a commercial bank, getting access to resources offered by households, companies, foundations, cooperatives, government branches, by means of current and saving accounts. In case the bank had issued bonds, it would have also drawn funding from investors in the capital market. But those variegated tasks pose daunting problems:

a) Does the Board of Directors usually assess any prospective loan not only matching the Central Bank regulations, but also constraining its members to the duties of loyalty and care?
b) Is the bank tunneling resources from depositors and bondholders' accounts so as to fund its subsidizing mission, or the other way around?

Looking more deeply into such problems, two types of dysfunctional habits arise: rent-seeking and soft-budget constraints.

On Rent-Seeking

From a political viewpoint, the state-owned bank must be regarded as the place where contestant groups of interest try to extract rents for their own benefit (rent-seeking). For instance, business firms in pursuit of subsidized loans, with longer maturities than similar ones granted by private banks, albeit they bear substandard risk qualifications; or the bank's oversized bureaucracy that is ready to claim, through its trade union, a slice of any increment in operational cash flows.

On Soft-Budget Constraints

The state-owned bank comes down as a double-edged instrument that nurtures opportunistic behavior with guile:

Firstly, as the bank lays claim on its subsidizing instruments, cash flows are allocated with an underlying pledge to rescue the beneficiaries facing any predicament on their loans and endorsements already granted, even to the extent of concealing any budgetary misdoing by means of creative accounting.

Secondly, since the bank cannot go bankrupt (this being a provision in its own Charter), there is a primary soft-budget constraint that becomes functional to the sustainability of the institution, which wedges a gap open to mismanagement, even to abuse of power.

Lastly, managers and the bank's staff, not bearing tight budget constraints and with the trade union on their side, encourage and advocate the opening of new offices as well as the increasing of their staffs.

Clinical Report on Conflicts of Interest in a State-Owned Bank

Part 1: Diagnosis

There are infringements to the fiduciary role, accountability and transparency whose consequences were enlarged in the prior sub-sections, in particular the following ones:

- Opportunistic behavior through rent-seeking and soft-budget constraints might lead to corruption practices.
- Incoming and outgoing cash flows from the commercial bank are mingled with the ones from the subsidizing branch by hiding these transactions through creative accounting and blame avoidance concoctions.

Part 2: Therapy

In section 3.7, we set forth a proposal intended to furnish any state-owned bank with a new type of governance. Needless to say, the following therapeutic guidelines will draw from such design.

It must be enforced the *Separation Principle* that requires for the commercial bank to be separated from the subsidizing branch. This principle is to be included in the bank's statute of governance.

The Board must consist of independent directors, appointed by agreement with the Congress, so that members of social, business, education and trade unions could be chosen in all fairness.

The bank's charter and its statute of governance must establish how the bank will be held accountable for operating the subsidizing branch.

The bank has to manage its commercial financial statements, compliance risks reports, and the statement of sources and applications of cash flows independently from the ones appertaining to the subsidizing branch, and the other way around.

The management and staff ought to be appointed by public contest and their career in office articulated to a law or statute on civil service. The CEO of the bank cannot be Chair of the Board, only executive director.

Acting as a commercial organization the bank must perform its activities on equal foot with its counterparts in the private sector.

A pair of compliance functions should be enacted: one for the commercial bank; the other to deal with compliance risks that stem from its subsidizing role.

Under no circumstances, incoming and outgoing cash flows from the commercial bank should be commingled with the ones from the subsidizing branch, and the other way around.

The Statute of Governance Applied to a State-Owned Bank

Within the dual governance that we have advocated for state-owned banks, the following principles and practices nest together. However, the sample is only a blueprint, and under no circumstances it intends to be portrayed as the best or the only one available. Bear in mind that the following is the statute embracing the whole organization. It goes without saying that some divisions of the bank could require their own statutes of governances, like we saw in chapter 2, section 2.7, when we referred to compliance risks.

Related to the Charter

Principle 1
The state-owned bank stands for a legal entity that is able to perform as a commercial bank.

> *Practice 1* The bank Charter will spell out its commercial tasks as a lender and borrower, also allowing it to manage investment funds on behalf of its customers (fiduciary funds, trust funds, and the like), foreign currency transactions, credit and debit cards on behalf of its customers, safe-deposit boxes, and the like.

Principle 2
The state-owned bank enters into a covenant with the State so as to establish an agency relationship regarding the subsidizing branch, which will be devoted to accomplish social goals and commitments.

> *Practice 1* The features of the partnership covenant broached in the principle above should be included in the bank's Charter.
> *Practice 2* The funding of the subsidizing branch stems from the Federal Annual Budget of the country, or the bank's accumulated earnings from previous periods, by apposite allocation of resources.
> *Practice 3* The state-owned bank is not allowed to either allocate funds or withdraw funds from the subsidizing branch to favor the commercial bank, or the other way round.

Practice 4 In practice, the subsidizing portfolio will be managed like a mutual fund.

Practice 5 The bank protects separate entitlements for the commercial bank and the subsidizing branch, without any overlapping of tasks between them.

Related to the Board of Directors

Principle 3
The Board of Directors in the state-owned bank must consist of a majority of independent and non-executive directors.

Practice 1 Membership is restricted to qualified and proficient people, recruited from non-governmental organizations, business chambers, universities, trade unions, and practitioners. Membership on the grounds of exclusive political affiliation is strictly forbidden. The total number of directors sitting on the Board must be even.

Practice 2 The only executive directors in the Board will be the CEO and the vice-presidents of the commercial bank and the subsidizing branch.

Practice 3 Tenure for non-executive directors is granted for three years, with only one renewal option. The choice of three years insures overlapping with successive governments[71], whereas a mechanism for staggering directors is encouraged, as it happens in many companies around the world.

Practice 4 The Chair of the Board must be an independent director and cannot belong to any Auditing Committee. None of the executive directors can be appointed as Chair of the Board.

---

[71] This span of time holds for government whose tenure in office follows a four-year pattern, and it was only chosen for the sake of illustration.

Principle 4
The Board of Directors must comprise two Auditing Committees, one for the commercial bank, the other for the subsidizing branch.

Practice 1 Both Auditing Committees are independent of each other, and no member in one of them can perform as director in the other.

Practice 2 Neither the CEO nor the vice presidents of the commercial and the subsidizing branch can belong to any of the Auditing Committees.

Related to Accountability

Principle 5
The Charter and by-laws must spell out, in detail, which are the commitments and responsibilities of the state-owned bank, either for the commercial bank or the subsidizing branch.

Practice 1 Directors and managers will be held accountable for their deeds, during and after tenure, in the terms of judiciary, administrative and control institutions. Their tenure in a state-owned bank qualifies as a duty to public service.

Practice 2 Stakeholders must get access to full disclosure of a considered performance report of how well or badly officials and directors meet their commitments and responsibilities.

Practice 3 The Board can request, and the bank must pay for, the so-called *"fairness opinion"*[72] from independent gatekeepers,

---

[72] A *Fairness Opinion* consists in a report submitted by an independent gatekeeper at the request of the Board. It certifies fairness to stakeholders, or the fulfillment of fiduciary duties, for any prospective transaction for which the Board could feel afraid of becoming liable eventually if due care and prudence were not granted in dealing with the transaction.

any time an accountability issue should arise, casting doubts on certain decision-making project still in progress.

Related to Transparency

Principle 6
The state-owned bank must disclose material information to the public in full.

Practice 1 The commercial bank and the subsidizing branch will release, independently from each other, their financial statements, clinical reports on conflicts of interest, and their compliance risks reports, all of them duly certified by external auditors.
Practice 2 All information disclosed by the bank, and certified by external auditors, will also elicit the certification and liability commitments from all members of the Board of Directors, including the Chief Executive Officer.
Practice 3 Investors and analysts, watchdogs and regulatory agencies will gain access to the full review of credit and risk ratings; such information will be disclosed once a year.

Related to the Management

Principle 7
Under no circumstances, the Chief Executive Officer can be Chair of the Board.

Practice 1 The CEO must be appointed among the members of the current management, although it can also be hired outside the bank, as it happens in the corporate world. He cannot be a political appointee.

Practice 2 The Board of Directors handles the package of remuneration and incentives to the management, by appointing a committee consisting of independent directors only.

Related to the Compliance Function

Principle 8

If compliance risks matter for private banking, this should become an issue of the utmost relevance for state-owned banks on the grounds of their dual governance structure.

Practice 1 The CEO's office will submit two Statutes of Governance Risks[73] to the Board for their approval and afterwards, make both of them enforceable: one for the commercial bank, the other for the subsidizing branch.

Practice 2 The state-owned bank must set forth and make operational two compliance functions: one for the commercial bank, the other for the subsidizing branch. Such functions, whose main objective is to cope with compliance risks, have to be independent areas reporting to the CEO's office but also, whenever is material, to each of the Auditing Committees in the Board of Directors.

CONCLUSION

The starting point of this chapter showed the main characters on the stage of any organization as well as their playing fields; among the former,

---

[73] In chapter 2, section 2.7, a sample of this statute was provided in full.

we pointed to claimants, stakeholders, complainants and discontents; among the latter, to transactional environments. Following an unconventional perspective about conflicts of interest, we made the contrast between cooperative and adversarial conflicts, moving on next to introduce the subject of multiple conflicts facing contexts of mutuality of interest; afterwards, it was given heed to agenda building, agenda setting and the thorny issue of factions. Taking advantage of such spadework, it followed that any organization or government agencies can be regarded as political conflict systems.

Governance not only grows older, but also dysfunctional, ailing, or deviant. Coming across these events prompts for solutions, treatment and cure, or a radical change of the former governance. To cope with many-sided conflicts pervading organizations, it was put forward the so-called clinical approach to governance, which employs two promising application tools: the clinical report on conflict of interests and the statute of governance.

Because dual governance carries weight with state-owned firms and social democracies, the subject was enlarged not only on meaning, but also in consequences. Last but not least, a new proposal for state-owned banks was set forth, including samples of their clinical report on conflicts of interest and statutes of governance

Chapter 4

DYSFUNCTIONAL GOVERNANCE, THE CAPTURE OF THE STATE, AND CORRUPTION

ABSTRACT

This chapter starts with the notion of dysfunctional governance, moving on later to opaque constructions. Next, it deals with regulations, gatekeepers, and connivance. State-capture is the subject that comes after, focusing on groups of interest, clientelism, corporatism, fascism, populism and corruption. Lastly, the main vehicles of state-capture are brought to light: namely, rent seeking, soft-budget constraints, and tunneling.

INTRODUCTION

The running of organizations and governments in real life raises many puzzles, among which the following one is conspicuous: what happens if certain organization deserts from working well, or forsakes its own governance? To shed light on this predicament, two remarks seem timely:

- firstly, any organization carries on a distinctive governance, from plainly designed ones as it happens with small companies or start-ups, to complex architectures as those conveyed by transnational corporations or government branches;
- secondly, any organization turns out to be a social arrangement dependent on its particular kind of governance.

Dysfunctional governances are a fact of life; something is wrong, out of order, unfitting, and it must be fixed. Nevertheless, and very often, they evolve on purpose, to take advantage of opaqueness that allows for a new and hidden governance to replace the older and visible structure. To what extent this substitution can be successful? The answer points to the regulators and gatekeepers who may connive with deviant organizations and branches of government. The capture of the State is strongly related with the leniency of the watchdogs and this turns out to be the reason why powerful organizations lay siege to institutions and co-opt the government so as to keep themselves away from control, blame and punishment. The end result, commonly known as corruption, is linked with a cluster of stepping-stones that bring such detrimental process into completion: clientelism, corporatism, populism and fascism. Lastly and for the sake of a telling picture, the chapter concludes with the main vehicles of state-capture: rent seeking, soft-budget constraints and tunneling.

4.1. DYSFUNCTIONAL GOVERNANCE

Each organization evolves, changing for better or worse; at times, the consequences of certain mutation disrupt its workings, even threatening its survival, in which case we say that *its governance has become dysfunctional*. And what happens with the underlying organization? In the face of such process, there are several contingencies to consider, among which we point to a couple of them: a) either the variation is brought about by factors beyond the control of the organization, like turmoil in the markets, latest regulations, impending government crisis, sweeping changes in international relationships; b) or the disturbance stems from within, either because the organization has grown beyond the old governance, or it has been spoilt by management mishandling. Let us give heed to three likely avenues on the side of internal mutations.

Failing Governance

As long as the organization develops, it needs to adapt itself to new circumstances, more complex and demanding than the prior ones. It may also be the case that the primitive governance does not fit any longer, that is to say, it has become dysfunctional.

To give an example suitable for small companies, we can delve into the problem of the founder's retirement, which means that the current governance should be superseded by a different one. The founding father will be followed by his inheritors, an event that raises a thorny issue: we could confront the reluctance of the old man and his staff to change, or perhaps they wish to close the company ever. Bear in mind that over his active life, he managed the firm on the grounds of his self-proclaimed wisdom and experience, without any contest or threat springing from any quarter.

How could the gap be narrowed between the old style of government and the one brought in by newcomers? It won't be surprising to know that most of the small- and medium-sized companies do not survive beyond the first or second generation. In other words, the dramatic shift from the time-honored parental governance towards a new one that puts up with disagreement or innovative strategies, it uncovers the fact that the former has become outmoded, whereas the latter stems from negotiating with siblings, in-laws, cousins, professional managers and consultants. If the company can't cope with this challenge, it will certainly be looking for trouble.

Failing Internal Politics

When carrying on its daily job, the management or the supervisory board may not keep up to expectations, and things may go from bad to worse. The failure ought to be tracked down to the way governors mishandle their organization; in other words, it's not the governance that should be blamed, but the politics, the craft of governing any social arrangement.

Unfortunately, examples of this kind of dysfunctional governance are countless, not only because of the sheer number of mismanaged organizations but also their blatant disregard of the law and fiduciary duties they ought to have complied with. Enron and Lehman Brothers in the United States are regarded as epitomes of how malfeasance and fraud can ultimately lead hundreds of companies to go under.

A Mockery of Governance

The implosion of the Soviet Union at the beginning of the 1990s entailed consequential outcomes to be confronted by Russia and her former confederate states; for instance, they realized that if they wanted to go through the road of representative democracies and capitalist markets, forceful decisions had to be taken on their state-owned enterprises: namely, how those huge concerns might look for financial support from international lenders, and how to build up a locally dependable capital market. For this to be accomplished, the companies had to converge towards the styles of governance western firms had been using for decades, with at least two connotations:

To begin with, companies had to issue tradable shares, set up boards of directors and a professional management, hold Annual Shareholders Meetings, take into account compliance risks, submit themselves to credit-risk ratings, and likewise.

By the same token, the former state-owned enterprise had to be shaped up like a limited-liability company, with a foundational charter and provisions to abide by the prevailing legislation in New York, London,

Zurich and Tokyo, to name some likely locations suitable for making public offers of stock and bonds[74].

As the vaunted privatization process took off, it showed how wanting the new enterprises stood in complying with regular standards of good faith, care and diligence; but this would not be so amazing if we recalled the incumbent government inherited what amounts to an authoritarian strand pervading the history of Russia for centuries, with utter disregard of law, accountability and transparency.

Although the governance of new companies was experimental for the time being, it triggered off widespread corruption with the connivance of the main players in the Western markets, giving rise to the infamous outpouring of the Gang of Oligarchs who had formerly been prominent members of the Russian elite (Nomenklatura), and now were struggling for the highest echelons of economic power. Instead of functional governances, this early development brought to light what can be called "the governance of mockery and shame"[75].

4.2. OPAQUE GOVERNANCE

After reviewing the implications of dysfunctional governances, we can address a key concept in this chapter[76].

---

[74] Naomi Klein's book (2008) on the devastating consequences for many countries in the 80s and 90s following the ill-advised plans devised by neo liberal technocrats working for international organizations and conservative think tanks, it comes down as a must-read. We will return to Klein in chapter 6, when dealing with her viewpoint on the so-called "disaster capitalism".

[75] Hoffman's (2011) book is an extremely useful work on the uprising and thriving of the gang of oligarchs.

[76] Up to our knowledge, the first operational definition of the expression "opaque governance" in the current literature can be traced back in Apreda (2012).

Statement of Meaning 1 – Opaque Governance

By *Opaque Governance* we mean a substitution process whose main features and outcomes are the following:

- there is a persistent and purposeful design for misconstruing the original governance of the organization;
- such process hinges upon three sustainable procedures: the accountability structure is shadowed, transparency morphs into mere window-dressing, there is a systematic flouting of fiduciary duties;
- the original governance of the organization is taken over by a new one, whereas the organization counterclaims that no change had taken place in actual fact.

As we can ascertain from the foregoing paragraph, opaque governance amounts to a complex blueprint for deceit and glaring neglect of truth, accountability, transparency and reliability. Nevertheless, one must bear in mind that we can have organizations with dysfunctional governance but without entering in the process of substitution that leads to opacity[77]. Contrariwise, if the governance were opaque, then it would be dysfunctional.

There are several contexts that perform like enablers and facilitators of any opaque governance, and we intend to display a couple of them: one that nurtures deviant behavior like rent-seeking, soft-budget constraints, tunneling, which will be handled in section 4.5. Another that fosters criminal behavior, like drug dealing, terrorism, smuggling, criminal offshore arrangements, financial misdeeds and, increasingly, ecocide; they will be worked out in next chapter.

---

[77] For instance, let us consider a family-owned company that must solve the transition from the "founding father" model towards one focused on inheritors.

Example

Imagine that in your town there is a well-known chain of stores which is owned and controlled by the same family, catering for households and offices that need their clothes and sheets to be washed, dried and ironed. We are speaking, of course, of a chain of laundries. Their governance exhibits two levels: the lower one runs each store; the higher level refers to the company that owns all the stores, what entails a more complex design of governance, with an organization charter in compliance with the regulatory framework for this sort of business. Last of all, as the owners are updated managers themselves, they have thought up and enforced a statute of governance[78], so as to have an edge in a very competitive market. Their going concern has been growing successfully for the last five years, enjoying an extremely loyal customer base.

One day, however, the owners were persuaded to sell the whole business to a powerful group of entrepreneurs who were determined to keep the structure and purposes of the former organization, inclusive of staff and managers, the network of branches, and the old building where their main office had been located through those years. Furthermore, employees and professionals who had been working for the former company received a remuneration package much more advantageous than the one they had been paid up to that moment. Nevertheless, two changes were introduced: firstly, they contributed with another building for the location of the new company's headquarters, leaving the older place to exclusively handling the affairs of the laundry concern. Secondly, a small group of new employees and professionals were accommodated at the new venue and provided with state-of-the-art equipment. The majority of this staff came with impressive qualifications, including lawyers, accountants, financial analysts, computer-system wizards, and some scientists; these human resources were paid handsomely and their workplaces met first-rate standards.

There was another innovation brought in the organization by the new owners. They designed a second type of governance, carefully hidden from

---

[78] This issue was enlarged in chapter 3.

outsiders (among them, the customer base of the laundries, their former suppliers, and the Internal Revenue Service) and insiders (mainly the former employees and managers). This second governance was handled from the new headquarters, and its real business consisted in laundering money from drug dealings. For the pair of governances to cohere at the end of the day, a new set of invoices, bills and receipts, with the logo of the former laundry were issued to record incomes from the drug business. Afterwards, the financial statements required by regulations would conceal a proportion of the newly printed bills (let us say, fifty per cent of them) as if they were coming from a largely fictitious customer base, whereas the huge increase of expenses were disguised as salaries and fees for staff and directors, additional investment in cutting edge technology of laundering, and the refurbishing of branches and the older premises. It goes without saying that a promiscuous portion of the earnings from the drug business didn't need to follow this accountancy road, being tunneled instead by the company towards offshore locations, with countervailing expense receipts from fake suppliers and phantom staff (for instance, by using the remaining printed invoices to mask fictional and countervailing earnings). Hence, one slice of the drug earnings was embedded into the financial statements of the core laundry business, while the remnants of such income were allocated into an offshore black hole. The harvest from laundering ended up in banks under the guise of saving and premium investments accounts, whereas the tunneling of resources (handled by the same banks, as a matter of course) was cloaked into offshore societies.

It is not surprising that this story of swindling and crime unveils what I am going to call in next chapter "governance of the organized crime". What is outraging, however, is the ease by which these concoctions are put into use, with the connivance of investment and commercial banks, lawyers, accountants, business consultants, financial advisors, regulators, judges, and politicians. By the same token, parallel stories could be told about chains of hotels, commercial airlines, land-transport companies, container carriers, shipping companies and the like.

4.3. REGULATIONS, GATEKEEPERS, AND CONNIVANCE

In this section, and for the sake of illustration, let us start with some well-known features ingrained through the financial system, to shift afterwards into more far-reaching contexts of application.

One thing is to realize that the global financial system actually feeds internal mechanisms that lead to instability. But quite another thing seems to admit that internal players, loopholes in the regulation framework, as well as pervading scheming among governments, investment banks and portfolio managers, gatekeepers, consultants, and even stakeholders, all of them bring damage to households, enterprises, pension funds, and taxpayers over whole economies; if in doubt, look back on the meltdown that took place in 2007-2008. It was Hyman Minsky (1986) who researched since the 1960s the nature of financial stability. However, academics and practitioners derided his work until the meltdown in 2007 proved him to be correct. Minsky was an outstanding macroeconomist, a staunch critic of unbridled financial capitalism, and not only a witness but also a victim of conspiracies to which professionals, journalists and academics, likely in the payroll of financial institutions, universities and think tanks, eagerly engaged themselves in campaigns of slur and slandering[79].

Therefore, it seems plausible to argue whether the regulatory framework ought to have prevented abuses of the so-called "financial system in the shadows", a subject matter that triggers off relevant issues to be discussed here in a much broader framework than the one previously related to banks:

- What are the differences between regulatory and discretionary governance?
- What is the extent to which regulations can become enforceable?
- How should regulations be shaped up?
- What can be said about the deep-seated hypocrisy of the Preacher's waiver?

---

[79] The same sort of despicable attack was launched in the 1960s against the great environmentalist Rachel Carson, financed by multinationals in the business of ecocide, as we are going to notice in chapter 5, sections 5.5 and 5.6.

Regulatory and Discretionary Governance

Broadly speaking, governance portrays a two-tiered structure. On the one hand, it is what regulators request as a matter of fact; on the other hand, directors and managers, as well as governors in the public sector enjoy the advantage of improving the governance of their organizations beyond the scope of regulators. *In the former case, we speak of regulatory, whereas in the latter of discretionary governance.*

Whenever an organization comes into existence, it will come up against a complex body of regulations regarding its peculiar type of activity. For instance, a public company must be incorporated, which gives it a law-abiding corporate personality comprising both rights and liabilities. Henceforth, a well-defined kind of information has to be released in a compulsory way, either at the incorporation date or, from that moment onwards, under the guise of periodic disclosures established on accountancy and fiscal duties, as well as claims from stock exchanges or ultimate lenders in the banking system.

To say the least, regulatory governance adds up to decision-making constraints. In the incorporation procedure the company unveils its ownership structure, the board of directors composition, the frequency they will arrange for their meetings, the rights of block-holders and minorities, the way directors and managers discharge their fiduciary duties, the assortment of commitments and responsibilities falling upon directors or managers, and the like.

If the organization does not match the corporation model[80], being a cooperative for example, the regulator will tell the founders how to design such particular architecture, what type of internal supervisory body will be required, how extensive will be the latitude of managerial functions, and how to cope with the conflicting roles of owners or beneficiaries in their usually strained relationship with the senior management.

Nevertheless, regulatory governance only amounts to established viewpoints about a variegated collection of organizations, leaving to the

---

[80] Hansman (2000) seems a worthy reference about the nature of a wide sort of alternative organizations.

discretion of owners, directors, and managers the fine-tuning of their governance systems. Such degree of freedom must be welcomed since it allows any organization to make a difference with its competitors, establishing more reliable ties with stakeholders, fostering both transparency and accountability, and nurturing a culture in the workplace that would increase the social and commercial worth of the going concern. However, more often than not, discretionary governance turns out to be an apt device for deceit and malfeasance, through opacity or, still worse, the engineering of organized crime.

What Is the Extent to Which Regulations Can Become Enforceable?

In most countries, there are several institutions in charge of interpreting and making regulations enforceable for organizations according the type they belong to. For the sake of illustration, let us discuss financial institutions. They have two main regulators: central banks and securities exchange commissions. In the first case, regulation consists in a legal structure that determines when and how a financial institution is allowed to exist, and a battery of resolutions or decrees by which the central banks set operational restraints to lending, borrowing, investing and transacting in domestic and foreign currencies. In the second case, securities and exchange commission deal with listed banks that place their equity and bonds through the public offer mechanism, as well as with qualified intermediaries, from brokers to dealers, engaged with publicly primary and secondary placements.

A striking feature that stems from reviewing the role of regulators is that they busy themselves with banks and their customers, mainly listed companies, what amounts to brushing aside the bulk of corporate actors that meddle, produce, exchange and distribute goods in the down-to-earth economy. There is no denying that usually regulators even skip some players in the shadowy financial system, for instance investment portfolios and offshore companies. It's worth delving into this matter in greater detail since such behavior is not blameless but complicit with a political system that disregards law and fairness.

Non-listed companies, by far the majority of organizations all around the world, remain technically closed firms, most of the time being family-owned enterprises, under the guise of small, medium or large companies; whereas in the Anglo-Saxon tradition both public offers and capital markets are well developed, nine out of ten countries in the world do not follow this tradition and their companies currently borrow from institutional investors and banks, whose loans can be assimilated to privately placed debt (Carey et al. (1993).

There are financial intermediaries that run their businesses in the so-called [81] *"shadowy financial system"*, which embraces a host of non-regulated corporate actors shielded from the control of any central bank or security exchange commission; within such that variegated group, we must spotlight the following big players:

- non-regulated financial intermediaries running their transactions either in the so-called Eurobond Market for deposits and bonds[82], or in offshore locations;
- institutional investors that engineer conduits for private placements;
- investment funds that offer both offshore locations and a motley assortment of financial vehicles to investors and borrowers alike, in particular Hedge Funds.

Many companies borrow or lend money through offshore locations or special purpose vehicles (SPVs; that is to say, financial instruments that are issued by putting previous ones as collateral) in pursuit of some definite objective, by means of private placements that skip over the overlooking of central banks, securities exchange commissions or internal revenue services in their native onshore locations.

---

[81] An expression used in the Basel Bank Report on Special Purpose Entities (2009). They are also referred to special purpose vehicles.
[82] On the Euromarket's nature and consequences, see Palan's book about offshore locations (2003).

No wonder then, after reading this list of makers and users, that the majority of transactions are not regulated or controlled; or still worse, that financial systems frequently evolve towards instability, so persuasively described by Minsky (1986). In point of fact, such appalling circumstances can be regarded as the offspring of neo liberalism, conservative governments (Thatcher, Reagan, and the Bush) and the lobby carried out by bank, hedge funds, and multinationals. Adding insult to injury, is it not shocking that the above-mentioned engineering brings about huge profits from opaque governance concoctions that so shamelessly flout the rule of law?

How Should Regulations Be Shaped Up?

To answer this question, two political procedures are open to discussion and implementation: either current regulation is improved, or new ones will be created. This is of the essence, albeit there are always risks in the enactment of regulations. Firstly, let us deal with the options, and later with the risks.

Improving Current Regulation

Something is wrong with regulations in most political and economic fields of practice. And there is a growing awareness that the problem doesn't lie only in private and public activities, but also is compounded by how regulators ultimately do their job. It goes without saying that regulators have to upgrade their own governance.

New Regulation to Fight Connivance

Regulations must be streamlined to deal with compliance risks by meeting two requirements: they must be simple to understand and put to use; and they must be enforceable.

The reader will think that such approach is easier said than done, but we have to bear in mind that a skeptical attitude on this subject has been nourished on purpose along decades. Firstly, by a lasting connivance of bankers, lawyers, accountants, economists, businessmen, politicians and lawmakers, who have been crafting blame avoidance vehicles, lenient laws and off-shore locations; secondly, by their capture of the state through corruption, rent-seeking, and opaque governance. This has been the way the ball bounced back: by laying the foundations of a connivance counterculture hostile to better governance. Surely, we must fight the battle against criminal complacency and secrecy, once and for all.

The Risks of Regulation and the Missionary's Zeal

Regulators ought to redress wrongs, but they also commit wrongs on their own, mainly when they undertake their job with what I call the 'missionary's zeal' *whereby they assume that the more regulations are enacted, the better the world becomes.* A clinical approach to regulatory organizations conveys a self-evident diagnostic and treatment: firstly, upgrade their governance and, secondly, make them more accountable, transparent and diligent.

Lack of Incentives and the Revolving Door

Notwithstanding the disgraceful failure of gatekeepers and sometimes their tilted complicity with regrettable practices, we can't help thinking of the lack of incentives offered to officials working for regulators, bringing about a perverse mechanism, the "revolving door", that was featured by Thomas Sowell (1996) under the following chain of assertions: staffs in the regulatory bodies are overworked and underpaid; organizations which are monitored by regulators promise people in the staff to employ them after their retirement or any time they resign from their agency; they grant them much higher salaries and fringe benefits; it is a foregoing conclusion that some public overseers become more and more lenient with their future employers.

The Deep Hypocrisy of the Preacher's Waiver

Not only regulators are to be blamed for outrageous mistakes; hence we must also bring to light the role of the remaining cohort of gatekeepers.

Most of them earn a lot of money by apparently watching over banks, companies and government agencies, rating their credit performance, advising on governance issues, being opinionated on financial tools of which they barely know their nature or their risk profiles in depth. For the sake of an example, investment banks and financial dealers usually pretend that they are natural gatekeepers to companies issuing shares and bonds. The meltdown in 2007-2008 witnessed how misplaced became their outspoken mission.

However, the most disgraceful feature that gatekeepers have been upholding for decades consists in the Preacher's Symptom, a pattern of behavior that could be briefed this way: *always preach others what to do and how to behave, but be serious enough never to follow what you preach.*

In agreement with these remarks, three likely paths of action ought to be expected, on behalf of good governance and better practices:

a) If private and public enterprises are urged by gatekeepers to disclose their activities, why could we not request the same from the gatekeepers themselves?
b) If regulations are enforced to upgrade and control the governance of companies, either public or private ones, why should be the gatekeepers exempted?
c) If gatekeepers advise corporate actors in the private and public realm to grow more accountable and transparent on behalf of their fiduciary duties, why should they not set an example?

There is wide and longstanding empirical evidence about the failure of gatekeepers. For the sake of illustration, we can refer the reader to Professor Coffee (2002) indictment of their joint performance when he wrote, in the aftermath of Enron's demise a paper with the provocative title *Understanding Enron: It's About the Gatekeepers, Stupid*.

4.4. THE CAPTURE OF THE STATE

By *State-Capture* is meant the purposeful efforts of business groups, trade unions, political parties, even non-governmental organizations, to shape and influence the underlying rules of the game, mainly through the passing of laws, regulations or policies that could benefit them, in spite of being detrimental to other sectors in society.

In general, there is a trade-off of reciprocal favors between these stakeholders and the incumbent government officials, mainly under the guise of electoral and financial support for oncoming political campaigns, public works allocations, business licenses or exemptions, and the like. To understand this collusion of private and public interests in pursuit of rent, benefits, reputation and impunity when handling monetary resources of the state, it will be advisable to split the discussion into four overlapping topics: groups of interest and clientelism; corporatism and fascism; populism and governance; and, finally, corruption.

Collective action is a force to be reckoned with, through the competition of well-defined behavior like those pursued by political parties, veto-players, and gatekeepers. Their main task is to exercise voice in the natural inputs of any political system (for instance, the demands and support of the constituency; or the wide array of claims and counterclaims of political coalitions) as well their outputs (decisions or policies carried out by the government; also, the empowerment of minority rights). It is in this context that we are going to stress the role of groups of interest, mainly when they shift towards political deviances like corporatism, populism, and corruption.

Groups of Interest

The activity of groups under the guise of social and political networks, was systematically discussed for the first time by Arthur Bentley in his path-breaking book *The Process of Government* (1908):

> All phenomena of government are phenomena of groups pressing one another, forming one another, and pushing out new groups and group representatives (the organs or agencies of government) to mediate the adjustments. It is only as we isolate these group activities, determine their representative values, and get the whole process stated in terms of them, that we approach to a satisfactory knowledge of government. (p. 269)

Groups of interest disclose two adversarial courses of action worthy of being examined:

- On the one hand, some of them actually help social endeavors making a substantial contribution to the common good. In this assortment, we can include NGOs, educational institutions, cooperatives and foundations, professional bodies, the media, churches, sport-related activities, learned societies, and minority groups.
- On the other hand, so as to fetch the connotations intended for this section, other groups of interests are instrumental in the capture of the state by the exercise of power, influence and money, embezzlement, political advancement, swindling and theft, to the extent of buying laws from political leaders and law-makers. The participants in this game share a well-shaped purpose: to earn money and favor their own businesses by precluding the whole society or minority groups from enjoying resources to which they are entitled by law and fairness.

Political Clientelism

This expression refers to the use of public funds to back political ventures, hence rewarding party loyalty or groups of interests that behave like staunch supporters of the party in office; to finance electoral campaigns, buy legislation, provide with employment in the public sector to followers and grant business chambers with favors in exchange for their endorsement. In this way, clientelism can also be mapped onto a cluster of connected patterns of conduct, on behalf of groups of interest hiding and thriving along the corridors of power.

Nevertheless, this sort of development consists in a double-way path. The government can stage its own performance as a group of interest of their own; for instance, through the following schemes.

Firstly, by allocating resources to loyal municipalities or states[83], instead of distributing them among other states in the hands of political opposition, only because the government needs to influence the former ones so as to reap electoral advantages out of their backing.

Secondly, a long-standing tradition among many politicians seems to be the assumption that because they devote their lives to "public service", once in office they must claim discretionary power over monetary resources of the state. In fact, they behave as if those resources were theirs and, hence, they shouldn't be held accountable on how they were ultimately allocated; that is to say, they prepare their private pension funds for the rainy days, with the taxpayer's money.

Corporatism

It was since the Middle Ages that certain social arrangements secured for themselves a bundle of peculiar features:

---

[83] In some countries, states are referred to with the word "provinces".

- the right to associate on behalf of common skills and labor qualifications for the sake of increasingly demanded jobs and crafts;
- the entitlement to grant the entry, training and exit of its members, as well as rewards and sanctions;
- the recognition of their existence by authorities in cities and governmental bodies.

The concurrence of these developments gave rise to "guilds" or primitive corporations, whose range would include craftsmanship groups, religious sects and churches, universities, and professional bodies. We must bear in mind that those associations were primarily groups of interest but with a further advantage: they were built around membership dividends like convenient wages, widespread reputation, and political activism. Step by step, they developed an *Ethos*[84] that nourished the cradle of corporatism.

As time went by, this basic and pervading social segmentation grew more and more political: firstly, by building up endurable relationships with the state and deeper commitments with the ruling elites; secondly, by slowly becoming proficient in the path that leads to state-capture. After the 1850s, the increasing empowerment of the foremost corporatist actors can be abridged this way:

Industrial capitalism attained voice and authority to influence governments' decisions on their behalf but to the detriment of other social groupings, mainly the lower levels of society. This movement was fostered by the joint performance of capitalism with the fetish of the liberal market system, as it will be unveiled in chapter 6.

Professional bodies achieved the role of self-regulated entities, which amounted to the monopoly of professional practices as well as their control. More often than not, however, they systematically ended up in protecting those accused of malfeasance and connivance.

Trade unions, which are a sect of themselves as regards corporatist assumptions, became friendly partners with labor-prone political parties that

---

[84] That is to say *the set of beliefs, ideas, etc. about social behavior and relationships of a person or group*. (Cambridge Advanced Learner's Dictionary, fourth edition 2013)

only in some cases were democratic systems, whereas in many other examples were authoritarian, populist, or non-democratic political structures.

Organized religious bodies, which have been bearing witness to an utter disregard of accountability, transparency and good practices; in fact they had been operating like secret societies most of the time[85]. Not a minor fact to be missed, most of them acquired huge amounts of wealth performing as real estate brokers, thanks to endowments, bequests, or granted privileges. The Catholic Church, for instance, promoted a "social partnership" among government, employees and employers, which was in fact antidemocratic and corporatist, laying up the foundations for fascism as it was forcefully marked by John Ralston Saul (1995).

Fascism

Which are the most likely traits that conclusively shaped fascism? Let us disclose a minimal list of them, taking advantage of Saul's perspective:

- vindication of corporatism, nationalism and anti-democratic claims;
- a staunch belief in basic and unquestionable assertions, not to be acquiesced but imposed;
- a simplistic view of the world that boosts social arrangements while despising individual freedoms;
- a fundamentalist standpoint that splits the world into friends and enemies (a dichotomy advocated by Karl Schmitt, a catholic, anti-Semite and Nazi supporter, as we remarked in chapter 3, section 4);
- a paranoid stance which points out to social groups or ethnic minorities that secretly conspire against the nation, and hence must be persecuted and stripped of their rights.

---

[85] We expanded on secrecy and governance in chapter 2, section 2.9.

For corporatism to blend with fascism, the foregoing features must coalesce with the mindset of sociopaths, whereby the corporatist players (government, business, political parties, and trade unions) set up a covenant for the absolute capture of the state[86].

Capitalism, Corporatism and Fascism

Capitalism bears the costs and shortcomings of mid- and long-term business cycles, unexpected ups and downs, persistent financial instability so courageously decried by Hyman Minsky; lurking inflation and exchange rates volatility; commodities surpluses and slumps; the Schumpeterian "creative destruction"; recessions and the closing of national economies; wars and international political conflicts; migrants waves disrupting local economies. Briefly, capitalism turns out to be dynamically fragile and, with the help of the liberal market-system it has been fostering organized crime, corruption and ecocide; hence, we can't help thinking that it is not only fragile but also inherently wayward and ailing.

As from the dawn of capitalism in the fifteenth century, business groups relentlessly pursued strong partnerships with governments and workers; until the end of the eighteenth century such fellowship involved business and workers guilds, state cities, and nation states alike. It was in the nineteenth century that the alliance among production, work and government deepened, by setting up industrial bodies and commerce chambers to shield the interests of producers, distributors, sellers and shippers. Little by little, support for guilds was on the wane, being replaced by trade unions and professional associations. By the middle of the nineteenth century, there were ultimately three big actors discernible by their influence, power, scope and size: capitalists (industrialists, business leaders, financial tycoons, land owners, state purveyors, stock- and bond-holders, and the like), workers (from trade unions, medical and lawyers associations, farmers groupings, government employees and officials, also including

---

[86] The increasing importance of this sociological tool of analysis for political analysis will be developed in chapter 5, section 5.2.

military staff), and the State branches (at local, regional, federal, and international levels).

It is not surprising that the movers and shakers listed above, each of them distinctive groups of interest on their own realized that they had common interests beyond their particular ones. The main concern of these players laid in the fragility and illnesses of capitalism whose consequences were so detrimental to their businesses. Consequently, they attempted a variety of disreputable solutions like the next below.

Mussolini Labor Charter of 1927[87]

For the sake of our line of argument, let us pick up some articles of the infamous Labor Charter of 1927, introduced in Italy by Benito Mussolini, and designed by Giuseppe Bottai, Undersecretary of State in charge of the so-called corporations. The following articles[88] speak for themselves and portray the worst features of corporatism as an antidemocratic coalition of the government, businessmen and workers, with a strong sponsorship of the Catholic Church. Bear in mind the foregoing features of corporatism and fascism as underlined by John Ralston Saul (1995).

Article 1 *The Italian nation is an organism,* having aims, life, and means of action superior to those of the single or grouped individuals who compose it. *It is a moral, political and economic unity which is completely realized in the Fascist State.*

Article 2 *Labor in all forms, intellectual, technical and manual, is a social duty.* In this sense, and in this sense only, it is protected by the State.

Article 6 Legally organized trade organizations assure equality between employers and workers, maintain the discipline of production and labor, and promote its perfection. *A corporation constitutes the organization of one field of production and represents its interests as a whole.* Since the interests of production are national interests, corporations are recognized as state organizations by virtue of this representation.

---

[87] www.archive.org/stream/FascistLaborCharter .
[88] Italics are our own.

Article 9 *The intervention of the State in economic production takes place only when private initiative is lacking or is insufficient, or when the political interests of the State are involved.* Such intervention may assume the form of outside control, encouragement or direct management.

Article 23 Labor exchanges (employment bureaus) shall be controlled by the Corporations. Employers shall be required to engage workers through these exchanges, *with freedom of choice among names inscribed except that other things being equal, preference must be given to members of the Fascist Party and of Fascist syndicates in order of seniority or registration.*

Article 24 Professional trades associations *must practice selective action among members for the purpose of increasing technical skill and moral value.*

Populism and Governance

By the end of the nineteenth century, the word "populism" started to be used linked with the defense of expectations, preferences, and living conditions of ordinary people, and those claims turned out to be the banners of the Populist party in the United States by the 1870s, as well as the platform of a collectivist movement in Russia (called Narodnik, which means populist). As long as the twentieth century evolved, the populist ideas were tied to progressive parties like Democrats in the USA or the Labor party in the UK. It was from the First World War thereafter that the label was also attached to political movements or parties that spoilt, step by step, the older democratic meaning at the cost of demagoguery and corruption. Nowadays, Populism has become widespread and contentious all around the world. A considered point of view has recently been held by Jan-Werner Muller (2016) that points to the meaning of a populist political actor and to key angles on the populist-governance:

- *A political actor qualifies as populist* if he is critical of elites; anti-pluralist (supports an exclusive representation); he is loyal to an unambiguous form of identity politics; he contributes to put in danger the democratic idea.

- *The populist governance* exhibits three topical characteristics: it tries to capture the State; it resorts to corruption and mass clientelism as the right way of doing politics; it attempts to suppress civil society.

As it can be witnessed from obnoxious examples, populism is harbored both by the Right or the Left; in the former case, we can watch Trump's government, whereas the latter offers plenty of examples, mainly in Latin America and Africa.

Corruption, Politics and Governance

Generally speaking, *corruption* means the use of public office for private gains, either financial or political, in blatant disregard of duties required in office. Not surprisingly, this concept comes down as essentially contestable, whereby it has undergone many connotations over time [Warren (2004); Brooks (1909)].

Example[89]

Let us assume that John is a public-office holder who will henceforth be called the Agent, whereas Peter is the owner of a building company that deals with investment and construction projects in public works. Peter (or his company) will be labeled Principal 2, whereas John's employer is the Ministry of public works, which will carry the tag Principal 1.

The first stage in this story begins with John favoring Principal 2 when handling procedures, payments or the granting of new projects from which the company could gain the best schedules and money allocations to public works. Soon Peter realizes that John deserves to be rewarded so as to keep him loyal to his company, and sets off to pay the public official on a monthly

---

[89] This example will be enlarged and suitably modified for the sake of accuracy, in chapter 5, section 5.3.

basis whereby John will qualify from that moment as a broker for the two principals. Later, a second stage ensues when Peter enters into a closer relationship with the Minister himself, and advises the latter to promote John to a more convenient place for the fulfillment of their common interests. Therefore, John comes to be regarded as a reliable partner in transactions whose volume become sensitive enough to be kept hidden from insiders at the ministry and outsiders as well. In other words, Principal 2 has bought services from the Minister and John, whereas the company will be paid with public funds, floating the rules of competitive bidding by getting rid of any standard of accountancy and transparency; that is to say, the government pays the contractor much more of what is due, figuring out a grossing up to get the final price, from which a discount delivers the bribe as promised.

Principal 1 and Principal 2 are, in fact, a key case of multiple accountability and mutuality of interests. In some regards, the former is truly a principal in this agency relationship, but the other way around it also holds true.

In conclusion, corruption entails, at least, the conjoint efforts of three parties: the corruptor, the corruptee, and the broker[90]. The whole enterprise succeeds when the governance of each organization becomes more and more dysfunctional. Politics enters in this plot because the corruptor and the corruptee are political actors who undertake commitments that bid for power and money.

4.5. THE MAIN VEHICLES IN STATE-CAPTURE: RENT SEEKING, SOFT-BUDGET CONSTRAINTS, AND TUNNELING

It is frequent for a concept in any scientific development that, albeit it may spring from a particular domain of knowledge, sooner or later it makes inroads over other branches either in the same science or others. This has

---

[90] In other circumstances, instead of an insider broker like John, it would be for an outside broker or lobbyist to play the role of mediator.

been the case with a group of concepts that were born and have been widely used in the realm of Public Finance since the 1970s, but afterwards they have spread over and come in handy to other fields of learning and practice as well. We are speaking about rent-seeking behavior, soft-budget constraints and tunneling, prominent vehicles in the capture of the state, to which we now move on by turns.

Rent Seeking

Tullock (1967) notionally introduced the phrase, but it was Krueger (1974) who later coined the term. It primarily conveys the idea of rational and self-seeking behavior that redistributes resources available to society. Tullock highlighted that lobbies are emboldened by the government to secure wealth transfers on their behalf. This purposeful sort of behavior seems ubiquitous nowadays, and rent-seekers hire and pay for the complicity of lawyers, accountants, public relations experts, lobbyists, politicians, to fulfill their expectations by and large. It's time for us to shape up an operational meaning attachable to this concept.

Statement of Meaning 3 – Rent Seeking

By rent seeking is meant any sort of consistent and purposeful behavior in organizations, to the advantage of managers, groups of interest, or government officials, with the following central features

- *knowing that there are economic rents to grab, they systematically compete for them with guile;*
- *they appropriate more cash flows from the organization or government than could be claimed otherwise;*
- *or redistribute cash flows, damaging other stakeholders in their rights to those cash flows;*

- *in doing so, they prevent the organization or government from achieving sustainable growth and value enhancement, as well as the completion of their commitments.*

When going by the book, the contest for cash flows is at the core of any profit-seeking organization; hence, equaling the latter with rent seeking should be utterly misplaced. From the definition above, rent seeking hinges on opportunistic behavior with guile, which trespasses property-rights boundaries claimed by other stakeholders and, sooner or later, it brings out losers among them, even to the extent of sinking the organization in the course of time (Baumol, 1990). Contrariwise, profit seeking turns out the conventional driver of business activity.

Soft-Budget Constraints

This expression refers to the following environment: *an unprofitable and failing organization is bailed out either by the government or the company's creditors, regardless whether it is a company in the private or the public sector of the economy.* In other words, instead of keeping a tight budget, managers can soften the underlying constraints because additional cash flows are likely to come out of the government or creditors' pockets, hence discouraging a culture of budgetary discipline. It was Kornai (1979, 2003) who stuck the knife into this issue regarding the context of socialist economies belonging to the former Soviet Union, a critical approach that was later extended to capitalist economies (an updating can be found in Maskin, 1999).

Kornai defined a budget constraint as *hard* when exerted with strong discipline: the firm can spend only as much money as it has, and credit is only available on the grounds of prudential banking procedures. The budget constraint is *soft* whenever the state and even the company's creditors (in capitalist settings) help the firm out of trouble. The state encourages firms to soften their budget constraints whenever it confers subsidies, tax exemptions, hidden price increases, credit on lenient terms, even to the extent of nationalizing failing private companies. It does not come as a surprise, as Kornai explained, that whenever a soft-budget constraint becomes a current malpractice, it is for the state to ultimately perform as an insurance company. In order to apply it sensibly to governance issues, however, we must tailor the notion to embrace the private and the public sector together.

Statement of Meaning 4 – Soft-Budget Constraint

We are going to understand by Soft-Budget Constraint any systematic and purposeful behavior within organizations whose core features are:

- *budget constraints and their cash-flows statements are merely declamatory;*
- *cash-flows are opportunistically shifted from apportioned targets towards rent-seeking allocations[91];*
- *growth and value enhancement are not tied to the current and future financial situation of the organization;*
- *failure or malfeasance arising from the former procedures are met by a bail-out process following a chain of consecutive stages:*
  - *the buck stops below the bottom line;*
  - *in case of financial trouble, creditors and governments are asked to foot the bill and keep the company running;*
  - *whenever things turn for the worst, creditors and governments are asked to take over the disposals.*

Comparing Rent Seeking with Soft-Budget Constraints

It is useful to make a contrast between rent seeking and soft-budget constraints. In the first place, let us give thought to a core similarity, to go on with some differences afterwards [Apreda (2005)].

---

[91] This assertion actually yields a pragmatic link between soft-budget constraint and rent-seeking.

The basic likeness rests on the fact that both are examples of consistent opportunistic behavior enacted by some parties to the detriment of their counterparts.

The first difference is to be found in how distinctive each behavior becomes. Whereas rent seeking can be pursued from operational, tactical or strategically perspectives, the soft-budget constraint hinges on cash-flows leniency that could become functional to rent seeking eventually. However, seeing soft-budget constraints as a mere particular case of rent seeking would be misleading, because soft-budget constraints may also be found in many organizations that foster a culture of inefficiency, mediocrity, sheer waste, or managerial mindlessness, without becoming dysfunctional or corrupt eventually.

The second difference that matters lies in the way we can track down the ultimate players. Broadly speaking, rent seeking is a game with many participants that hold a stake in the organization. In contrast, it is for the governors of the organization to carry out the soft-budget constraint. In this regard, however, a striking contrast arises when we follow up how this behavior evolves either in the public or the private sector; in fact, two varieties are worthy of being noticed:

In state-owned companies or government agencies, any time the public-office holder in charge expends and invests beyond the budget constraint, he does not feel obliged to meet neither efficiency nor efficacy targets, since he is aware that indulgence goes hand in hand with lack of accountability (Whincopp, 2000).

For private companies, it is for the government to foster the running of their business within an environment of soft-budget constraints [like in many emergent countries, being Argentina a disreputable example (Apreda, 2001, 2009)]. If such were the case, private managers follow the same behavior that public servants, oblivious of any competitive thrust, innovation, even accountability to their stakeholders. Instead of economic fairness, politics intrudes in markets to lead business into a path of corruption and malfeasance.

Tunneling

Tunneling stands for the hidden deflection or the outright expropriation of resources from certain organization to another one, for the sake of government officials, lawmakers, the judiciary and political parties, union leaders, owners, businessmen, managers, and politicians alike. In order to successfully perform this activity, the organization must channel assets as if working under tunnels to prevent the outside world from knowing what is actually taking place. It goes without saying that such mechanism requires opaque governance to outlive the duality of what is the real and what the fictitious.

Among the courses of action employed by tunneling, we can point out to the following strategies of concealment:

- to remove physical assets from one organization to another, in the purposeful attempt of depleting the former of their rightful resources;
- to transfer human resources from one industrial plant to another located in a different place, in search of cheaper labor costs;
- to relocate a whole division of the organization and gain tax rebates or exemptions;
- to take advantage of "transfer pricing" so as to undervalue or overvalue assets or services transferred from one organization into another by resorting to window dressing when disclosing their financial statements;
- to sell its own shares, or exchanging them for shares from a counterpart;
- to buy an off-shore location that allows for secrecy, tax evasion, and blame avoidance[92].

---

[92] Hoffman's book (2011) is a must reading on how the Oligarchs in Russia after the implosion of the Soviet Union, distributed the spoils of privatizations among themselves.

Example

Conflicts of majorities and minorities within family-owned companies are usually dispelled in the Latin or Germanic governance paradigms by means of organizational forms named "pyramids" by which the family seizes the political power albeit not the bulk of dividends that flow instead towards minorities. It goes without saying that a pyramid could be a legal and reputable enterprise (as it happens in France, for instance), but we are interested here in the widely used variety from which the family benefits by means of dysfunctional governance.

For example, if the pyramid is to follow the rule "one share-one vote", and the family as block holder had 51% of the company A's stock, and the latter the 51% of the company's B stock, and this one the 51% of a third company C, then 100 million dollars of dividends coming out of the last one would be apportioned the following way:

49 million to C's minority, and 51 million to B;
25 million to B's minority, and 26 million to A;
12,74 million to A's minority, and 13,26 million to the family.

Therefore, the family actually gives up 86,74 millions in dividends on behalf of minorities, keeping only 13,26 millions, but it controls all the pyramid components instead, which amounts to political power by and large (appointing directors and managers for the whole construct, holding discretionary authority in transfer-pricing, tunneling physical and human resources at will, having the last say in strategic decisions and the business plan pertaining each component in the pyramid, and the like).

This subtle engineering also applies, almost verbatim, to state-owned firms. In the illustration given above, it is enough to substitute the state firm for the family-owned company.

Conclusion

Dysfunctional governance is a fact of life, either because the organization ages, gets ill, can't adapt to environmental changes, or fails to update itself. These developments might be natural, even under no control from the organization; but they could arise out of purposeful behavior with guile that sets up a sort of opaque governance that cloaks deviant behavior, although working under the shadow of the old one.

The apparent leniency and immunity of opaque governance uncovers telling connections with regulators and gatekeepers, mainly through connivance and complicity. Changes needed to curb malfeasance and crimes were advocated in detail.

There is a strong partnership between opaque governance and the capture of the State by groups of interest, corporatism, fascism, populism and corruption. Last but not least, three essential vehicles to accomplish such capture were described; namely, rent seeking, soft-budget constraints, and tunneling.

Chapter 5

THE GOVERNANCE AND POLITICS OF ORGANIZED CRIME AND ECOCIDE

ABSTRACT

Our purpose in this chapter consists in dealing with organized crime and ecocide, whose underlying organizations convey dysfunctional, opaque or rogue governances. Section 1 will address the so-called Elephant in the Room Metaphor, whereas section 2 will do the same with the mindset of sociopaths; both are valuable tools for the diagnostic and treatment of deviant governances and politics. In the following two sections, connections among governance, politics and organized crime will be brought to light. Lastly, section 5 will introduce ecocide, whereas the closing one will move on the meaning and consequences of ecocide.

INTRODUCTION

Since the earliest social groups settled down on Earth, there has been crime, murder, and plunder all of which took place on a revolving stage where the main actors were always found on antagonistic sides: kingships fighting their tribal quarrels; factions contending within cities; warlords disputing borderlines; empires clashing among them. Also, we discover how power struggles among chiefs of armies and religious movements usually ended up in malfeasance and butchery. By the same token, alongside the oldest groupings there have been crooks working on their own or in small blocks, just to damage and steal other people, even to murder them. In a way, they didn't support any alliance or loyalty: they were crime-seekers, even specialists in crime, without any higher aim than increasing their personal wealth by taking away from others whatever they regarded as covetable possessions.

As from the late Middle Ages, governments and powerful groups of interests found out the advantages of being organized. Therefore, the allocation and assortment of resources started to be handled by means of a rational viewpoint systematically employed in daily affairs: armies and government partnered with civil and commercial teams that became suppliers of food, weaponry, financial and commercial know-how, technical knowledge (ship building, trade fairs, accountancy procedures, numerals and geometry, architecture and engineering), the blossoming of professional guilds, administrative methods applied to governments or private business concerns, and the like. It goes without saying that large organizations had not been foreign to human achievements earlier in the past: prominent examples were the Confucian Chinese State; older empires like Egypt; Greek and Roman cities bringing about impressive logistics for securing territorial expansions with their armies and navies; also little states in the Fertile Crescent in the Middle East[93]. But the novelty consisted in the rational pursuit of secular objectives blended with habits of purposeful social action, fostering competition and success; hence, it was from the thirteenth century that the seeds of the Modern World were sown in friendly soil.

There was another unprecedented event: the emergence of nation-states after the Peace of Westphalia in 1648 from which the idea of organization spread over manifold social arrangements, to the extent that the process also gave rise to criminal parties whose main purpose was to extract rents and steal assets from society by mastering administrative skills as if they were

---

[93] The reader is referred to Finer's masterpiece *History of Government* (1999), as well as the book written by Frankopan (2016), about the past Silk Roads and their pertinence for our day and age.

business enterprises. In contrast, pilferers, thieves, pickpockets, blackmailers, smugglers and murderers remained in the shadows of their craftsmanship, because they were, in a way, self-employed and lonely actors.

Remark on Basic References

This book brings forwards a heterodox treatment of politics and governance; hence, we take advantage of the following references which frame historical analysis in unconventional fashion: a) Clive Ponting, *World History: a New Perspective* (2001); b) S. E. Finer, *The History of Government*, 3 volumes (1999); c) Peter Watson, *Ideas: a History of Thought and Invention, from Fire to Freud* (2005); d) Clive Ponting, *A New Green History of the World* (2007); e) E. Hobsbawn, *The Age of Revolution: 1789-1848* (1996), *The Age of Capital: 1848-1875* (1996), *The Age of Empire: 1875-1914* (1989) *The Age of Extremes: 1914-1991* (1996); f) F. Braudel, F, *Civilization and Capitalism $15^{th} - 18^{th}$ Century* (volumes 1, 2, and 3) (1981, 1992) ; g) R. Fitzgerald, *The Hundred-Year Lie* (2007); h) R. Carson, *Silent Spring* (1966); i) J. Diamond, *Collapse* (2011); j) P. Frankopan, *The Silk Roads: A New History of the World* (2016); k) N. Klein, *This Changes Everything (2015);* l) Peter Watson, *The Modern Mind (2001)*; m) J. Diamond, *Guns, Germs and Steel (1997, 2017);* n) M. Moss, *Salt, Sugar, Fat: How the Food Giants Hooked Us (2014)*.

Before setting about our chartered task, however, two diagnostic devices will be introduced. The first one hinges upon the so-called "the Elephant in the Room" metaphor, a time-honored tenet of social enquiry, which has been remarkably spelled out by Eviathan Zerubavel (2006). The second delves into a pattern of behavior that shapes the interpersonal engagements of any sociopath, which has been accounted for by Martha Stout (2005) in her persuasive book on the subject. It is my contention that both viewpoints are consequential for understanding organized crime and ecocide, either from the side of politics or that of governance.

5.1. THE ELEPHANT IN THE ROOM METAPHOR

There are topics over which a family or people at their workplaces persistently refuse to acknowledge their existence. Still worse, such behavior can also be tracked down to villages, kinships, religious communities, professional associations, even society at large. The common feature exhibited in those groupings is the knotting together of fear, denial and avoidance, through a concealed covenant to not see, hear, or speak about an embarrassing social development. This kind of experience has been linked up with the metaphor of an elephant in the room: although everybody knows what is going on, they act as if the painful topic were not there, just to steer clear of any suffering, as sociologist Eviatar Zerubavel (2006) asserted in his clever analysis of conspiracies of silence.

Be that as it may, such social pattern becomes deeply ingrained into organized crime. Not surprisingly, several skills and devices are employed: avoiding and hiding, learning to ignore, separating the "relevant" from the "irrelevant", setting the political agenda, blocking information, co-opting local (even federal) government. It is my contention that this dark side of real life contributes to the expanding of organized crime globally.

Example – Bolivia

As we all know, Bolivia is one of the most conspicuous producers of coca leaves in the world. Most of the peasant population is engaged in the sowing, harvesting, and processing of the plant that will be traded and shifted to the farthest locations in the drug global market. However, nobody seems to acknowledge the deadly consequences in the recipient country for the health of consumers and the shattering of their families, the lives of victims who blow the whistle on criminal activities, the security officials slain dead when attempting to crack down on dealer's networks, or the murdered investigative journalists that bring to public light the nuts and bolts of criminal undertakings. Still worse, politicians running Bolivia carefully deny and silence all criticism, allegedly for the sake of employment rates and the balance of trade. The former allows thousands of families to be nourished in this nasty way, instead of rearing other labor alternatives; the latter gives the country's economy the hard currency it needs to allocate funds for public works, utilities, and the payment of salaries and hidden bribes at government level. There is nothing to see, to speak, or to hear when dwelling with the ghosts of evil and corruption.

5.2. SOCIOPATHS AT THE GATE

The American Psychiatric Association regards an individual as likely to be a sociopath when he exhibits at least three of the following seven traits[94]:

i. failure to conform to social norms;
ii. deceitfulness and manipulation;
iii. impulsivity and failure to plan ahead;
iv. irritability and aggressiveness;
v. reckless disregard for the safety of self or others;
vi. consistent irresponsibility;
vii. lack of remorse after having hurt, mistreated, or stolen another person.

According to the psychiatrist Martha Stout in her impressive book *The Sociopath Next Door* (2005), the foregoing list should be enlarged to also contain three supplementary features:

i. they are seductive, showing glib and superficial charm;
ii. they are risk-takers; fond of lying and conning; they build up parasitic relationships with "friends";
iii. they are noted by the shallowness of their emotions and their well-known callousness.

---

[94] Stout (2005), pages 6 and 7.

Briefly, sociopaths behave as if they did not have conscience of their bad deeds; they are prone to do anything without guilt or regret. Therefore, it would be worth taking stock on this fruitful diagnostic mechanism by means of a timely example.

Terrorist Networks

Organized terrorism has grown from isolated and simple cells operating at their own peril to full-fledged associations that allowed them to benefit from technological innovation. If anyone can use their cell phones to exchange messages worldwide through concealed or encrypted channels, it is not surprising that criminal organizations followed suit by availing themselves of all sort of powerful gadgets for sharpening their interpersonal communications.

Terrorism comes down to an insane concoction of loyalty, bigotry and fanaticism that resorts to violence for political purposes. That is to say, they fight, endure, and die on behalf of lofty and farfetched ideals, in spite of deprivation, hazard or personal injury.

Let us notice some of their antisocial features. To begin with, they harbor a deep hatred of cultures, societies, ideas, government, or religious beliefs, through the logic of the "friend-enemy" dichotomy so widely worn and torn in human history, which was rationalized, among others, by Carl Schmitt[95]. Hence, terrorists "fail to conform to social norms", betray their "irritability and aggressiveness", "display reckless disregard for the safety of self or others", show "lack of remorse after having hurt, mistreated, or stolen another person", and "they are noted by the shallowness of their emotions and their well-known callousness", just to excerpt some traits from the prior list. And we should add another one: they feel the need of killing their enemies and traitors; still worse, they are ready to kill them outright.

Furthermore, because they work underground, many strategic and tactical schemes used by them resemble the ones employed in most countries

---

[95] On Schmitt and his political leanings toward Nazism and anti-Semitism, see chapter 3, section 3.4.

by intelligence services: surreptitious search of information; excelling in cybercrime (enlisting hackers to rig elections or military and security databases); making connections with stealthy informants; performing sensitive surveillance of places, people, and organizations; funding special operations (contracting killers, for instance). In other words, "they are risk-takers, fond of lying and conning"; they "build up parasitic relationships with friends"; moreover, "they have glib and superficial charm, they are seductive"; again, we are quoting particular traits qualifying a person as being a sociopath. We cannot forget that in a representative democracy, coercion is an exclusive resource of the State to protect their citizens and country. Terrorism shares the employment of illegal coercion in collusion with paramilitary bands, private armies, or intelligence agencies.

5.3. GOVERNANCE AND ORGANIZED CRIME

Although the notion of organized crime seems common knowledge today, mainly because of its unrelenting exposure through the media, we are going to put forward an interpretation grounded in political analysis and sociological concerns, albeit if might run at variance with old-time and rather outmoded judiciary precepts.

If we looked up in an authoritative dictionary, like the Concise Oxford (2009), crime comes defined this way: "*an action which constitutes a serious offence against an individual or state, and is punishable by law*". This assertion conjoins two separate clauses: the one related with "a serious offence against an individual or state"; the other requiring that the action "is punishable by law"; the latter clause is effective for the offence to be contested in court. Nevertheless, it is when we deal with the notion of criminal organization that a more agnostic and embracing semantics will be needed.

Statement of Meaning 1 – Crime

By crime is meant individual actions or organized activities that display the following features:

- *they entail a serious offence against individuals, social groups, corporate actors, environmental locations, minorities, or the state;*
- *whereas some of them are punishable by law, others are not;*
- *even when they are not punishable by current law, they infringe human rights..*

The centrality of human rights in our day and age provides the rationale behind the third assertion in the statement above. The historian Niall Ferguson (2012) regards the following list of human rights as a comprehensive one: the right to life; protection from torture; slavery and forced labor; the right to liberty, security and a fair trial; protection from punishment without law; the right to respect for family and private life; freedom of thought, conscience, and religion; freedom of expression, assembly and association; protection of property; freedom from discrimination; the right to education, housing, health care, a decent job, and a clean environment. Later in chapter 7, we will lay bare the intrinsic connection between social democracies and human rights.

Our next step is to join up this sociological and political compact with the workings of organizations that become criminal at the end of the day.

Statement of Meaning 2 – Organized Crime

By organized crime is meant any kind of organization and their networks whose most important purposes are to purchase, produce, distribute or sell criminal goods or services, with the single design of making money from their underground activities[96].

---

[96] What about terrorist or insurgent factions? Albeit their main purpose is not related to profit, some of their back-office organizations make money to fund their primary goals; for instance, by engaging themselves in drug dealing.

Organized crime provides their customers either with goods (drug-dealing, weapons, faked drugs and medicines, smuggling of human organs and endangered animal species, counterfeit bills and passports, trading on immigrants, and the like), or with services (spying, blackmailing, protecting, or killing; embezzlement in government agencies; accounting and legal advisory on tax evasion or offshore locations). We must bear in mind that several well-known mafias, like Italian and Asian players, started their records as safety suppliers, sheltering small- and medium-sized companies from competitors or bands damaging their business concerns, and guarding well-to-do families in danger of being kidnapped or murdered[97].

As time passes by, these organizations blend management skills, time and effort, human and monetary resources, by following two complementary courses of action: either they tie together lesser units so as to grant a sweeping control of production, distribution and selling; or they affiliate both the branches delivering goods and the ones supplying services into the structure of a multinational syndicate.

Not surprisingly, the defining features of a sociopath[98] are imprinted in the mind of each member of these disreputable associations. But there is one among those features that stand out eventually: lack of responsibility, that is to say, "no conscience" (Stout, 2005). Hence, the rejection of any responsibility seems inherent to a human being who betrays neither conscience nor moral commitments. It is in the nature of organized crime to keep their members away from any outside claim of accountability or transparency, among other reasons because their bosses and higher executives graduate themselves as well-bred sociopaths.

As any other commercial association does, criminal organizations profit from a governance structure, although far beyond from conventional business, since they operate in the darkness by tunneling their activities in utter contempt of law and social restraints.

---

[97] Further evidence and expansion are found in Gabetta (1996) and Varese (2005).
[98] This topic has been furthered in section 5.2.

Statement of Meaning 3 – Governance of Organized Crime

By governance of organized crime is meant the governance of organizations exhibiting the following features:

- they are criminal organizations;
- they choose their governance among three main alternative styles of design:
  - *the makeshift variety, that takes advantage of the current meaning attached to governance, but with a purposeful rejection or lessening of some defining characteristics;*
  - *the opaque variety, that sets up an opaque governance so as to carry out their tasks in utter concealment;*
  - *the rogue variety, that draws up a set of assertions conveying principles and practices that enable an architecture intended for the flouting of regulations and human rights.*

The three styles of design perform as conceptual types; it goes without saying that in real life, criminal governances mingle the components of this triad in fuzzy structures through overlapping functions. As time goes by, we can see how each organization swaps alternate styles of survival and growth at their convenience.

The Makeshift Variety

For the sake of illustration, take a pharmaceutical laboratory which sells one product without due diligence procedures, neglecting harmful side effects and leaving out the necessary safety trials before releasing the product into market. Although the remaining areas stick to a good corporate governance, the branch in question mocks accountability, transparency, fiduciary roles and the rule of law to favor a faulty product which is sold in underdeveloped countries with a different pharmaceutical brand of origin, a design that conveys purposes usually found in the mindset of a sociopath. In other words, the counterfeit medicine, although produced by the real laboratory, it is distributed and sold through the label of a phantom laboratory established in an off shore location. Once the side effects bring about the expected symptoms of a serious disease, the real laboratory behind the scheme offers the government one untainted medicine to save thousands of lives, pouring a lot of money into the pockets of office-holders. The marketing strategy consists in selling the faked item at astonishingly low value, intended to cure a variegated sort of minor illnesses (toothaches, headaches, sore throats, stomach inconveniences), whereas the savior medicine is supplied at preposterous prices that the government is ready to pay on the grounds of political opportunity (for instance, by pretending they care for people, while waiting for oncoming elections). Needless to say, public hospitals are to provide the healing medicine without charge to the victims[99].

Furthermore, a conspiracy of silence is set into motion within the company. First, to hide the situation and the real causes of such negligence, bad faith and disloyalty towards patients; second to mask the motivations of such behavior: repulsive greed, cooking up numbers at the bottom line of the financial statements, and boosting the market valuation of the company's stock. Once again, let us quote some traits that point to sociopaths in the Board, the CEO's office, senior executives and the scientists involved in the scheme: "they are noted by the shallowness of their emotions, and their well-known callousness"; "restless disregard for the safety of self or others"; "consistent irresponsibility"; "lack of remorse after having hurt, mistreated, or stolen another person". There's no denying that in many underdeveloped countries, pharmaceutical laboratories are able to avoid punishment from the local Federal Health Agency by conning each medicine written specs and bribing public officers at the agency as well as their political bosses.

---

[99] Background on these strategies can be found in Naim (2005).

The Opaque Variety

Criminal organizations that resort to the opaque variety frequently grow out of a partnership between the private and the public. Construction companies involved in public works and utilities[100] provide a noticeable illustration. Two of the most blatant and shameless examples have lately been uncovered by effective investigative journalism and serious work from a few courageous judges in Brazil and Argentina. The architecture of this type of dual opaque governance comprised the following stages:

The Public Works Ministry headed by the Minister and a loyal staff adjudicated contracts to a small number of companies interlaced with the Minister's gang by a loyalty covenant. For this concoction to be successful, governments[101] were allegedly in the knowledge and up for grabs by means of contrivances that also poured money to ministers, businessmen and trade union leaders, also benefiting to judges, federal court members, customs officials, police forces and intelligence services. Needless to say, companies that engaged themselves in this criminal arrangement won almost all the public works tenders. By marking up final prices, the government sent money collected from tax-payers to confederate companies which gave back the minister a settled slice of the mark-up, oiling the wheels of a distribution mechanism that favored the presidency and ministry, as well as their whole cohort of corrupt officials.

For this scheme to work smoothly, there are two correlated opaque governances at play. Firstly, the government distorts its normal and expected public governance, by building another one that was functional to the grab, tunneling, and pillage of the country resources. In the meanwhile, the old governance provides with blame avoidance mechanisms so as to trespass accountability, transparency, fiduciary duties, and the rule of law. Secondly, the company in charge of public works also puts up its own opaque governance in pursuit of illegal monetary rewards as partner or customer of

---

[100] In section 4.6, we gave an introductory example of this type of corruption.
[101] A recent book on the case of Brazil is Damgaard (2018), whereas for Argentina stands out the book written by the investigative journalist D. Cabot (2018) in Spanish, although by 2019 it was not still available in English.

the government, mainly through a syndicate of companies performing as a special purpose vehicle to be registered offshore. It has been proved that in many examples the building contractors not only grabbed their bribes, but also never finished the works or, still worse, not even started the projects. In this way, they left numberless disadvantaged communities without roads and bridges, electricity grids, schools and hospitals, drainage, sewage and waste treatment plants, drinking water facilities, and sanitary-ware. It is not surprising that the sociopath nature of corrupt politicians and businessmen has a bearing on any considered analysis of the subject.

The Rogue Variety

If we imagine the worst-case scenario, when the former two types of design do not fit with the organization's purposes, there will be another blueprint whereby the assertions that define governance are formally kept in their entirety, but emasculated through their negatives on illegal contexts of application. We are going to provide an instance of the rogue variety based on the track record of criminal syndicates like the sort found in the Italian *Camorra and Maffia*, Chinese *Tongs*, Japanese *Yakuza*, Hong Kong *Triads*, and Russian *Mafiya*. The reader interested in getting further information is referred to remarkable contributions made by Varese (2005), Gabetta (1996), and Naim (2005).

With this goal in mind, let us assume that a member belonging to a notorious drug-dealing gang is captured by the American DEA and testifies in court how his comrades actually designed the governance of the organization. The federal attorney submitted the judge the admission of the defendant and how he answered to each assertion contained in the statement of meaning that defined governance in chapter 1, section 1.2. It goes without saying that the following text intends to be didactic but it should not be merely regarded as fiction; instead, it matches the evidence conveyed by investigative journalism and acknowledgements rendered by infamous culprits.

Assertion 1

- *the search of principles, rules, procedures and good practices that allow organizations or countries to be run within the constraints of evolving institutions and changing regulations;*

Answer

Our principles consist in producing, distributing, selling, and making money from drugs. The rules and procedures are coercive when negotiating with suppliers, distributors, sellers and customers; but if that course of action fails, we will become nasty with our antagonists. Of course, we don't give a fig for institutions and regulations.

Assertion 2
- *the design, implementation and follow-up of functional social-action mechanisms for participation, representation, opposition, negotiation, conformity, dissent, voting, countervailing monitoring, by means of inducements, learning, and standards of performance;*

Answer

We are a state-of-the-art organization which employs a highly qualified group of accountants, lawyers, chemists, financial analysts; former members of the military who are experts in strategy, combat, and counterintelligence; officers in the police echelons; and political analysts. They have taught our senior staff how to design, implement, and follow up mechanisms of social action that strengthen a friendly context for our business. That is to say, they help us with the appraisal of production technologies and logistics, as well as of the stuff demanded from different groups of income; also with the recruitment of street-sellers, including teenagers eager to work for us to earn their food, shelter and drugs. Participation is not voluntary, but coercive: that is to say, neither their entry nor exit is innocuous for any of them.

Sales representatives are chosen carefully, according to neighborhood, county, town, state, nation, or our own global branches around the world. Opposition means that some members may become adversarial but their rate of physical survival is astonishingly low. Negotiation with customers and suppliers may be tough, because we are price setters and they are price takers. Conformity is good value, whereas dissent and voting are constrained to the board of bosses only. Our monitoring system is highly sophisticated and we employ counterintelligence expertise and electronic surveillance methods; in fact, we have a whole division in our organization where first-rated computer analysts and hackers carry out their tasks on our behalf. As regards to inducements, we reward professionals and executives with better appointments and higher than market salaries, providing them with Medicaid, lawyers' advice, pension allowances, and good education for their offspring. Learning is widely acknowledged in our organization, and we hold seminars and workshops in sensitive issues (legislation and law; blame avoidance skills; logistics and distribution; electronic networking; forgery of documents, bank notes and passports; chemical or pharmaceutical advances, and the like), whereas standards of performance measure each member capability and contribution; nevertheless, if they were not well-rated they would be demoted but kept in the organization under a sort of probation regime; otherwise they would take their last stroll to the graveyard.

Assertion 3
- *the fostering of accountability, transparency and fiduciary duties, as well as the management of conflict of interests among natural persons, corporate and political actors.*

Answer

Accountability is of the essence for us: membership entails commitments that demand responsibilities. But we understand a very narrow sort of accountability: it is constrained to workers, staff, and the board of bosses. Similarly, transparency is a cherished value, but restrained to the internal operations of our company: you must work outside the company enveloped in secrecy, but can't hide anything material for the society to your bosses. What could I say of fiduciary duties? They are at the root of our governance: good faith among us; care in the doing of our business; and loyalty, which amounts to what our Italian brothers call the code of Omerta[102]. Conflicts of interest are easily managed: either you reach a good settlement for the company, or you suffer an accident. That's why I appealed for special custody, and testified as a protected witness.

5.4. POLITICS AND ORGANIZED CRIME

As long as organized crime designs governances on behalf of their own businesses, a complementary thread runs through their leagues: the search and procurement of political cover-up. It stands to reason that governance is not enough, unless internal and external politics follow suit.

Internal Politics

The day-to-day life of these enterprises is ruthless; their members realize that their survival depends on stringent skills to put up with a background of threat, treason or countervailing forces coming out of competitors and watchdogs. It follows that there ought to be authority lines which would not be contested; influence to be gained by deeds and not words; control in the hands of bosses and senior executives of the whole structure so as to ensure no leakages of information or waste of resources; power so as to get loyalty and accomplishment from membership, and to obtain submission and dread from outside suppliers, customers, and protectors. In short, these organizations become political systems out of necessity[103]. It's certainly a risky way of living, although very profitable, but the partners in the gang suffer from stress and strains which they endure by nurturing and mastering the mindset of a sociopath.

---

[102] This expression involves connivance, conspiracy of silence, and binding loyalty.
[103] On political systems, the reader is referred to chapter 1, section 1.3.

External Politics

Whenever they go past a threshold of scope and scale, these associations discover that to take any step further will require the connivance of political actors who could bestow on criminals a structure of complicity and freedom from punishment. The most conventional path to follow consists in building a safekeeping network, starting at regional levels, through linkages with police officers, judges, mayors, politicians, and street-workers. When the syndicate grows over and above the local area of influence, they must co-opt higher officials working in the government, customs, police headquarters, justice agencies and courts, journalists, bankers, trade union leaders and businessmen. Organized crime needs protection and pays lavishly to their patrons for the supply of political and judiciary clout; in point of fact, they could attempt to gain admission to politics straightforwardly, by endowing certain members of the gang to run up for local, state, and even federal elections. It goes without saying that they can pick up candidates easily, from their own stock of well-respected characters living up the double-role of being a good citizen but also a hidden criminal. This is their crowding achievement since it perfects the pivotal web of intrigue and collusion needed for the success of the syndicate.

But the pursuit of political involvement can't be restricted to purchasing protection only. In fact, globalization and the astonishing enlargement of their enterprises, led these organizations to deepen their involvement with communities. Let us highlight some courses of action from which criminal syndicates profit in daily life. At the village level, they contribute to the building of the local primary school, as well as the rural hospital and sports center, exhibiting in that way their concern with people's needs and living conditions; by the same token, they set up "clean enterprises" not linked to their current trade, albeit their funding would come from the latter; such "clean companies" provides local people with employment and social benefits; likely, all neighbors in the village are in the knowledge, but the "Elephant in the Room" metaphor grants denial and avoids any sort of embarrassment. If the pace of their business hastens, bosses in the syndicate sharpen up their partnership with mayors in country cities and governors in state capitals; this linkage conveys the diversion of huge amounts of money earned in criminal engagements to be laundered eventually. In bigger cities, the criminal gang commits itself to more daring undertakings: they buy a football club, enter into real estate developments, the ownership and management of lavish hotel chains[104], shopping malls, freight-container shipping lines, antiques and art private galleries, private jetliner companies, universities and public libraries endowments, long-distance bus lines, or performing-arts locations. Since they need to further their political networks, it is not surprising they enter into the local or national media enterprises just to play the social influence game.

5.5. Laying the Groundwork for the Study of Ecocide

It is when we intend to cope with ecocide that several preconceptions come across and impinge our understanding of the problem. Let us introduce some basic statements over which we may agree so as to root out some of those prejudices, and move on towards a sensible analysis of one of the most pressing topics of this century: how the destruction of our environment and own lives is deeply bound to organized crime for the sake of big companies' earnings, in partnership with corrupt governments.

Settling Basic Statements on Ecocide

a) Firstly, we belong to a system of relationships whose main components are air, solar energy, land, water, minerals and fuels, plants, animals and human beings. Each component is interdependent on the most pervasive and ubiquitous way with the others, while building up articulated connections among them to grant subsistence and survival. *This kind of system is known as*

---

[104] Or appointing instead well established hotel names to manage their property.

ecological. Whenever a change takes place, amazing mechanisms set into motion so that adaptation and adjustment follow to protect such particular ecological area. The healing process could be successful or not; in the latter case, disarray comes next, even the shattering of interlaced habitats of life, because the older partnership among the different constituents of the system has being damaged.

b) Secondly, looking back on history we perceive that environment destruction had started well before mankind gained entry into this world. *In other words, human agency is not the only cause of ecological damage.* Natural development, from higher to lower temperatures, rains and fires, flooding and illnesses, earthquakes and volcanoes eruptions, meteorites and gales, glacial periods followed by retreat, the collapse of ice shelves, genetic mutations in crops or animals, droughts and hurricanes, deforestation and soil erosion, have all been unremitting factors of evolution without any human agency.

c) Thirdly, to make bad things worse, *the rise of human beings was a disruptive influence in degrading the ecological harmony.* It is true that in ancient times men and women improved the environment by sowing a beneficial cereal or taming a wild beast; but more often than not, people paved the way to unintended consequences, mainly because an apparently innocuous action like building their homes out of lumber produced irretrievable harm to the subtle relationships the ecology and geography of the place had been nurturing for centuries, as the biologist Jarred Diamond explained in his books *Collapse (2011)*, and *Guns, Germs and Steel* (1997). Still worse, plagues and diseases spread by human action have killed millions of people. We can point to the influenza pandemics soon after the end of the First World War, which left a death toll of more than thirty million victims, much higher than the total number of deaths during the whole war.

d) *But one development was of paramount importance in creating a cleavage between human beings and their environment: the emergence of big cities.* This evolution raised unknown problems that couldn't be managed at the end of the day, whereas a group of them perhaps had no solution ever. *The growth of big cities entails at least three wearisome outcomes: the inhabitants must be fed, their waste must be cleared, and dwellers must be sheltered and protected.* Up to this level, although the partial solutions claimed human agency, the environment was certainly damaged without any other purpose than granting the survival of thriving urban populations. Strongly related with the expansion of bigger cities over the landscape to establish densely populated suburbs and country areas in the nearby, we must add up some pervasive and harmful side-effects: pests, defective mechanisms of waste disposal, waves of hunger, social unrest, depletion of natural resources and drinking water springs, decimation of dietary basic staples, and the like.

e) *As from the fifteenth century, another evolvement held the floor with unforeseeable consequences for the world: we mean capitalism*[105]. It was a long-winded experiment that would be going to shape new social, political and economic regimes. This sweeping upheaval in the human psychology and the cultural environment of the Western World brought about a deep belief in progress, self-interest, material wealth, the search of income and profit, the ascent of competitive markets, colonialism and wars, slave trade and peasants migration towards cities where they lived in appalling conditions, the Industrial Revolutions of the eighteenth and nineteenth centuries, the scientific dominance of the next century, and the age of information networking nowadays.

f) *Simultaneously, the onset of industrialization in capitalist and non-capitalist countries unveiled offensive and malicious patterns of economic and social behavior.* Industrialization took off both in capitalist and non-capitalist countries by the end of the eighteenth century. For capitalist countries, the process ensued from entrepreneurial, managerial and technological drivers; and it was

---

[105] We are going to enlarge upon this weighty issue in chapter 6.

fostered by huge governmental interventionism, under the guise of subsidies, monopolies, tax advantages, colonialism, wars, and hegemonic policies. For non-capitalist countries, the progression was emboldened by authoritarian regimes, copycatting and smuggling Western technology and science, strong militarist interests, and a bid for power, mainly in Asia and Russia. The success of industrialization widely rested on sheer underpaying of poverty-stricken workers, exploitation of natural resources, and indifference of businessmen regarding environmental and social issues.

g) *Lastly, and mainly after 1850, industrial innovations coalesced with capitalists' unconstrained selfishness and greed.* The final outcome was pollution and toxic slug. The former was fostered by chemicals of every sort poured out over farms and natural resources, to prevent them from being damaged by plagues, pests, and other natural threats, avoiding on purpose any ethical or scientific assessment of their consequences for plants, animals, and human beings. The latter consisted in the throwing out of waste and residual toxics into refusal pipelines, rivers, lakes, lands and seas, destroying whole eco-systems forever. Both developments frequently commingle and overlap because some pollutants turn out to become sludge, and the other way round [on this, see Stauber and Rampton (1995)]. They share a common albeit regrettable fate: both are toxic; they sicken, cripple and kill human beings.

Driving Away Some Misleading Assumptions

Now, let us draw up a short list of frequent misconceptions that prevent a considered debate from being started eventually. We are going to attach counterarguments intended to dismiss partisan errors or farfetched assumptions.

- Only human agency spoils the environment.

    False, because of what we have argued in statements a) and b) above. For conclusive evidence of non-human agency in the environmental damage prior to human beings, the reader is referred to Ponting (2007, 2001) whose books should be credited as masterpieces that broaden the mind in connection with their subject matters.

- Human agency is behind environmental destruction.

    True, because of what it has been asserted in statements a), c), f) and g) above. To drive away doubts on this issue, we can avail ourselves of research set about, among other scholars, by Diamond (2011), who noticed how environmental problems could be sorted out in several groups: on natural habitats, wild food sources, biological diversity and soil; ceilings on energy, freshwater and photosynthetic capacity; on toxic chemicals, alien species, and atmospheric gases; last but not least, on the increase of human population.

- The real and only culprit of the environmental havoc is Capitalism.

    False. Industrialized non-capitalist, authoritarian and non-democratic regimes have been as instrumental in bringing environment wreckage as capitalist ones[106]: Spanish conquerors in the sixteenth century, Japan under the Tokugawa shogunate, the Soviet Union during and after Stalin genocidal industrialization programs, China since the infamous times of Mao Ze Dung. Be that as it may, capitalism certainly appears as a conspicuous offender of the global ecosystem, as it follows from statements d) and e) above. On this Pollan (2000) provided grieving experiences from dietary habits based in toxic chemicals, pollutants, and widespread diseases affecting animals and crops.

---

[106] Ponting (2001) describes the texture of events, facts, assumptions, and ecological damage throughout human history.

- The environmental debate is ideological and clearly leftist.

  This is utterly false and spurious. On the one hand, we can notice that assertions d), e), and f) point towards technological and social contexts of discussion, apart from right or left stances. On the other hand, if ideological features permeated the discussion (and how could such thing be avoided?), then we should balance left- and right-winged viewpoints together. The former has been brought to light by Hobsbawn's masterwork (1996, 1989), whereas the latter was thoroughly unveiled in the impressive history of Capitalism by Braudel (1981), both providing countervailing but invigorating approaches to this relentless debate.

- In our own century, commitments and improvements in the way big companies have been coping with environmental problems largely make up for past failures.

  False and feigned. Firstly, the arguments in statement f) above are fairly conclusive. Secondly, as from the date when it was published *The Silent Spring* by Rachel Carson (1962), this misconception has become shameful and outrageous, to say the least[107]. And later on, books like *Toxic Sludge is Good for You* (1995) by Stauber and Rampton, heaped proof upon proof against this sort of libeling and slandering campaigns, paid by big companies to shelter their vested economic interests.

- Ecologists and their supporters stand out against progress, innovation, and the betterment of life conditions brought about by entrepreneurs, engineers and scientists.

  False and mischievous. No sensible person stands out against progress, innovation and the improvement of life quality. Quite the opposite, the bone of contention lies in two unfolding processes that Naomi Klein (2015) indomitably described in her book: firstly, the outrageous consequences for the environment and living creatures of pollution and sludge, global warming and pesticides, oil spills and

---

[107] If in doubt, read the introduction to her book written by Linda Lear, who spells out the slurring campaign that Monsanto and other multinationals in the business of ecocide launched against Carson.

acid rain, carcinogenic food and waste water, urban ecocide and neurotoxin-transmitting devices, and the like; secondly, public relations agencies hired by multinationals, their complicit professional chambers, and lavishly funded think-tanks contrive propaganda discourses on behalf of the actual offenders of ecosystems and human lives, distorting facts and denying harm, for the sake of blame avoidance and outrageous profits reaped from consultancy fees.

5.6. ON THE MEANING AND CONSEQUENCES OF ECOCIDE

What does "ecocide" stand for? The Concise Oxford English Dictionary renders a pithy explanation: *destruction of the natural environment, especially when willfully done*. In my viewpoint, the entry in the dictionary turns out to be a good starting point, but it requires several fixing remarks:

If we agreed with the first part of the assertion, ecocide would stem from both non-human and human agency. The former amounts to a sort of suicide or self-damage committed by Nature itself, through geological, physical, chemical or biological factors. In contrast, human agency turns criminal organizations and conniving governments as partners in ecocide.

The second part of the assertion deserves further qualifications: destruction may happen by negligence, or unintended consequences that ensue when there has been dumbness, ignorance, technical miscalculations, or accidents; it is the case of a faulty dam building that begets the flooding and disappearance of native villages by depleting the nearby ecological system; but destruction also follows from willful design, when related to urban expansion, the waste disposal system, farming engineering, the tracing of roads and waterways, to the in-built pollution of big cities, and the global warming triggered off by industrial activities and transportation fed with fossil fuels; all of them come down to resolute decision-making in the knowledge of intended consequences that result in environment debasement. We must be aware of the real problem of ecocide: it mostly brings about irreversible damage to the environment. Taking advantage of the foregoing comments, we move on to those organizations that participate in purposeful ecocide.

Statement of Meaning 4 – Ecocidal Organizations

By an ecocidal organization is meant any organization that purposefully commits itself, takes part or brings to completion activities leading to ecocide.

It goes without saying that these organizations become criminal in the context of the statement of meaning 1 in this chapter.

We muster up legal and illegal organizations together in their carrying out of ecocide. In point of fact, there are criminal deeds toward the environment that have not been outlawed yet in many countries, and this lack of enforcement is often a deliberate achievement of corporate activism, political lobbying, with the connivance of lawyers and public relations agencies, as Naomi Klein (2015) forcefully decried in her book.

On the Governance of Ecocidal Organizations

Whereas criminal organizations not involved in ecocide usually choose either the rogue or the opaque varieties of governance, ecocidal ones show a preference for the makeshift variety. There is a commonsensical rationale behind this sort of pecking order: although many companies may be well regarded in their activities, in some distinctive subsidiaries or divisions they behave in utter contempt of law and environmental demands. Hence, they resort to deviant governances so as to disguise their purposes in pursuit of commercial malfeasance, mainly when carrying out their businesses in underdeveloped nations. It is the case of African countries where multinationals from developed countries (among which China clearly stands out), destroy or deplete natural resources, strategic minerals, and rainforests. Still worse, they experiment pharmaceutical products in human beings that would be utterly forbidden in their own countries, or engage themselves in large-scale weapon smuggling. They play the mockery of first-world governance at headquarters, while following a makeshift variety through infamous foreign subsidiaries. For example, mining firms usually profit from this type of dysfunctional governance, setting up an international syndicate of companies with untainted reputations in their own countries[108], and playing the game of being good fellows abiding by the law, while advertising their devotion to a green way of life.

The way things are, it would be an ill-advised strategy for a well-reputed company to carry out ecocide and being named as a criminal organization by public opinion and investigative journalists. This is a job that calls for an independent player, a criminal organization that masters the skills needed to bring about ecocide in full scale. Hence, "good companies" outsource handy "felon partners" that build up a rogue governance eventually; such scheme resembles the counterpart transaction of hiring a killer.

On the Politics of Ecocidal Organizations

Overwhelming evidence shows that in ecocide concur big names of the business world. It follows that their entanglement with politics traverses a two-tiered level of deliberate action:

Firstly, they take up some courses of action similar to other criminal organizations that seek political clout and connivance, mainly because they are destroying natural resources over widespread spates on the planet, comprising rivers, lakes, springs, seas, land, farms, forests, fuel fields, glaciers, prairies, and the modification of food quality without any serious scientific studies about the downsides and consequences for human beings, plants and animals.

Secondly, as their political action is often deployed in locations and countries where companies bring criminal offence to the environment, they need to draw up deterrent strategies at their headquarters. Therefore, they arrange a framework of blame avoidance, connivance and conspiracies of

---

[108] This seems ironic, but the fact is that they avoid executing mining projects in their countries of origin, perhaps following the precept "not in my back yard", or NIMBY in short.

silence by expending huge budgets in hiring professionals who give them protection from public opinion outcries, green activists, investigative journalists, politicians and judges that could denounce, indict, and send to jail their owners, directors and managers.

Environmental Wreckage and Health Ravages

The contribution of human agency to environmental wreckage and health ravages since the industrial revolution of the eighteenth and nineteenth centuries has become a disreputable fact of life. One thing is to nurse development and growth in developed or non-still-developed countries by coordinating capital, labor, technology, education and government partnership. Quite another to pauperize vast expanses of the world, shatter ecological systems, draw up the gap between poor and rich to the extent that one percent of the global population holds back more than ninety percent of global wealth. At the root of those evils we find a disquieting paradox lying in the pathway of both capitalist and non-capitalist industrialized countries. On the one hand, they must develop and grow; accumulate wealth; increase political and military prowess; give better education and health care to the elites of power and their families; make entrepreneurs, managers, stockholders and government officers more and more affluent. On the other hand, they impoverish the bulk of population; debase their education, health care and unemployment entitlements; impair upward social mobility, smash their environment, spread illness from poisoned food and toxic sludge; pollute drinking water and breathing air. The resolution of this looming paradox might be of the essence but, as we are going to contend in chapters 6 and 7, it would entail the demise of capitalism and the endorsement of a post capitalist governance and politics.

In the following list we find several examples concerning air, land and water pollution, intertwined with the related issues of waste and the enhanced greenhouse effect.

Air pollution and waste: gas emissions, forest fires, soil fertilization (nitrogen fertilizers), deforestation, motor vehicle pollution, industrial waste (nitrogen and sulfur oxides, ozone, heavy metals), airports pollution, acid rain (sulfuric and nitric acid), smog, air pollutants (sulfur dioxide, nitrogen oxide, methane, carbon dioxide), authorized landfill sites (decomposed organic matter produces methane), nuclear pollution, paint removers, synthetic furniture, disinfectant sprayers, dust (asbestos and silica), noise, window and carpet cleaners, toxic chemical flame retardants (electronic appliances, furniture, carpeting).

Land pollution and waste: domestic pollution (household waste and detergents spilled into waste water), industrial pollution, intensive husbandry (animal dung introduces large quantities of nitrate in the soil that filter into the water table), nuclear pollution, agricultural pollution (large scale use of fertilizers and pesticides), intrusive fertilization (certain pollutants seep into the soil), and landfill sites.

Water pollution and waste: industrial waste (lead, mercury, arsenic, cadmium, hydrocarbons, acid deposits); intensive farming with pesticides and herbicides (sinking into the water table and water courses); household waste in septic and sewers systems; oil pollution (leaks from refineries, offshore drilling platforms, ships emptying their fuel tanks at sea, oil spills); degreasing agents and household bug-killers; dumping excess prescription drugs and hazardous substances from hospitals and cleaning of waste from hotels, restaurants and laundries into septic and sewers systems, rivers, lakes and streams.

Enhanced greenhouse effect: fossil fuel; hydraulic fracturing methods to extract gas and oil (fracking); intensive farming (chemical fertilizers); air conditioning systems; motor vehicles pollution; industrial waste; intensive husbandry (methane emissions by raising ruminants in huge numbers); airports pollution; acid rain; air pollutants; nuclear pollution.

The Dreadful Bid for Shelf Life and Convenience Food

We cannot help thinking in the expanding global process linked to the food and beverages industries, which hinges around what could be labeled "the bid for shelf-life and convenience foods". It goes without saying that those industries fight a hard battle against expiration dates in what we eat and drink; still worse, they contrive the notion of convenience food, in utter disregard for nutritional and health features. It's worth making a contrast between explicit goals and concealed motivations of such strategy.

Among the explicit goals, we can point, firstly, to the pursuit of producing, distributing and selling of goods with longer lives, mainly those whose production takes place in farther locations. Apparently, this would seem a commendable setting, good for consumers when choosing their daily needs, and still better for supermarkets and neighborhood small stores that otherwise ought to dispose of expired articles in shorter times. Secondly, they intend to help households and employees to get access to processed food that saves time and effort in cooking, suitably convenient to tired and overworked men and women when going back their homes, or employees that eat at their workplaces. On this thorny subject, Moss (2013) book is a mind-opener that brings to light the criminal endeavors of industrial food processing and their immoral use of salt, sugar and fat to grant convenience and shelf life.

Regarding the concealed motivations of such strategy, there is a hideous problem, strongly related to the "Elephant in the Room" metaphor we dealt with in section 5.1. To stretch out the life cycle of any product beyond what Nature establishes, we have to alter and reframe the maturity of the produce. We can, and will do it, by using chemical substances like foodstuff preservatives, flavor enhancing substances, chemical coolants, salt derivatives, pesticides, fertilizers, pasteurization, chemical stabilizers (bread making, cookies, dairy products), radiation, freezing and genetic manipulation, among other technological devices to stop food and beverages from decaying. All this comes with a cost when the people start to fall ill, intoxications spread over, crippling and deaths follow. In the meantime, swindlers look to the other side, paying for blame avoidance professionals, who wall up conspiracies of silence pervading the environmental wreckage and health ravages, as Zeruvabel (2006) put forwards in his book on everyday self-denying.

To close this section, let us notice the chemical or mechanical concoctions that food and beverages industries resort to. We only need to pick up the more grievous and damaging:

- widespread harm to the biodiversity of crops, water, forests and trees;
- toxic feeding to cattle, poultry and fisheries;
- dairy products in general must be fortified because their production and processing depleted them of most of their nutrients;
- a huge amount of synthetic food and candies addressed to children and adolescents contain savoring and addictive substances;
- managerial and marketing unconcern about mishandling the proportion of sugar, fat and salt when selling processed food;
- contaminated vaccines by the usage of toxic preservatives;
- chemical stuff replacing wholesome foods;
- products advertised by highly expensive publicity campaigns that shape consumer tastes and impulses, with the connivance of public relations agencies which work on behalf of their patrons, in utter disregard of health consequences in the market;
- as from the 1940s, technologies for processing food and beverages reached new stages of innovation by means of the development of some chemical breakthroughs for the worse of human health; on this regard, Randall Fitzgerald (2006) is a must-read book;
- last, but not least, witness the appalling pandemics brought about by the craziness and revolting greed of the offending companies: obesity, diabetes, heart attacks, cancer, allergies, arthritis, infectious diseases, neurological impairments, crippling, pathological ageing, reproductive damages, mental diseases, and death.

CONCLUSION

At the beginning of this chapter, two weighty analytical tools to deal with organized crime and corruption were introduced: the Elephant in the Room Metaphor, and the mindset of a sociopath. For the first time, both are included in a book on governance and politics because they shed light in our line of argument.

Afterwards, connections between governance and organized crime were brought to the fore. Criminal organizations were clearly depicted, as well as the three kinds of dysfunctional governance they resort to: makeshift, opaque and rogue varieties.

Next, the relationships between politics and organized crime were shown, featuring the external and internal habitats where criminal gangs intend to be politically cloaked for the sake of their business.

Ecocide was set forth in section 5.5, settling down a collection of statements that intended primary agreements from which misleading assumptions might be argued and dispelled. Lastly, in section 5.6, ecocidal organizations were highlighted to ponder how their governance and politics allowed environmental wreckage and health ravages.

In short, this chapter has conveyed a bleak picture of capitalism and the liberal market-system, both of which have proved to be a booster and partner of organized crime, corruption and ecocide, eventually. At this juncture, it will be worth wondering how and when we should be entering the age of past capitalism. It will be for chapter 7 to head for a political alternative, grounded on the welfare state and social markets, shaped as social democracy.

Chapter 6

THE DAY OF RECKONING FOR CAPITALISM AND THE LIBERAL MARKET-SYSTEM

ABSTRACT

This is a chapter that strongly disapproves of capitalism and the liberal market-system because of their deep contempt for social issues, the common good and environmental damage. In section 1, a distinction will be made between political and economic liberalism, outlining the role of historical context and impermanence. Next section will delve into capitalism, Marxism and post capitalism. Afterwards, an analysis of markets in general will be developed, in contrast with the preposterous metaphor of the liberal market-system. Section 4 will argue against the alleged coalescence between capitalism and democracy. Lastly, it will be depicted the so-called "disaster-capitalism model" and the shock discipline advocated by scholars and practitioners from neo liberal quarters, a worldview which had brought so much misery to so many underdeveloped countries.

INTRODUCTION

At this stage of our inquiry, it's worth pulling together the threads that run through former chapters, by setting apart two opposing packages of assertions and developments. In the first bundle (chapters 1 to 3) we find a comfort zone that binds the realms of good governance and better politics, although their boundaries grow movable, adjustable, and dynamic. But in the second bundle (chapters 4 and 5) we enter the domain of dysfunctional and deviant roads along which bad governance and worse politics strengthen organized crime, corruption and ecocide. The disparity of both alternatives brings about a disturbing question: Why did such shift take place, allowing for the degradation of institutions and social behavior? In other words, why did governance and politics turned sour? Seeking for plausible answers, let's give heed to the interlaced performance of some explanatory factors.

To begin with, and most importantly, the liberal market-system and its variants paved the way to organized crime, corruption, and ecocide by furnishing them with the same toolkit of resources used in legal circuits and markets, either within democratic or non-democratic governments which do not make any noticeable attempt to curb and crack down on such activities. A telling example took place when, after the fall of the Berlin wall and the implosion of the Soviet Union, capitalism disrupted the social texture of new emerging countries, giving location, timing and power to crooked politicians and tainted multinationals ready to grab at dirty money.

Benefiting from the established economic worldview, the industrial revolution nourished an ideological framework that was shaped up as liberal economy in the nineteenth century and branched off later into neo liberalism (a misnomer, since it is shamelessly conservative) and the disgraceful Consensus of Washington.

In the meantime, a feigned fairy tale has been taught in universities for decades to any student enrolling in the introductory course widely known as Economics 101, in the belief that its contents put forth an unerring narrative of the real world. We should bear in mind that Economics 101 is taken up by many students following different syllabuses, among them future lawyers, journalists, businessmen, political scientists, sociologists, historians, accountants, and the like, who will later make his professional decisions with such scanty knowledge. James Kwak (2018) recently denoted this type of behavior *economism,* pointing out that such anti-social approach has ultimately led to bad economics and rising inequalities all around the world.

Last of all, two intertwined intellectual programs designed in the 1950s, made inroads into conventional wisdom, with the overt purpose of acquitting capitalism and the liberal market-system not only of their brazen misdeeds but also their outrageous social consequences. The first program consisted in assuming that capitalism and the liberal market-system would coalesce in the end with representative democracies. The second program claimed that taking advantage of crisis and disasters grieving many underdeveloped states sympathetic to the former Soviet Union, would lead them to representative democracies and a friendly habitat where the seeds of neo liberalism could be sown successfully, just from scratch. It was taken for granted that nations ought to be treated after disasters as if they were so weak that their social capital and culture could be erased, hence getting a blank slate without past identities and allegiances, easing the way to their political and economic conversion. Such was the proposal of the Chicago School whereas their sect of neo liberal evangelists tried to carry out anti-social experiments followed by devastating wreckage to the detriment of so many countries around the world.

6.1. HISTORICAL CONTEXT AND IMPERMANENCE: THE CASE OF LIBERALISM

As time passed by, both capitalism and liberalism conveyed different things according to their inception in the public mind. That is to say, they showed historical context-dependence. Therefore, we have to avoid the delusion that regards some issues as if they were permanent, unchangeable and truthful. Indeed, capitalism and liberalism have not been invariant or fixed: both entered the common knowledge of scholars, politician and chroniclers not before the sixteenth century. Hence, who can grant whether they will last for long or be impervious to consequential changes? Moreover, liberalism has borne dissimilar meanings in different times; on this regard, it was in the nineteenth century that two different and overlapping branches stemmed from it: political liberalism and economic liberalism.

On Political and Economic Liberalism

The expression "political liberalism" points to the viewpoints of Scottish and French philosophers, as well as the ensuing social awareness of values, expectations and beliefs grounded in the principles of freedom and citizens´ rights; on the other hand, "economic liberalism" pertains to the blending of that political philosophy with the mainstream economic ideas started by Adam Smith, lately argued by any utilitarian guided by Jeremy Bentham, carried on by David Ricardo, and coming to a head with John Stuart Mill. At this point in history, capitalists and entrepreneurs, tradesmen and bankers, politicians and stockholders, government officials and the members of the military-industrial complex of those times, realized that by contriving the political tenets of liberalism with the pragmatic achievements of capitalism, they could gain access to a friendly system of thought so as to play their game of self-interest, profit, greed, and power without any guilt or regret. In other words, economic liberalism became the mindscape of the ruling class.

The First Step

In fairness, although we cannot deny the fact that most of the criticism against economic liberalism has come true since the 1950s, even reaching our own century, political liberalism has stuck up for worthy ideals and fought remarkable battles in favor of freedom, toleration and the enhancement of human lives. Many scholars, John Gray (1995) among them, point out to Locke as the founding father of liberalism, with his advocacy of security, property rights and equality, at least for the upper-middle and higher classes of the British society; after Locke, the Scottish Enlightenment was instrumental to support individualism, self-interest, free trade, education, faith in the progress of society and moral austerity; by the same token, the Constitution of the rising United States endorsed the division of powers, representative democracy and limited government[109], whereas the French Revolution did the same with the Rights of Man and secular independence from the Church.

Along the nineteenth century, philosophers and economists worked out the tenets of a new political philosophy that mixed the economic metaphor of a self-regulating market-system[110] with freedom, property rights, and endless faith in progress. This was the junction point between capitalism and liberalism. At the apex of what has been known as classical liberalism we meet the towering figure of John Stuart Mill who, paradoxically, also contributed to the grinding down of liberalism by opening the gateway to social participation and bolstering the activities of cooperatives, mirroring requests put across by the radical movements of socialists and Marxists[111]. In the span of time when Mill's most influential books were published, countervailing appeals against liberalism were disclosing its failures and out-of-this-world economic assumptions, an evolving process that led to the welfare state and several successful social democracies.

The Second Step

It was in the twentieth century that liberalism split up into disparate factions: any European liberal became a right-wing political actor, whereas many left-wing politicians and followers took the path of socialists, Marxists, or radicals. In the United States, as from Teddy Roosevelt, those who formerly embraced liberalism turned out to be progressives, a trend that hardened during the New Deal under Franklin Roosevelt, so that any Democrat, from the viewpoint of conservatives, came down as being a synonym of left-winger. In contrast, countries in Latin America regard

---

[109] The Founding Fathers were widely influenced by the masterpiece *The Spirit of the Laws* (1748) written by the French political thinker Montesquieu.

[110] As we are going to make explicit in section 6.3, the market-system should not be mistaken with the variegated meanings attached to the expression 'markets'.

[111] On this regard, it's worth reading Chapters on Socialism, included in Mill's *On Liberty and other Writings*, Cambridge University Press, 2010.

liberals as right-wingers while progressive militants have swung among populist, pro-labor parties and fascist political movements. Last but not least, wide-ranging changes in society and politics have been so ubiquitous, that "liberal" was ultimately emptied of a lasting meaning, hence losing scope and appealing.

Assessment

Liberalism, with its apparent endorsement of individual rights and freedom, has steered itself clear of social demands from the poor and dispossessed, almost by definition; otherwise, liberalism might have pierced a bleeding gap between their cherished self-contained conjectures and the composition fallacy: how to make social concerns the grounds of political action without destroying the confidence and selfishness of each and every human being? This conflict, unsolvable within the liberal frame of mind, was instrumental in shaking up its foundations. Be that as it may, we must avoid narrowness and bigotry, trying instead a sober assessment of liberalism.

There is no denying that liberalism has lost the influential role it played for almost a hundred and fifty years, and curtain calls seem to seal its historical relevance forever; nonetheless, the history of ideas bear witness that the core of any time-honored thought system survives and ends up embodied in the social capital of civilization [by the way, two books by Watson (2005, 2002) are masterpieces on the subject]; in the case of liberalism such core embraces the defense of human entitlements to freedom, education and literacy for increasing majorities, limited government and checks and balances, the universal granting of the voting franchise, the abolition of slavery, "the vindication of the rights of women"[112] and minorities; accordingly, when speaking about the downfall of liberalism, capitalism or the liberal market-system we have to keep an

---

[112] This is a due reference to the feminist masterwork by Mary Wollstonecraft (1797) *A Vindication of the Rights of Woman,* Cambridge University Press, 2009.

agnostic mind: even if they were to fail inescapably, their heritage would not.

Henceforth, let us face the harshness of our current age, where capitalism and liberalism still put up with their impermanent meaning and self-defeating dynamics.

6.2. Capitalism

Capitalism can be regarded like a process of interlocked sources and overlapping developments, as from the fifteenth century, which we are going to connect by using two clusters of connotations, the first focused on its material conditions, and the second on its cultural features. Under no circumstances we could assume either list to be complete or the best available; they are tentative and were chosen for the sake of a didactic purpose.

First Cluster of Connotations: The Material Conditions of Capitalism

- The growth of cities and the coming into view of new crafts and services;
- the expansion of commerce that adjoined cities, ports and regional trade fairs;
- shipping innovations and the conquest of remote lands across the oceans;
- the Silk Roads, the economic battlefields between Muslims and Westerners that spread out from the Fertile Crescent to the Mediterranean Sea, the frantic pace that the Crusades triggered off in trade and commerce, the rise of Mongols, the ravages of the Black Death, all these were unfolding hallmarks in the landscape of earlier capitalism;

- scientific and technological breakthroughs that bolstered manufacturing, efficiency and higher productivity;
- the invention of the printing press, diffusion of accountancy methods, design of new financial instruments, the ascent of money as vehicle of exchange;
- the production of goods and services that paved the way to the ownership of the means for such production in the hands of a new social class that got access to fixed assets (factories and plants, office buildings, machinery, ships, tools), division of labor and learning of technical skills, distribution networks and the setting up of foreign branches; not surprisingly, the whole development allowed the rise of entrepreneurs and producers, hoarders and project developers, investors and wholesalers, explorers and purveyors, bankers and inventors, ultimately framing the profile of 'the capitalist' as the mover and shaker of this unstoppable process.

Remark

The Black Death is nowadays regarded as a pivotal turning point in History whose consequences led to a complete reshaping of the Western World, nurturing self-discipline and long-term viewpoints, entrepreneurship and technical innovations [see chapter 10 in Frankopan (2015)]. On this crucial unfolding of events towards a full-fledged capitalism, the student can profit from volume 1 of Braudel's classic (1992); also the recently updated approach of historian Frankopan (2015) on the Silk Roads, which cast many doubts on the conventional wisdom held by former scholars about the rise of capitalism.

Second Cluster of Connotations: The Cultural Features of Capitalism

- A down-to-earth view of the world stemming from the Renaissance with an overwhelming stress on secular and individualistic values;
- the expansion of dissent through the Protestant schism and a systematic non-conformist behavior in science;
- the pursuit of wealth as an end in itself, which praised earnings-seeking, unbounded greed, self-interest, even contempt and manipulation of law;
- the contractual and property rights approach designed by English and Scottish liberal thinkers as from the Civil War (1642) and the Glorious Revolution (1688);
- the constitution of groups of interest thriving for political connivance and clout in pursuit of capturing the state;
- the unrelenting clash between government, business and workers;
- the design of new kinds of organizations and a complex financial engineering to fund them; the development of a geopolitical worldview by the end of the nineteenth century (from neoclassical streaks to neo liberal distortions of common sense) that endorsed vested interests of governments, entrepreneurs, economists, politicians, managers and colonialists.

Step by step, capitalism expanded from being, firstly, a commercially successful endeavor in continental Europe and Great Britain, also comprising the United States later; secondly, it became an international industrial complex without precedent in human history, drifting into global colonialism, and reshaping itself for the sake of administrative skills and mass-production innovations along the First and Second World Wars; lastly contributing, as from the 1960s, to a new economic order grounded in the economy of information, their related technologies in computers and the world wide web of Internet.

It couldn't be denied that after each of those stages capitalism improved the living conditions of middle classes, albeit it was not able to hide the darkest side of its blossoming: social unfairness, labor unrest, unemployment, arms race and wars, appalling working conditions, and a business class indifferent to poverty, lack of opportunities, and malnutrition of the dispossessed in the less endowed countries. Not surprisingly, in spite of scientific and technological enhancements, the seeds of discontent were planted. As more and more enfranchised people gained admission to casting their votes rewarding or punishing governments, social democrat parties and reformist movements smoothed the way towards the welfare state[113] whose purpose was to equalize incomes and redress wrongs that troubled too many people at the sight of such unfair wealth distribution on behalf of scanty but influential elites. It is worth slowing down here to deal with the development of elites and their advocacy of being promoted by merit only. On this account, the latest book by Markovits (2019), is not to be missed, pointing out to the meritocracy trap that becomes so detrimental to middle class and also harms so deeply to the elites themselves, and makes for a great divide in society throughout the increasing spate of inequality and the exclusion of poor and middle-class families from an up-scaled educational system that is designed in favor of well-to-do households, leaving for the former a substandard and demeaning system of schooling that curtails social uprising as well as keeping them away from decent incomes and incentives. Markovitz highlights how the meritocrats exert themselves following a logic of being trained in the most expensive educational institutions and being overworked in the most demanding professions, which gives them the best positions and salaries whereas middle class workers earn less and are prevented from qualifying themselves in the contest for better jobs. This is the trap that gathers the middle with the poorest classes, making freedom of choice and opportunities a social path available only to the meritocracy members and their children.

While capitalism moved on with alternating successes and failures, praise and indictment, their ideological supporters contrived a host of

---

[113] We are going to enlarge upon the welfare state in section 7.2, chapter 7.

magical metaphors to keep the whole process under a benevolent appraisal from the public mind, and to imbue a cohort of university students for about a hundred and thirty years with indoctrination and evangelical zeal against the facts of life and in favor of models that would substitute mathematical settings for political economy in the real world. As regards magical metaphors, the following cannot be missed: perfect competition; efficient markets; minimal government; freedom of choice; a self-regulating market system[114] and competitive trade. However, in the real world, we only see trusts, holdings, big companies setting up syndicated ventures, cartels and monopolies; through groups of interest and their professional bodies big companies collude with their competitors so as to fix prices; markets are segmented and differentiated in pursuit of opportunistic rents to the detriment of consumers; in most cases, instead of markets we face authoritarian, almost fascist transaction habitats, in connivance with the government, trade unions, financial and business groups. The Australian economist Steve Keen (2011) carried out an overwhelming indictment of those fairy tales, as well as their underlying mathematical fetishism; it is worth reading his thought-provoking essay that debunks farfetched neoclassical and neo liberal contrivances.

On Marxism

On the whole, our book deals with deviances on governance and politics that allowed organized crime, corruption, and ecocide to thrive as never before in human history. Therefore, we don't attempt to expand on Marx's influential criticism of capitalism as it was taking place in England and some European countries in the nineteenth century; there are distinguished authors who had carried out such task; by all means, Marx's writings are a towering acknowledgement of his talent. The student who wants a first reading of Marx "Capital" can take advantage of the Penguin Edition in three volumes,

---

[114] In section 6.4, we take a step further on this metaphor by means of a withering viewpoint advanced by Karl Polanyi.

with an introduction and references by Ernest Mandel (Penguin Classics, 1990, London). Mandel himself extensively wrote about Marx.

By the same token, Paul Mason (2017, chapter 5) gives an updated assessment of Marx's contributions and heritage, disclosing some surprising insights written by Marx in *Grundriss: Foundations of the Critique of Political Economy (1858)*, which only came to light by the 1960s in Europe and the 1970s in England. There is an essay in that book, called *Fragment on Machines,* in which Marx highlighted that the key force out of production is knowledge embedded through the machines which eventually turns out to be social. It was a far-reaching foresight of Marx showing how the knowledge ingrained in social capital would mean sooner or later the demise of capitalism because workers would ultimately become ancillary to the process of production, and the class struggle would be superseded by a sort of knowledge economy. Unfortunately, it was a breakthrough not taken into account until a century later and, still worse, nobody can give a sensible explanation why Marx did not follow up with this innovative idea further.

Be that as it may, there is a broad agreement that after the First World War the scope and relevance of Marxism started to wane because of some irreversible circumstances, namely:

- the spreading of communism and leftist ideologies in the 1920s worn out and forsook the fundamental tenets of Marxism;
- the world evolved farther and farther from the historical and sociological context on which Marx built up his system, one that was intended to run clockwise;
- the implosion of the Soviet Union in the 1990s and the switch of China to a managed proxy of market economy, apparently left many marxists without their conventional narrative;
- technological advances, the welfare state, the increase in the size of middle classes, the pervading influence of education and science, huge migratory waves, the global interdependency of countries and social networks, have been instrumental factors in shaping a world thoroughly different from the one in which Marx lived and put forth his otherwise gifted assertions;

- in point of fact, Marxism might have become a view of the world that people no longer hold.

Henceforth, we will focus and deal with those features of capitalism and the liberal market-system that have contributed the most to harbor organized crime, corruption, and ecocide, making plausible Schumpeter's prediction (1942) that capitalism convey the seeds of its own demise, preventing itself from survival while moving countries unrelentingly towards variegated alternatives to socialism.

On Post Capitalism

In the twenty first century, capitalism seems to be on a slippery slope whereby its political articles of faith have been fading away. Mason (2017) pointed that three consequences of the current technology may bring forward the downfall of capitalism.

Firstly, information technology makes difficult to know where to draw the boundaries between work and free time; by the same token, impressive changes are erasing the connection between work and wages.

Next, information goods prevent the market from setting reliable prices because information is not scarce; as a counterpoint, markets resort to monopolies, outrageous levels of concentration with higher barriers of entry for newcomers. Their attempts are doomed to failure sooner or later because of diminishing costs, copycatting, internet profligacy of technological protocols, the faking of trademarks rights, and the carrying out of secret intelligence to the detriment of competitors, hence bestowing market participants with cheapness, affordability and duplication.

Lastly, an increasing collaboration in the production of goods, services and the design of organizations collide with time-honored principles and rules of the market, to the extent of rejecting managerial hierarchies, predatory practices, and most of the scrap that Business Schools are still teaching.

When asking himself for the aftermath of capitalism, Mason put forth a couple of alternative courses of action[115]: either a new form of cognitive capitalism based on other sort of firms, markets and networks would stand to supersede the older order; or the sources and legitimacy of the liberal market-system ultimately collapse and post capitalism would ensue eventually.

6.3. MARKETS IN GENERAL AND THE LIBERAL MARKET-SYSTEM

Markets are part of a system of interactions, although not all of the latter end up in buying or selling goods and services. For example, when Tom and Helen go to the shopping mall in their neighborhood just to look around and not to buy anything, at least on that date, they interact with sales assistants, exchanging information with the latter and also revealing them the couple's preferences about tastes, their budgetary constraints and cherished fads; the same could be stated when Tom and Helen search for bargains in Internet. It goes without saying that their shopping interactions take place face-to-face, whereas in the Web virtual counterparts carry out their transactions, hence selling or buying products through active networking.

From the oldest human societies till our day and age there have been markets where prices were not of the essence and haggling went on among small numbers of agents gathered in very constricted places instead. Let us give semantic boundaries to this ubiquitous notion, in pursuit of clarity and common ground.

Statement of Meaning 1 – Market

By market we mean a compact of relationships with the following features:

---

[115] This point will be the subject matter of chapter 7.

- *there are locations, either physical or notional, where people carry out their trade by shopping around or exchanging goods and services;*
- *at each location, some people produce, distribute and sell goods or services, whereas consumers are ready to purchase or hire them;*
- *there are conventional terms of trade that allow suppliers and consumers to bring their exchange to completion, agreeing either with non-monetary values or monetary prices;*
- *these social networks become persistent, repetitive and reciprocal; in fact, they arise out of needs and opportunities; and eventually coalesce in formal or informal fields of interaction subject to rules and constraints, that is to say, to institutions.*

The most helpful inference that we can draw from the meaning conveyed above consists in dispelling the farfetched idea of the free and self-regulated liberal market-system. In the real world we can find and assess an impressive list of markets that do not follow the neo liberal fairy story; to wit, the following ones:

Household coordination, which is the hub of countless market daily transactions paid in kind, mainly in villages and subsistence primary economies, either within a single household unit or an unplanned network of family units.

Collective enterprises or corporations, that should be regarded as distinctive command markets; on this issue, we should bear in mind that Ronald Coase (1937) established how corporations in their internal operations behave like repressive and authoritarian actors, managing their main functions the same way peremptory markets are used to.

Social markets, that have developed through three dynamical social drivers, from the 1750s through up our own times:

- civil society, which coordinates collectivities (charities, mutual societies, affinity clubs, foundations) as a result of trust, social fairness and cooperation in producing and distributing goods and services;

- regional cooperatives and social movements as from the nineteenth century that have proved there are available coordination constructs to take the place of the liberal market-system; an outstanding enlargement of these social experiments led to the idea of communitarian politics, whose markets grew in opposition to liberalism and Marxism varieties;
- from the 1870s henceforth, a network of social assistance and redistribution of resources, spread over European countries that ultimately brought forth the welfare state.

Popular markets, which are conspicuous arrangements in the less developed countries where wide-ranging unemployment and poverty might threaten the social peace; they resort to innovative procedures to bolster informal economies mushrooming by the side of the formal ones and granting the survival of handicapped social groups. A classical reference is Hernando del Soto's inquiry into the Peruvian informal economy (2002, Basic Books, New York).

The government, which prevails as a big producer, supplier and consumer of goods and services; also performing as a social distribution machine of monetary transfers and social assistance in favor of the poorer sectors of society, which leads to the so-called welfare state.

On-line networked markets that, since the 1990s, have enjoyed an unprecedented growth in what amounts to a pervading and ubiquitous transactional habitat, by which millions of sellers and buyers meet together virtually, by using their computers or alternatives gadgets, regardless of their nationality, place of trade, or cultural cleavages. These are highly molecular markets (their participants are countless) whose marginal costs are falling on slippery slopes, and their transactions settled without direct money exchanges, weakening the time-honored role that monetary prices have conveyed until recently.

Copycats and fakers' markets, whose ancestors were bands of smugglers who eagerly set up surrogate markets for goods hard to be purchased otherwise. In other words, smuggling was a transportation system to illegally carry merchandise from one place to another, a tunneling mechanism so as to trade in the shadows through the assistance of black or informal markets. Unfortunately for smugglers, newcomers arrived by the end of the nineteenth century, who were able to produce and sell counterfeits goods in competition with the original ones. These newcomers resorted to the same logistics, technology and manufacturing employed by the originators. Instead of offering in Kenya a legitimate appliance smuggled from Italy, now any Kenyan was able to buy from Turkey a copycat or fake of Italian merchandise.

For such markets to thrive (and they have succeeded straight away) it was not enough to bestow old networks of smugglers with far reaching contacts and money to grease customs officers and border patrols. Among other things, distribution and transportation costs had been increasing as much as the risk involved in doing such kind of business; on the other hand, circumstances were seasoned for subduing the practice of mere smuggling to ancillary types of trading activities in the shadow. Therefore, entrepreneurs handling their business in the black economy set up factories, laboratories, storage facilities, while developing scientific research, management skills, compliance with the host country regulations, paying taxes, and the like. In other words, copycats took advantage of a governance more suitable to the one which any smuggler were used to employ in their time-honored profession.

Lastly, a distinction can be drawn between faking and copycatting, although boundaries may become fuzzy in real life. Broadly speaking, by faking we reproduce certain product (a painting, clothing items, jewelry). *Faking does its best out of retailing, catering for up-markets. Copycatting refers instead to big business that cares for wholesale and mass markets; in a figurative way, it is the final stage of the industrialization of faking.* Furthermore, many branches of the copycatting industry became fully legal in the host country and as such exported to foreign countries; for instance, Asian electronic gadgets and pharmaceutical proxies selling cheaper and flooding world markets.

Command markets, which are notorious in authoritarian political systems, and are ruled by federal or local governments which handle systematic schedules of production and distribution from top to bottom; they prioritize targeted quantities. In other words, command markets are locations where suppliers decide which are the goods and services to be consumed. We must bear in mind that the expression "suppliers" in this context stands for government agencies, party officers and factory managers. These kinds of exchange habitats have successfully performed in many places and times, outstanding examples of which are to be found in ancient Egypt, China, and the Fertile Crescent societies, as well as Russia and China nowadays.

Markets of organized crime, corruption, and ecocide also stand as alternative markets, regardless of how despicable they are[116].

The Liberal Market-System

It was Charles Lindblom (2001) who furnished a critical approach to "the market system"[117], an economic structure he defined as a system of coordination of human activities that don't follow from command but from interlaced interactions under the guise of transactions.

This kind of perspective deserves some remarks to fit the context of our book. Firstly, the expression "market system" comes down as a misnomer. To all intents and purposes, we cannot assimilate it with the expression "market" as if they were synonyms, because they aren't. The former entails the ideological concoction of economic liberalism; the latter, instead, refers to a wide spate of alternative arrangements in the real world that successfully match the statement of meaning we gave above. Still worse, the expression "market system" is also a misnomer on quite a different ground: all markets encompassed in the actual life are systems, that is to say, structures evolving out of components, relationships and purposes. That is why we label the liberal contrivance "market-system" with a hyphen.

Secondly, "market-system" actually stands for "liberal market-system", as we rather like to call it henceforth, because it predicates a self-adjusting

---

[116] They were dealt with in chapters 4 and 5.
[117] In section 6.4, we are going to expand on Karl Polanyi's criticism of the self-regulating market. Lindblom acknowledged his debt with Polanyi in page 283 of his own book on the market system.

market mechanism which automatically clears up prices by assuming a perfect competition environment without interference, even precluding government, intermediaries and transaction costs, as they can only be found in text-books or the eldest Swiss villages in the quiet Switzerland from where Leon Walras, among others in his time, wrote about this fairy tale by the end of the nineteenth century.

Finally, contrasting the market-system with a command economy as Lindblom advocates, it would prevent the vast majority of alternative markets enlisted in the foregoing section from being noticed and qualified.

In any case, and more importantly, let us move onto a subtle argument posed by Lindblom: according to his opinion, the market-system would require of two coordinating devices to become successful, one to grant peacekeeping and the other to foster cooperation. Not surprisingly, in the context of liberalism this viewpoint nourishes an inner contradiction.

Coordination by peacekeeping: such process would involve the government as a prominent setter in the demand and supply of goods or services, also assuming the role of an umpire who overlooks and constrains the players to peacefully comply with rules, among which contracts, costumes and laws are conspicuous examples. If this were the case, the market-system would not be self-adjusting.

Coordination by cooperation: the whole arrangement would call for voluntary and concerted efforts of labor, entrepreneurs, households, capitalists and the government in producing, distributing, consuming, or accumulating wealth. Cooperation is necessary to articulate in a lasting way the interactive texture that keeps markets replenishing the daily needs of their participants. If this were the case, the market-system would not be self-reliant.

The Inner Contradiction

If the market-system needed of coordination by granting peacekeeping, there would raise an essential contradiction for liberalism and capitalism alike, because the mechanical structure predicated by liberal economists couldn't be managed without an overwhelming role of parental care expected from the government. If the market-system needed of coordination by cooperation, such setting could not be granted down to earth, unless the government became a crucial player, because suppliers actually hold an adversarial relationship with buyers, households, and retailers of good and services, by fixing prices and handling the quality specifications without any control, setting up oligopolies and cartels, and preventing the entry of competitors by dint of barriers and exemptions. All in all, the market-system is internally flawed when we try to map it onto markets in the flesh, because the assumptions of the model can't fit the facts of the world. In the end, peacekeeping and cooperation flatten out the road to the welfare state.

6.4. Capitalism, the Liberal Market System, and Democracy

All things considered, we must bear in mind that ill-advised people sometimes believe (or intend us to do it) that capitalism, the liberal market-system and democracy merge in the end so as to become a compact that falls short of distinguishing its components. It's worth slowing down here so as to face this implausible perception.

Broadly speaking, capitalism takes advantage of representative democracies by means of groups of interest trying to co-opt the State, fostering organized crime, corruption and ecocide by downgrading and corroding democratic institutions, as we dealt with in chapters 4 and 5. To uphold that capitalism and the liberal market-system blend with democracy seems at least preposterous whenever we watch what happens nowadays in most countries worldwide.

There are several governments that claim to manage liberal market-systems although we couldn't call them capitalists. Prominent examples are Russia, China, and other conspicuous Asian countries, after the 1990s, which administer what has been called state-capitalism. However, it must be doubted that they are run through a market-system in the sense denoted by

Lindblom; strictly speaking, central command is disguised by allocating decision-making on lower organizations, pretending a sort of ancillary coordination, within the political context of fake representative democracies.

We also find countries that could not qualify as democratic, being quite the opposite instead. Firstly, they don't favor the liberal market-system since they run their markets by command, with strong participation of the government in most of their economic decision-making; in general, they thrive in a barefaced rejection of the representative democracy tenets. As things stand, this uncovers the playing field for "rogue states" like Iran, Afghanistan, Cuba, Venezuela, Iraq, and several African states[118].

In our global village of today, massive and unaccountable market transactions don't take place in legal markets, but they happen in the underground for the sake of criminal organizations that produce, distribute, or consume goods and services[119]. In many nations the quality of democracy has been worsening, slowly debasing the interlocking institutions of democracy, economy, the rule of law, and civil society, as the historian Niall Ferguson (2012) has warned us in his work *The Great Degeneration*.

The Magical Metaphor of the Self-Regulating Market System

Looking into the nineteenth century, mainly in England, it can be witnessed how bankers, economists, entrepreneurs, capitalists, big companies, political writers, journalists, and politicians, contrived a compact of beliefs, assumptions, and statements that shaped a worldview called 'economic liberalism'[120]. It started as a veritable attempt to understand the complex connections inside the Industrial Revolution and to lessen the disruptions that had befallen over the real society. Ultimately, groups of interest made of economic liberalism an ideology, doomed to failure after two world wars which scourged several countries, sweeping away cultural assets, collective values, and cooperative stances on the life of democracy.

---

[118] This list makes sense by the time of this book publishing date.
[119] Really, they could be denoted as criminal markets; we have dealt with them in chapter 5.
[120] See remark on liberalism in section 6.1.

The root of such economic philosophy, which was to become so disreputable later, must be found in a well-known viewpoint that asserted that the market was self-regulating, a physical machine that fashioned human beings as disposable robots supplying the fodder that the industrial-commercial complex needed to increase its scope and scale. It was Karl Polanyi (1944) one of the first Western thinkers that pointed out to the devils of this magical metaphor that assumes human beings behave as maximizing profit machines and it takes apart the economic and political realms of society, by which people turn out to be subservient to the economic system; even worse, it deletes from the picture any entitlement to fairness, equity, and social concern.

6.4. THE DISASTER-CAPITALISM MODEL AND THE SHOCK DOCTRINE

After the great depression of the 1930s and up to the 1960s, both the Keynesian ideas and the practices of the welfare state were streamlined and highly regarded on behalf of the common good. It seemed that neoclassical liberalism was waning out, even in the Anglo-Saxon cultural habitats, and likely doomed to oblivion; at least, their loss of influence was a foregone conclusion.

However, two outstanding developments had been lurking and growing behind the stage, only waiting for the chance of stretching out their weighty arms with unforeseen consequences; we mean globalization and neo liberalism.

Globalization, Multinational Companies and the Bid for Malfeasance

There is no denying that globalization and transnational enterprises convey both good and evil. Let us handle this duality by turns.

Globalization is not a modern invention; in fact, there had been several similar processes in the distant past, for instance the one under Alexander's conquests; the evolving Silk Roads along a thousand years up to now; the Muslim spreading over the Mediterranean and Eastern Africa; the Western discoveries of new territories from the end of the fifteenth century; the Industrial Revolution and the colonial world. Nonetheless, what takes the current globalization process apart from their elder ones consists in overwhelming acquisitions that mankind achieved in the fields of logistics, transportation, communication networking, science and technology, information engineering and computing design, and the like. Never before was any civilization able to claim for so many concurrent capabilities. Regrettably, however, instead of profiting from such bountiful supply of new resources and products to improve fairness and social mobility, inequality soared to genocidal levels, whereas distribution of human capital and tangible riches ended up in one percent of the population owning ninety per cent of the world wealth, among them businessmen, owners of real estate, bankers, lawyers, accountants, corporate groups, portfolio managers, politicians, public relations agencies, economists, without missing shareholders, directors and managers of multinationals.

The darkest side of transnational enterprises can be briefed this way: they realized that globalization afforded them to take a quantum leap to hyper profits and lower taxes in underdeveloped countries, plunging production and distribution costs across different locations, not forgetting the ubiquitous contrivances that accountants designed to figure out transfer-pricing mechanisms which made feasible the tunneling of assets and human resources from one branch to another, a mechanism that improves or worsens the bottom line of the counterparts according to preferences enacted by their boards of directors and managers. Furthermore, as from the 1960s, capitalism and the liberal market-system fostered another devilish globalization: the one pertaining organized crime, corruption and ecocide, as we have delved into in chapters 4 and 5.

Neo Liberalism and the Mediation of Antisocial Thinking

Although the blossoming of economic prowess has been impressive and breathtaking, even in their outrageous consequences, there couldn't have thrived the way witnessed by facts and numbers if ideological support and psychological comfort had not been provided by thinkers, professors and lavishly paid think tanks. In the 1950s, well known scholars like Milton Friedman, Arnold Harberger, Larry Sjaastad, George Shultz, and the Austrian Friedrich Hayek (Friedman's mentor) built up a new frame of mind strongly rooted in economic issues only, as if there were not other features worthy of concern and political action. They were the inheritors of neoclassical economy and the Austrian School. Last of all, Friedman, Harberger, Sjaastad and Schultz belonged to the department of Economics at the University of Chicago[121], to the extent that the ideological network crafted by them was dubbed "The School of Chicago" approach, and their practitioners "the Chicago boys", both with deprecatory undertones.

In the former chapter we brought to light the bunch of metaphors they handed out packaged in textbooks, journals and newspapers, seminars and conferences. By means of generous fellowships[122] they trained lots of Latin American and Asian students to graduate in Economics, some of whom were appointed afterwards to several international agencies like the World Bank and the International Monetary Fund, whereas others built up powerful elites of bureaucrats and business consultants that applied in their own countries the teachings of neo liberalism and the consensus of Washington. But their most labored contribution consisted in setting up what Naomi Klein (2008) has so aptly described as *"disaster capitalism and shock discipline models"* which assumed a change of global and national governance for the worst.

---

[121] In spite of the disreputable political performance of this department and some of their graduates, we must acknowledge that the University of Chicago, mainly in the hard sciences and social sciences, has highly contributed to improving critical and innovative learning, research and teaching. It has been, as it is today, a harbinger of wisdom and scholarship.

[122] This took place mainly through the agency of the Ford Foundation.

The Disaster Capitalism and the Shock Discipline Model

According to common knowledge, the word "disaster" means something that brings about damage and a lot of harm, either in unintended ways (volcanic activities, droughts, flooding, tsunamis) or intended ones (drug-dealing trade, wars and terrorist fights, economic sanctions enforced by some countries against their rivals).

As from the 1950s, two complicit developments evolved in systematic and profitable courses of action: the military-industrial complex in the shadows of the Cold War, and the Chicago School teaching and evangelism. Both engagements entailed a new strategic scope and starting point which we are going to brief this way:

> How could some well-developed countries, mainly the United States, profit from disasters taking place in any place around the world, chiefly in those countries where governments were politically on the side of the Soviet Union and which, from the economic viewpoint, could be labeled as heretical deniers of the market-system, like the Keynesian and socialists or, even worse, followers of the welfare state beliefs and practices?

Although they put into use parallel approaches, in the end a surprising convergence was attained through decisions, facts, and consequences. Let us briefly look into this evolution, strongly referring the reader to Klein's book, backed up by ten years of research she invested in her line of argument.

a) *The military-industrial complex*, which consists in a pervasive and knotty partnership of the military, the multinationals devoted to military and security businesses, politicians and governments. As the Cold War was growing with alacrity and peril, those groups of interest tried to win the battle not only in the field, but mainly through the knowledge they could get from their enemies' weaknesses, taking advantage of disasters that might befell onto their opponents, namely epidemics, floods, earthquakes, climate havoc, widespread hunger, cities wreckage, and the like. Dreadfully, they realized that their toolkit for the cold war should include psychological disasters their opponents could suffer in the battlefield or within prisons, namely personality impairment, torture, brain submission by shocks and drugs; in short, the debasement of human condition[123]. The military-industrial complex funded universities and hospitals to do research on how people's minds could be rebuilt from scratch after long-term imprisonment, despondency, loss of conscience and purposeful injure of cognitive skills, as a matter of course.

Feeding back from these endeavors, two evil assumptions were lurking on behalf of the whole project: firstly, the Cold War was not only the fight against communism, but also a huge fountainhead to do big business in the global village; secondly, chances would arise to topple undesirable governments, mainly leftist, terrorist, or heretical, that were plunging into social and economic disasters, so as to detoxify them with the tenets of neo liberalism.

Big transnational companies engaged themselves in defense and security programs, increased their technological capabilities and secured a bountiful supply of government contracts, without any transparency or accountability, shielded not only by the military secrecy of their commitments, but also by the shift of conservative governments since Reagan and Thatcher, and followed by both Bush, senior and junior, towards the outsourcing of homeland security, military weaponry projects, cyber-warfare, and intelligence services in favor of friendly multinationals, mainly through shameful practices of crony capitalism, connivance and corruption.

b) *The Chicago School shock discipline*: the requirements of the military-industrial complex prompted Friedman and their apostles to hold the floor, arguing that the best path to rescue countries from devilish ideas like Keynesianism, social democracies and powerful

---

[123] Further details and plenty of references can be found in Klein (2008), chapter 1.

welfare states, consisted in starting their reconstruction from ground zero, in the aftermath of shocking disasters. Therefore, the didactic experiment should begin just when political and economic regimes shattered because of rampant inflation and unbridled foreign exchange devaluation, devastating stages of unemployment and poverty, disruptive financial instability, soaring government debt levels, fierce storming of protesters and strikers on the streets, terrorism, and the like. In such circumstances, the government should be toppled, and the unwarranted intrusion of the military should be allowed. This is the point of intersection between the military-industrial new approach to disasters and the Chicago model of wreaking havoc and doing business without any moral concern.

The kicking off of this heinous project was set into motion by Friedman when he started to exchange letters with the Chilean General Pinochet after the latter ousted President Allende from power. Friedman advised Pinochet how to start from scratch and the government main offices were crammed with graduates from Chicago University. Afterwards, the experience was exported to Argentina, Uruguay and Brazil, intermingled with military responses to leftist terrorism through the execution of the so-called Condor Plan and what was later called the "dirty war".

To all intents and purposes, we should raise the following query: *Which are the main programs set forth by this worldview that was called "neo liberalism" (which is a misnomer for neo conservatism)? There are three that should be regarded as primary in this ideology: privatization, government deregulation and huge cuts to social spending (a treatment also known as the shock discipline). And interlaced with the former question, we must ask to ourselves: How were they able to carry out such antisocial, disruptive and unpopular measures?*

The answer points out that in each country where the programs were tried and enforced there was a prior "state of disaster" over which they became the vehicles to perform magical cure by means of what was later dubbed "the shock discipline". Disasters fostered plenty of opportunities for big business, to the detriment of the inhabitants dwelling in the countries chosen as social laboratories. This was the deep connection between the military-industrial complex and the neo liberal gospel.

After the devastating tests carried on for the sake of fighting terrorism in Latin America, the Chicago Boys tried to became functional to new democratic governments elected in the 1980s. It was the second phase in the experiment, with even worse consequences. The whole process changed gears and instead of being grounded on military struggles against left-wingers and terrorists, it took a political and economic streak. Later on, the implosion of the former Soviet Union and the fall of the Berlin Wall at the end of the eighties ushered a wave of countries that lived in appalling conditions and were prone to manifold disasters[124]. The three main goals of neo liberalism were eagerly attempted to a vast swathe of new republics (we mean privatization, government regulation, and cuts to social spending). The consequences are familiar to us: discontent and grievances, political extremism, populism either from the right or the left, one percent of the world population owning ninety percent of the global wealth, organized crime, corruption, ecocide, outrageous levels of poverty and unemployment.[125]

---

[124] In her book, Naomi Klein contributed with critical analysis of the experiences undergone by Chile, Argentina, Brazil, Bolivia, Uruguay, Russia, China, South Africa, South Korea, Malaysia, Thailand, United Kingdom (under Thatcher), United States (as from Reagan), Iraq, Sri Lanka, and Israel.

[125] By the time this book was submitted to the publisher, December 2019, social unrest in Latin America came to the fore, entailing the outrageous consequences of neo liberalism as well as secular social inequality; to wit, Bolivia, Chile, Ecuador, Venezuela, Argentina, and a bunch of Central America countries showed worrying symptoms of instability and the upsurge of populism.

CONCLUSION

This chapter argued that the day of reckoning for capitalism and the liberal market-system is coming closer. Firstly, it was noticed how historic context and impermanence erodes the basic tenets of liberalism, either in the political or economic variants. Secondly, material and cultural features of capitalism were displayed, showing that Marxism is also doomed to pass away; both developments in the history of ideas are likely to be superseded by post capitalism, under the guise of social democracy as it is advocated in this book, or authoritarian regimes like the thriving ones of China, Russia, and other countries in the world. Afterwards, a considered assessment made a contrast between the many-sided examples of markets in the flesh and the far-fetched fairy story of the liberal market-system.

Last but not least, it was brought to light how misplaced seems the much-vaunted convergence between capitalism and the liberal market-system with democracy. Linked to the former issue, liberal think-tanks and preachers from the Chicago school developed the "disaster capitalism and shock discipline models" that was a notorious banner proposed and enacted by batches of their graduates, who became bureaucrats of the IMF and the World Bank, as well as office-holders in many governments of underdeveloped countries, and who tried to enforce the ill-fated policies of neo liberalism and the so-called Consensus of Washington. Needless to say, their policies only brought misery, unemployment, social unrest, discontent and hate, ravaging the lives and welfare of people all around the world.

Chapter 7

SOCIAL DEMOCRACY, SOCIAL MARKETS, AND THE WELFARE STATE WILL STAND FOR POST CAPITALISM

ABSTRACT

This chapter starts with social capital and cooperatives, deploying the deepest linkage there is between social capital and the common good; next, it expands on the welfare state, social markets and social democracy; afterwards, it shows that any political statement also conveys a moral assertion. It goes without saying that the failure of capitalism and neo liberalism points out that we are at the birth of a new viewpoint on governance and political action; bearing this in mind, it is for the last section to draw up the likely outline of post capitalism under the shape of social democracy.

INTRODUCTION

Something is rotten to the core when one percent of the population, also embracing multinationals, off shore locations, and investment funds, possess almost ninety percent of the collective wealth on earth. One could argue that never before in History things were different, although this would surely amount to a cynical statement, indeed. It could hold true if we looked how wealth was distributed in the fifteenth century and backwards. Amazingly, it was just from that junction in history that continental discoveries and colonization, the Industrial Revolution starting in the eighteenth through the nineteenth century, political and economic liberalism, technological and scientific breakthroughs, the growth of middle classes and the pervading influence of new professions, all of them were driving forces that ought to have improved wealth levels all around the planet. Regrettably, this was not the chosen course of events, and one percent of the population has been grabbing all the benefits, by fair means or foul.

Why has this unseemly development taken place? It won't come as a surprise that as this book draws to its close, we are able to stress that the root of the problem lies in the intended and unintended pitfalls of capitalism and economic liberalism. Uneven wealth distribution runs side by side with its shameful concentration. Stoking intended consequences, groups of interest tried and obtained from regulators the loosening of constraints to set up bigger organizations without adequate government oversight, all in the name of size, scope, and nationalism. But this process went beyond control when the managers of organized crime, corruption and ecocide became movers and shakers under the clout of capitalism and the liberal market-system, which brought about heinous unintended consequences.

The foregoing paragraphs cast doubt whether such a bleak depiction also holds true in countries where capitalism and the liberal market-system are not native to their mindsets. The answer is crystal clear: if we gave heed to what happens in China and Russia, for instance, the perspective would even be much bleaker. To begin with, there is no evidence that social mobility has been bolstered in those countries, albeit there is an increasing professional class grounded in strategic, economic, commercial, military and scientific reasons, but the bulk of the population remains in a social context that allows survival only, with widespread lack of opportunities and hopes. The picture is still more detrimental in India, the Philippines, also in Middle Eastern and African countries.

We are going to carry on our line of inquiry mainly through the Western World where most representative democracies strive to improve their fate.

Nonetheless, if we look into countries with non-representative political systems, criticism of capitalism and the liberal market-system also holds true because those countries intend to fake capitalism features and economic liberalism as a matter of convenience, albeit amplifying their deviant performance with even worse outcomes for their inhabitants.

7.1. SOCIAL CAPITAL AND COOPERATIVES

At this stage of our argument, it seems indisputable that capitalism and the liberal market-system, through their own dynamics, have been failing miserably in making lasting changes for the benefit of the have-nots and lower middle-class in society; to start with, by disregarding public education, health and retirement programs, which are basic stepping stones to social mobility.

More often than not, capitalism and the liberal market-system have taken no notice of two building blocks of participative democracy, which offer plenty of resources and applications to redress wrongs and bring fairness[126]. We mean, namely, social capital and the propping up of new varieties of cooperatives[127].

a) Social Capital

There are concepts, in social sciences, so embracing and suitable that they are able to ratchet up assertions and discussions with stronger foundations; such is the case of 'social capital'.

---

[126] Barber (1984) has been a staunch supporter of participative politics and his book seems a must-read one for any informed citizen concerned with political action and better governance.
[127] To the extent of regarding, in section b) below, any private company as being a creditors' cooperative.

Statement of Meaning 1 – Social Capital

By Social Capital we mean an arrangement of social assets, interactions, beliefs, and expectations that can be outlined this way:

- Human beings are embedded in manifold networks of social exchange since they are born, hence assimilating their cultural heritage, step by step.
- Those exchanges take place in successive informal settings, starting with the family place and, henceforth, evolving towards more formal and wider circles among which we find neighborhood acquaintances, church membership, schools and club gatherings, close friendship groups, colleges and, later on, jobs environments.
- Persistent social interactions provide the players with skills and techniques, attitudes as well as rules of the game, norms and habits.
- As long as this 'community knowledge', explicitly or tacitly, is acquired and handed down, people realize that trust and recognition, mutuality and loyalty, good faith and reputation, cooperation or punishment, acceptance or rejection of an increasing number of courses of action, might be regarded as natural payoffs deeply-rooted in their communal life.

Mind the fourth assertion in the statement of meaning above: it stresses the fact that the community resorts to explicit or tacit knowledge. The latter notion has been essential for social capital and was forcibly advocated by Michael Polanyi (1966) who pointed out that human beings can know more than they can tell, and this feature comes ingrained in human nature through survival skills learnt by trial and error, obliquity, lateral thinking[128], and heuristics. [By the way, Michael Polanyi (1891-1976) was a Hungarian-British chemist and philosopher not to be mistaken for his brother, the economic historian Karl Polanyi (1886-1964) who will also be referred to, later on this chapter]

---

[128] Readers interested in obliquity are referred to J. Kay (2010), whereas the classical book on lateral thinking is the one by Edward De Bono (2012).

Astonishingly, only in recent decades the topic of social capital has raised the interest of social scientists. Nevertheless, there were a cohort of classical novelists in the nineteenth century that laid the groundwork for social awareness, among them Jane Austen and Charles Dickens, in the English tradition; or Honore de Balzac and Emile Zola, in the French literature. Lately, it was sociologist David Halpern (2005) who has highlighted three constituents in the concept of social capital: firstly, a social network; then, connections among norms, values and expectations; finally, rewards or sanctions[129]. On the other hand, he hinted at reciprocal tiers of analysis: individual (micro-level); community and groups (intermediate level); nation and international affairs (macro-level). Besides, he singled out functional sub-types of social capital:

- *bonding social capital*, which is inward looking; it bears on exclusive identities and aims to improve the homogeneity of the group;
- *bridging social capital*, which is outward looking; it takes into account people across different social groupings;
- *linking social capital*, which could be regarded as a particular type of bridging, where the main issue consists in connecting sets of people with asymmetric power relationships, a characteristic of any political network.

Social Capital and the Common Good

It was when he delivered his presidential address at the American Political Science Association in 1911 that Woodrow Wilson rendered a memorable excerpt of what he understood by common good (*common interest* in his own wording), following a time-honored tradition in the United States set forth by the Founding Fathers at the end of the eighteenth century.

---

[129] In other words, Halpern shaped social capital as a dynamic system.

> Suppose we define business as the economic service of society for private profit, and suppose we define politics as the accommodation of all social forces, the forces of business of course included, to the common interest. We may thus perceive our task in all its magnitude and extraordinary significance. Business must be looked upon, not as the exploitation of society, not as its use for private ends, but as its sober service; and private profit must be regarded as legitimate only when it is in fact a reward for what is veritably serviceable, - serviceable to interests which are not single but common, as far as they go; and politics must be the discovery of this common interest, in order that the service may be tested and exacted. (p. 7)

Almost two hundred and fifty years after the independence of the United States, Robert Reich (2018) has raised the voice of that long-standing heritage to critically meet face to face how the pursuit of common good has worsened since the 1950s. He interprets the common good as a pool of trust living along generations, whose outstanding features consist of shared values, ideals we wish to achieve, consensus about which are the rights and the wrongs of society, as well as norms we abide by for the sake of our welfare; in other words, the common good is embedded in social capital. It is from his praise for the morality of the common good that we can draw a simple lesson: *your neighbor is your friend, and the other way around*.

Looking the enduring crisis and debasement that common sense has undergone in the United States (and in most representative democracies, by all accounts), Reich draws attention, under the guise of precepts in plain sight, to three patterns of political practices that have worn out social capital over the last decades:

Do whatever it takes to win politics, a course of action that enables the most powerful groups of interest to reap political gains, by co-opting the state and their institutions, an immoral behavior that fosters organized crime, corruption and ecocide.

Do whatever it takes to make huge profits, which turns out to be the most brazen contempt of stakeholders in society, by means of connivance, blame avoidance and sheer lies.

Do whatever it takes to rig the economy, which allows mighty groups of interest to steal people from all economic gains, and socialize the losses stemming from commercial failures and financial crisis carried out by criminal schemes of banks, portfolio managers and insurance companies, as the meltdown of 2008 bear witness to the outrageous and unforgivable bailing out of the culprits with taxpayers' money.

The foregoing remarks not only disclose the deep linkage between social capital and the common good, but also herald the day of reckoning for capitalism and the liberal market-system. It is my deep contention that the time may be ripe for the coming out of social democracy, social markets, and the welfare state.

b) Cooperatives

The ancestors of formal cooperatives can be traced back to the eighteenth century[130], but it was as from the nineteenth, mainly in England, when they attained sound legal entitlements and made significant inroads on fostering commerce and improving workers' welfare. In England, workers created the time-honored Rochdale Society of Equitable Pioneers in 1844, and wrote down a bundle of governance principles that have been guidelines for other cooperatives since then, including democratic control by their members, and distribution of earnings according to patronage. The underlying reasons for the existence and development of cooperatives were not only economic, but also political and sociological, so forcefully insisted upon by Perkin (2002). At this point, it will be worth making explicit what the expression "cooperative" stands for.

---

[130] In the United States, it was for Benjamin Franklin to found the first cooperative in Philadelphia by 1752, a mutual fire insurance company that is still running [Center for Cooperatives, 2012, www.uwcc.wisc.edu].

Statement of Meaning 2 – Primary Cooperatives

By a Primary Cooperative we mean a business association or civil society, both endowed with legal entity, whose main features are the following:

- members enter the organization to pool their own resources on a fully voluntary basis for the fulfillment of their mutual interest and benefit;
- members are owners and patrons; they hold only one vote, regardless of their equity holding;
- earnings are shared and distributed to the extent of the use (or patronage) that ultimately each member makes of the cooperative's services, either as consumer, producer or worker;
- only members can be appointed and trained as directors;
- members live, work and trade within, or in the nearby of, local communities.

It shouldn't come as a surprise that we enveloped primary cooperatives as being either business associations or civil societies. The expression "business association" might be misleading unless we recall that most cooperatives intend to do business in the markets on behalf of their patrons without becoming for-profit associations. If their operations at the end of each year earned good results, they ought to be channeled either by plowing back them into new investments or recorded like patronage dividends on behalf of their members, as it was explained in chapter 3, section 3.6.

Why have we chosen to define "primary cooperatives" instead of "cooperatives" in general? Because every other form of co-op evolves out of this primary notion, in the guise of one-, two-, or three-tiered arrangements.

- *One-tiered structure*: primary cooperatives performing as local single associations.
- *Two-tiered structure*: cooperatives built up out of primary cooperatives, albeit on a regional scale.

- *Three-tiered structure*: they arise out of two-tiered structures that join together to expand their range to national boundaries, although they have not been very popular so far.

Remark

As a matter of course, the transition from one-tiered to higher levels of organization entails increasing obstacles, being the three-tiered structure the most assailable to governance impairments.

On Cooperative Patrons

Let us focus on those stakeholders who actively engage themselves in the daily transactions that flow into and out of any cooperative; they are customers, suppliers, or workers, also acting as members and "social owners" of these organizations by which they are denoted *patrons*[131]. It is because of their featured roles and functions that we are led to a well-known and natural typology of cooperatives[132]:

- *Consumers cooperatives:* general retail (food, clothing, house conveniences); financial (cooperative banks, credit unions, insurance); housing and public works; health and social care (hospitals, rural dispensaries, pharmacies); utilities (electricity, water, telecoms); public services (child care, health centers); education (cooperative schools, technological institutes, universities).
- *Producers cooperatives:* farming, fishery, forestry; wholesaling supply to networks of member stores (either supermarkets, hardware workshops, groceries and bakeries franchisees, and pharmacy outlets); restaurants and coffee bars; catering for services needed by small- and medium-sized organizations.
- *Workers cooperatives:* owned and managed by their workers; also including law and accounting firms, household fixing and

---

[131] One of the earliest attempts to deal with the notion of patron can be found in *The Ownership of Enterprise* by Hansmann (1996).
[132] The list does not intend to be all-inclusive but representative only.

maintenance technicians, investment banking, engineering, security agencies, consultancy organizations, health and caregiver professions, and the like.

By the way, if we carefully looked at the prior list of cooperatives it would seem noticeable that several of them become essential in the fight against ecocide, as Naomi Klein (2015) underscored in her withering criticism of global warming and ecological wreckage; she highlighted the impressive performance of cooperatives in the field of utilities dealing with non-extractive sources of energy, as we can witness in Denmark, the Netherlands, Sweden and Germany[133].

Why Cooperatives Pose a Competitive Threat to Capitalist Companies

Would it be farfetched to regard the capitalist company as a cooperative? For most people who support neo liberal ideas such viewpoint may sound outrageous, to say the least. However, this approach was strongly advocated by Hansmann (1996) in his riveting book *The Ownership of the Enterprise*, where he asserted that capitalist concerns should be thought as cooperatives of creditors. Let us labor this point in more detail.

Although such a daring perspective was deemed a remarkably academic contribution, it shortly lost importance in neo liberal quarters and faded away eventually. Contrariwise, social democrats and progressives acknowledged the proposal not only as commonsensical but also ingrained in their time-honored assumptions.

There is no denying that translating the nature of a capitalist company into a cooperative setting, it will mean to be owned, managed and overseen by their creditors. On the other hand, it turns out to be feasible and promising in the context of social democracy provided that five changes, at least, might be brought into completion:

- the idea of profit and making money for its own sake must be replaced with the one that intends the pursuit of social earnings;

---

[133] In section 7.5, this chapter, practice 35 sets forth a more wide-ranging function for cooperatives.

- the notion of patrons, who receive patronage instead of shareholders dividends, is of the essence; it connotes that the old stockholders and creditors become social owners of the organization;
- interest and principal payments on debts must follow the pattern currently found in capitalist companies; in other words, interest over the principal are periodically paid, and the principal given back at maturity dates;
- when private companies turn out cooperatives, workers must gain access to their labor rights of joint management, membership in Boards, and profit sharing[134];
- their governance must be nearly akin to the one predicated for cooperatives.

7.2. THE WELFARE STATE, SOCIAL MARKETS, AND SOCIAL DEMOCRACY

To countervail the pervading deviances of capitalism and the liberal market-system, let us move onto a compact of remarkable and interlaced alternatives: the welfare state, social markets and, lastly, social democracy[135].

a) The Welfare-State

All over the nineteenth century, persistent social unrest among poverty-stricken workers and their families collided with Liberals and Conservatives (firstly in England, next in continental Europe). Hence, there were several attempts to help the poor and dispossessed, mainly through the agency of socialists, communitarians, Marxists, and revolutionaries of all sorts. The

---

[134] This will be principle 14 in the statute of governance for social democracies; section 7.5.
[135] As it will later be clear in 7.2.c), the meaning of social democracy also comprises social markets and the welfare state.

rumblings of anger and discontent frightened dominant groups in each country, to the extent that governments realized that something should be done to curb the mounting wave of violence and labor demands. In the end, the political answer consisted in setting up mechanisms of social assistance to the poor, the unemployed, and the aging (one of the earliest models was introduced by the conservative Chancellor Bismark for Germany in the 1870s). In the twentieth century, systematic efforts of governments, their opposition parties and social democrats on behalf of the have-nots would be strengthened by Keynes' major breakthroughs and contributions in the 1930s. Eventually, the welfare state came of age, entailing the following features:

- *unemployment safety-nets* to support the daily needs of people out of work, as well as retraining plans for deskilled or poorly educated workers;
- *universal pension programs* to grant the well-being of the aging after their working life; and social benefits addressed to ailing, handicapped and mentally impaired people, forlorn children, the poor and dispossessed, widows with children, and the like;
- *health care provision and public education* as a human right irrespective of age, family economic constraints, gender, race, religious affiliation, or nationality;
- *financial assistance to communities* hit by natural catastrophes, small- and medium-sized companies that might have become the losers of doomed regional economies, and workers downgraded by technological advancements.

The confrontational process between the liberal market forces, on the one hand, and social assistance measures, on the other, was remarkably explained by Karl Polanyi (1944), who called it "the double movement": firstly, he pointed out the workings of the self-regulating market, a liberal fetish covering up unbridled capitalism as if it were an organizing principle of society, bringing forth shocking levels of inequality as well as destitution. Secondly, there was an adversarial movement giving battle to the former, preventing the social texture from being wrecked; it was ruled by a principle of social protection that ultimately promoted the rise of the welfare state.

b) Social Markets

With the advent of capitalism in the fifteenth century[136], markets were increasingly being depicted like self-regulating systems under the guise of mechanical concoctions that were notoriously borrowed from Physics. As a result of a powerful blending that included capitalism and the liberal market-system during the eighteenth and nineteenth centuries, the market was regarded as the meeting place of free and rational individuals that sell, buy, produce, distribute and consume; they were assimilated to uncommitted participants[137] in a game that did not give time, room, nor money for social issues. In actual fact, the so-called perfectly competitive markets never prevailed beyond villages or counties trading commodities for matching their local needs, and they couldn't exist in the flesh, only being a magical metaphor at the mercy of an ideology. On this account, Barry Schwartz (2000) has given heed to what he called "the costs of living", meaning the increasing trend by which human beings relinquish cherished things of life (home time, friendships, cooperation, cultural and entertainment engagements, social values, community participation) because the market fashions commodities out of them. In contrast, social markets intend blending human assets or entitlements with daily market tasks and commitments.

In prior sections of the former chapter, we acquainted ourselves with the fact that the Industrial Revolution unleashed waves of protest, resentment, and discontent. To many serious thinkers and politicians, left- or right-

---

[136] Several scholars, even Braudel (1992) in some particulars, have been reluctant to attach a starting date for this consequential process, and argued that there were earlier contexts for the coming of capitalism. Recently, Frankopan (2015) brought the date further back before the tenth century in the Eastern World.

[137] As if they were molecules shifting and drifting in containers with heating gases or liquids, as physicists usually deal with in their dynamic models; eventually, this attempts actually grew up like pitiful examples of the "extrapolation fallacy".

wingers alike, circumstances brought them home to the fact that impending changes had to be carried out lest the social conditions should go from bad to worse.

The first step consisted in fiercely disputing that markets could become self-regulating machines, and this step was taken indeed, conveying a momentous perception and belief: the liberal market system was a social environment oblivious of poverty-stricken people by and large.

A distinctive second step smoothly followed: as the market was not a self-operating contrivance, and benefited only few individuals who were in pursuit of wealth and power, it was for the state to play the role of the decisive umpire who redresses social balance and fairness; that is to say, the state was to curb the evils of the market-system, and had to become a big producer, supplier and purchaser of good and services.

By the end of the nineteenth century[138] the welfare state replaced the economic contrivance of the market-system with new arrangements: *as from that moment, the expression "social market" stood for a network of cooperation, government assistance and redistribution of resources, not only from the haves to the have-nots, but also by investing in utilities and public works on behalf of the common good. Markets became living partnerships among producers, investors, consumers, and the government.*

On Social Markets and the Purposes of Any Company

Social markets reject neo liberal ideas about which are the goals any company should fulfill. For the sake of illustration, let us deal with two statements conventionally held as if they were true, albeit they are utterly wrong and misguiding eventually.

> *Statement 1:* For capitalism and the liberal market-system, the basic purpose of any company is to make money, on behalf of shareholders.

---

[138] We are thinking of Finland, Norway, Sweden, the United Kingdom, Denmark, Germany, Austria, the Netherlands and Switzerland; also, in some connection because of their outstanding social policies, Australia and Canada.

It seems sensible to absolutely destroy the pretense of such assertion because, if it were true, what would be the difference between a good company when contrasted with Enron, or a sweatshop which enslaves children and women; even worse a drug-dealing cartel? Regretfully, this humbug is still taught in many Business Schools. Contrariwise, social-market supporters advocate that a new statement should be framed as a principle of governance.

New Statement 1: In social markets, the actual purpose of any private company or state-owned firm is to gain earnings in the context of corporate social responsibility towards their stakeholders, and the full compliance of the law, regulatory habitats and human rights.

Closely related and also widely endorsed by economic groups, we frequently come across with another misplaced belief.

Statement 2: In capitalism and the liberal market-system, the corporation should not care whether it produces externalities[139] to the disadvantage of people (including children, disabled, or paupers), communities, minorities, countries, and environmental resources.

Disgracefully, this statement also infers that "those pitfalls amount to the costs of running business". Indisputably, companies do produce and release externalities that damage the health of people (even killing them), deplete natural resources, disrupt the balance between people and their environment, pollute cities and country sides, rivers and seas, lakes and valleys. Hence, the former statement should be rendered this way:

New Statement 2: In social markets, externalities produced by private companies or state-owned firms that could become harmful to stakeholders disclose a behavior grounded on the contempt of law,

---

[139] Broadly speaking, they are costs ultimately borne by external actors to economic or environmental activities that end up as detrimental to those actors; foremost among them, the costs of pollution.

human rights, and disregard of corporate social responsibilities, by which those companies must be prosecuted on federal charges.

c) Social Democracies

For all intents and purposes, social democracies were a natural response to hard times all over the nineteenth century in Europe. However, a distinction should be drawn between this sort of political system and the more radical ones like socialism and communism. Socialism and communism campaigned for the state ownership of the means of production, a mechanistic command market, and a harsh program of social assistance whose nature, mainly in the case of communism, was more akin to cattle management or to a style of living fashioned after slavery plantations. Contrariwise, social democracies evolved and remained strikingly different.

In the context of our proposal let us frame the notion of this political system as we expect it to develop as time goes by in our day and age.

Statement of Meaning 3 – Social Democracy
By Social Democracy we mean a political system whose main features are:

- *firstly, it is a representative democracy with periodic elections, opposition parties, independent government branches and full-fledged checks and balances;*
- *secondly, it advocates a strong state with a pervasive and quite effective reach through social markets;*
- *thirdly, the state cares for people, detaching itself from the sheer individualism and self-interest predicated by the economic liberal model; hence, it pleads for a welfare state in which private companies are encouraged to become creditor's cooperatives;*

- *fourthly, universal human rights are upheld as essential rights of individuals and communities[140];*
- *last but not least, it makes public education and public health top priorities; it handles political negotiations with trade-unions and businessmen; it shows responsiveness to citizens demands; it safeguards free thinking and the exercise of an independent and critical press.*

We lay stress on the first assertion in the statement of meaning. As from the 1960s, it has often been heard that political parties are on the brink of death, a viewpoint that ultimately would entail the disempowering of representative democracies. This seems an overstatement since such standpoint leaves aside other political systems from being assessed, narrowing down the topic to liberal democracies only, forgetting how resilient social democracies can be and how well they may do against all dooming expectations.

Only if we constrained ourselves to the political background of capitalism and the liberal market-system, then the waning out of political parties would hold true. Although such frame of mind led to Professor Mair's (2013) calling into question the legitimacy of political parties in liberal democracies, as soon as we make the contrast with social democracies counterparts we realize that the latter keep alive the seeds of cooperation, trust and commitment with social issues: those are exactly the values that liberal democracies and their political parties have been surrendering along the last century. Social democracies avail themselves of opposition parties to enliven the political debate and sharpen up accountability, because at stake is nothing much higher and more important than the common good of the whole society, instead of vested interests befriended by callous elites.

---

[140] Among them, the right to property (article 17, Universal Declaration of Human Rights).

Social Democracies and Human Rights

There is no denying that any social democracy intends to be sympathetic towards communitarian concerns almost by definition. But it goes further than that, to the extent of embracing human rights as a distinctive feature of their governance and politics, as it was portrayed in the statement of meaning given above.

When on December 10, 1948, the United Nations General Assembly proclaimed the Universal Declaration of Human Rights[141], it portrayed a structure of social cooperation, as it is highlighted at the Preamble of such declaration:

> whereas recognition of the inherent dignity and of the equal and inalienable rights of all members of the human family is the foundation of freedom, justice and peace in the world [...]

By the same token, it concludes the Preamble with the following assertion:

> Now, therefore, the General Assembly proclaims this Universal Declaration of Human Rights as a common standard of achievement for all peoples and all nations, to the end that every individual and every organ of society, keeping this Declaration constantly in mind, shall strive by teaching and education to promote respect for these rights and freedoms and by progressive measures, national and international, to secure their universal and effective recognition and observance, both among the peoples of Member States themselves and among the peoples of territories under their jurisdiction.

Needless to say, this was a momentous achievement in History. And it had far-reaching consequences for the governance of social democracies. It's worth slowing down here and take stock of this remarkable connection:

---

[141] The whole document is available at www.un.org .

a) social democracy is a political system engaged with the common good of their constituents, bringing an articulate bridge between the social markets and the welfare state;
b) human rights underscore social behavior impinged upon dignity, equality of rights and freedoms (article 2), entitlements, duties and cooperation; it also ascertains that human beings should act towards one another "in a spirit of brotherhood" (article 1);
c) social democracy becomes feasible and reliable because its political goals consist in the enhancement of people and society by acting as a gatekeeper for human rights; otherwise, how would it uphold not only social markets but also the welfare state?
d) it follows from a), b) and c) that, in contrast with neo liberal countries, authoritarian political systems or libertarian regimes, social democracies cannot connive with organized crime, corruption, and ecocide.

Following the line of argument upheld in this book, we are going to choose among those rights most directly linked with the subject of social democracy:

- right to life, liberty and security of person (article 3);
- recognition everywhere as a person before the law (article 6);
- everyone has the right to own property alone as well as in association with others; no one shall be arbitrarily deprived of his property (article 17);
- everyone has the right to freedom of thought, conscience and religion (article 18);
- everyone has the right to freedom of opinion and expression (article 19);
- everyone has the right to freedom of peaceful assembly and association; no one may be compelled to belong to an association (article 20);
- everyone has the right to take part in the government of his country, directly or through freely chosen representatives; everyone has the

right of equal access to public service in his country; the will of the people shall be the basis of the authority of government (article 21);
- everyone, as a member of society, has the right to social security and is entitled to realization, through national effort and international cooperation and in accordance with the organization and resources of each state, of the economic, social and cultural rights indispensable for his dignity and the free development of his personality (article 22);
- everyone has the right to work, to free choice of employment, to just and favorable conditions of work and to protection against unemployment; everyone, without any discrimination, has the right to equal pay for equal work; everyone who works has the right to just and favorable remuneration ensuring for himself and his family an existence worthy of human dignity, and supplemented, if necessary, by other means of social protection; everyone has the right to form and to join trade unions for the protection of his interests (article 23);
- everyone has the right to rest and leisure, including reasonable limitation of working hours and periodic holidays with pay (article 24);
- everyone has the right to a standard of living adequate for the health and well-being of himself and of his family, including food, clothing, housing and medical care and necessary social services, and the right to security in the event of unemployment, sickness, disability, widowhood, old age or other lack of livelihood in circumstances beyond his control; motherhood and childhood are entitled to special care and assistance; all children, whether born in or out of wedlock, shall enjoy the same social protection (article 25);
- everyone has the right to education; education shall be free, at least in the elementary and fundamental stages; elementary education shall be compulsory; technical and professional education shall be made generally available and higher education shall be equally accessible to all on the basis of merit; education shall be directed to the full development of the human personality and to the

strengthening of respect for human rights and fundamental freedoms; it shall promote understanding, tolerance and friendship among all nations, racial or religious groups, and shall further the activities of the United Nations for the maintenance of peace; parents have a prior right to choose the kind of education that shall be given to their children (article 26).

As we can conclude from the foregoing articles, the welfare state and the tenets of social democracies become fittingly endorsed by articles 17, 20, 22, 23, 24, 25 and 26.

In addition to what has just been said, three significant factors have made inroads into the texture and scope of human rights since the approval of the Declaration in 1948:

Firstly, from the end of the Second World War onwards, many states have entered the United Nations; today, we can confirm that the whole world has gathered around and into the United Nations.

Secondly, a new kind of globalization development arouse as from the 60s, mainly through unprecedented innovations in commerce, transport, finance, logistics, information, engineering, communication and computer technology; such background ultimately furnished with handy solutions to common problems shared by most countries worldwide.

Thirdly, a host of new nations became conversant with alternative political systems, chose among them, and coped with an overwhelming concern over human rights, which grew so influential to affect terms of trade in international commerce, financial assistance, investment projects and investigative journalism.

The process highlighted above gave rise to complementary resolutions by the United Nations. Outstandingly for the purpose of this book, we can notice the International Covenant on Civil and Political Rights, adopted on December 16, 1966, and enforced from March 23, 1976[142], whose aim is to make provision for the exercise of negative liberties (in the sense of being formal, defensive). Furthermore, the Covenant on Economic, Social and

---

[142] The whole document is available at www.un.org.

Cultural Rights pairs with the former covenant, whereas it makes provision for the exercise of positive liberties (with the meaning of being enabling, material). These covenants, together with the Universal Declaration of Human Rights, are regarded as the primary compact of human rights in the international community of nations. Thomas Meyer (2007), in his noteworthy book *The Theory of Social Democracy*, has enlarged upon deep connections of these covenants with the Universal Declaration of Human Rights.

7.3. BACK TO THE MORAL FOUNDATIONS OF POLITICS

It is often read and debated that politics has nothing to do with moral; even worse, that politics turns out to be an immoral, or at least amoral human enterprise; however, such standpoint comes down to an embarrassing mistake. Political systems and parties, governments and their opposition, scholars and practitioners, journalists and the typical man in the street, when putting forward their political discourse actually unmask and make known those things that they believe, expect or assume either as right and good, or wrong and evil; in other words, they bundle and predicate moral assertions into their political concerns.

The tasks of politics amounts to handling and disputing about what is good or bad for societies and political actors in certain historical context and cultural tradition; it goes without saying that *any political system must give account of what sort of moral assertions were chosen and to whom they benefit eventually, to sow the seeds of likely agreements and healthy dissent.* On the other hand, if governance intends to be the blueprint to attain good government, it can't steer clear of moral statements and social values, as neo liberals attempt under false pretenses, belittling the subject of moral and values to a mere trifling issue of immaterial consequences; indeed, this is a malicious narrative that only lends a helping hand to antidemocratic assumptions shared by deviant groups of interest worldwide.

The sway of moral assertions and social values in politics has been recognized since olden times by philosophers; later, it was cogently argued

Social Democracy, Social Markets ... 219

by Scottish and English thinkers in the seventeenth and eighteenth centuries, like Locke, Hutchison, Ferguson, Hume, and Adam Smith[143], among others. In our own century, cognitive scientists have started to contribute to the understanding of the so-called "political mind" [George Lakoff (2009)], delivering a warning about the pervading role the subconscious has in political action and how human beings subordinate their assertions to mindscapes shaped in the past, without realizing that most of them might have grown out of date, a standpoint that echoes of David Hume (1751, 1748) and Keynes (1935, p. 383) insights[144].

7.4. AT THE CROSSROADS OF A NEW KIND OF GOVERNANCE AND POLITICAL ACTION

In the first part of the book, from chapter 1 through chapter 3, we have expanded on the upsides of governance and politics, by putting forth some key statements and proposals:

- governance is the blueprint for good political action and better government[145]; accountability and transparency are social learning processes;
- as any organization frames itself as a political conflict-system, dysfunctional governance takes place and remedial courses of action may be required; hence, we designed a clinical approach to make a diagnosis and follow up a treatment for regaining the health of those structures;
- for each organization, either private, public or global, even the whole government, we can draw up a covenant that entails

---

[143] It is often disregarded, or suspiciously forgotten by conservatives, that Adam Smith was a prominent professor of Morals at the University of Glasgow.
[144] Jonathan Haidt (2013) put forward a compelling argument on the role of Hume's moral mindscape in modern sociological and political analysis.
[145] Literally, this was precisely the subtitle of my book on Public Governance [Apreda (2007), Nova Publishers, New York].

commitments and responsibilities (accountability) and help stakeholders be aware of what is happening within the organization (transparency); we called such device *the statute of governance*, which comprises principles of governance and good practices;
- the gist of governance and politics rests on social capital, that is to say, community values, cultural achievements, the citizens' demands to government and the moral heritage of social groups, minorities, and civil society.

So far so good, we could say. But chapters 4 and 5 disclosed how easily bad governance and worse politics shifts to corruption, organized crime and ecocide; it would be deceiving to predicate that these undesirable outcomes can only be tracked down to human malfeasance in search of impunity. Quite the opposite, the blooming of organized crime, ecocide and corruption must be sought in the dynamics of global capitalism and the liberal market-system, both of which empower criminal organizations to meet their objectives by engineering courses of action like the following ones:

- organizations are set up in offshore locations by means of lenient and opaque governances; crime syndicates hire (and handsomely reward) accountants, financial experts, scientists and lawyers to frame their roguish contrivances;
- those syndicates foster sympathetic relationships with politicians and regulators, by co-opting officials in the government, the Judiciary, the Congress and security officials; in other words, organized crime and corruption go hand in hand;
- in the case of ecocide, as we have already seen in chapter 5, criminal organizations lavishly pay public relations companies, spin doctors, journalists and political advisors who produce and distribute deceptive images on behalf of their undertakings to avoid the public outrage and the threat of investigative journalists who may uncover their secret operations;
- criminal gangs keep pouring huge amounts of money to commercial and investment banks that lend their own customers at their

headquarters with laundered money [to put it bluntly: if criminal earnings were channeled into offshore locations, who but bank managers would be the beneficiaries of dirty money at their receiving end, as professor Palan (2003) has insisted upon in his remarkable book on the subject];
- lastly, we can't help being amazed about the extent to which organized crime had been profiting from politically supportive habitats like those provided by authoritarian, populist regimes and right-winged governments in developed countries.

We are certainly in great need of a new governance and politics to supersede capitalism and the liberal market-system fetish. The considered enlargement of this line of argument will become topical in next section.

7.5. TOWARDS A STATUTE OF GOVERNANCE FOR SOCIAL DEMOCRACY

More than ever before, societies are wanting in a minimal set of measures for the furtherance of the common good. It is my contention that such arrangement would pave the way to post capitalism in the guise of social democracy, social markets and the welfare state. At this juncture, it will be worth slowing down and taking stock about the proficiency and resilience of social democracy against the triad of organized crime, corruption and ecocide. To start with, we have to handle the following question: to what extent would social democracy be able to redress the wrongs brought about by the triad and their main accomplishes? There are two courses of action worthy of being taken:

a) On the level of principles, a statute of governance must be embedded in the country's Constitution so that the triad above-mentioned turns out to be incompatible with the tenets of a social representative democracy.

b) As from political practices, they must uproot the capitalist and neo liberal black holes that have supplied the triad with leniency and connivance in their criminal endeavors so far.

Needless to say, that we will only focus on those principles and practices linked to the main topics conveyed in this book: how capitalism and the liberal market-system shamelessly helped organized crime, corruption and ecocide. This entails that overhauling the governance and politics of any country lies in many other factors that do not come under the purview of this work; such would be the task of a whole national statute of governance embracing the underlying political system as well as its institutions, its social capital and Constitution. Nevertheless, the principles and practices listed below will be part and parcel of such national statute.

Methodological Remarks

- Next list doesn't claim to be complete or the only one to be chosen.
- *On footnotes*: easing up the reader's bearings, each principle and practice will be joined by a footnote that locates the chapter and section where proper details and extensions could be found, or refers to some author for complementary reading.
- It should be noticed that social democracies are a particular kind of representative democracies. Nevertheless, we wish to press home that certain principles or practices advocated below holds for social democracies albeit they may not entirely stand firm in other types of representative democracies.

a) Governance Principles

The assortment of governance principles that will follow actually stem from the main inferences put forward in this book, and intend to prevent social democracies from being co-opted by organized crime, corruption and ecocide. Hence, we will focus on the basic architecture for that governance, encompassing its moral foundations, social capital, ownership and property rights, welfare state and social markets

On the Basic Architecture

1. In representative democracies, the founding covenant for governance and political action largely consists of their Constitutions[146];
2. In representative democracies, the rule of law is both condition and consequence[147] of democracy whereas accountability, transparency and fiduciary duties are cornerstones of their governance and politics[148];
3. In social democracies, the Universal Declaration of Human Rights and their covenants must be unconditionally embedded in their Constitutions[149];
4. The core principle of any social democracy lies in the pursuit and sustainability of the common good[150]; contempt of this principle must be charged as flouting the constitution, triggering a federal indictment;

On Moral Foundations

1. for governance and political action to be efficacious, their underlying moral assertions must be brought to light[151] and explained;

---

[146] In some countries, like the United States, there is also a bill of rights and amendments attached to the Constitution, hence enlarging the basic covenant.
[147] This amounts to "democracy if and only if rule of law", as Norberto Bobbio (1987) has argued.
[148] We refer the reader to chapter 2: *How accountability and transparency become social learning processes*.
[149] This key point was discussed in section 7.2 c). See articles 1, 2, 3, 4, 18 and 19 in the Declaration.
[150] The notion of common good was introduced in chapter 1, introduction.
[151] On the moral foundations of the social texture: section 7.3, this chapter.

2. in social democracies, corporatism is a lurking and detrimental threat to the common good; one thing is the democratic and legitimate interaction of groups of interest; quite another if the activities of those groups further the growing of non-democratic, opaque sects or fascist political groupings[152]; by far, any type of fascism must be outlawed;
3. freedom of press and opinion through any kind of media and websites must be regarded unrestricted, barring those activities that could slur or debase constitutional rights and entitlements of single or collective political actors;

On Social Capital

1. trust networks, cooperation, responsiveness, and participation must be rated and practiced like building blocks of social democracy[153];
2. political parties, communitarian groups, trade unions, social networks, schools and colleges, free press, and civil associations are the means by which debate, opposition, negotiation, control, and agreement[154] nourish social capital and representative democracies;

On Ownership and Property Rights

1. In social democracies, private ownership rights are fully bestowed to individuals, families, small- and medium-sized companies, cooperatives and other arrangements in the civil society[155];
2. Property rights are to be regulated on behalf of the have-nots and social peace; house ownership is a human right; the welfare state

---

[152] John Ralston Saul (1995) wrote a must-read book on the subject of corporatism and fascism. See also section 4.4 in chapter 4.
[153] Trust networks were dealt with in chapter 1, whereas social capital and cooperation in section 7.1, this chapter.
[154] More on this matter is available in chapter 1. Furthermore, Barber (1984) is a key source on participatory politics.
[155] Article 17 of the Universal Declaration of Human Rights; see section 7.2.c).

Social Democracy, Social Markets ... 225

must provide each poor family with their own household; peasants must get their own land to work and live in[156];

3. Social democracies request from business companies' reliable commitments with social markets and the welfare state; on these grounds, they foster the viewpoint that private enterprises should be encouraged to adopt the structure of creditor's cooperatives[157];

4. In social democracies, there must be enacted a *Law on Inheritance and Transmission of Assets*, by which inheritance bequests and transfers must be tightly restricted, whereas their underlying inheritance taxes will be highly exacting on behalf of social needs and fairness entitlements; the ensuing resources must be allocated to public utilities and works, social housing, public health and education; even the development of backward regional economies[158];

5. In private companies, workers must be entitled to their labor rights of joint management, membership in Boards, and profit-sharing programs[159];

On the Welfare State, Social Markets and Social Democracies

1. Social markets convey a governance and politics deeply-seated on social values[160];
2. The welfare state is the precondition for organized societies that intend to safeguard the well-being and independence of their inhabitants[161], in good and bad times;
3. In social democracies, the actual purpose of any private company or state-owned firm is to gain earnings in the context of social responsibility towards stakeholders, and the full compliance of the

---

[156] Article 25 of the Universal Declaration of Human Rights; see section 7.2.c).
[157] See section 7.1 a).
[158] These hard measures on behalf of society and the have-nots have been currently enforced for decades in some northern European countries.
[159] Germany has been the leading case on this issue.
[160] Groundwork on social markets can be seen in section 7.2, this chapter.
[161] The welfare state was dealt with in section 7.2, this chapter.

law, regulatory habitats, and human rights[162]; otherwise, their activities must trigger off federal crime indictments.

b) On Political Action Practices

In any social democratic country[163], the measures set forth below attempt to fight opaque governance, corruption, organized crime and ecocide; it goes without saying that they ought to be enacted by the Congress; we also have to take into account other kind of practices about health care, education, and market alternatives.

On Criminal Governances and Corruption

1. Organizations are political conflict-systems and their dysfunctions should be diagnosed, treated, and healed by means of a clinical approach interlocked with binding statutes of governances[164]; independent compliance functions are to be compulsorily enforced in private and public organizations, as well as in government branches[165];
2. In representative democracies, there should be enacted a *Law on the Funding of Politics*, establishing hard demands for the funding of electoral campaigns, mainly from private and corporate contributions to political parties; on top of that, the statements in the law ought to be interlaced with regulations of the Internal Revenue Service pertaining sources and applications of funds from individual or corporate contributors[166];

---

[162] Further details can be found in section 7.2.c) this chapter.
[163] A comprehensive treatment can be found in chapters 4 and 5.
[164] This was the main content of chapter 3.
[165] We refer the reader to chapter 2, where compliance risks and the compliance function were introduced in their relationship with accountability and transparency.
[166] Intertwining the Internal Revenue Service with the financing of political parties is of the essence to prevent organized crime, corruption and ecocide from laundering money and capturing legislatures and governments, as we saw in chapters 4 and 5.

3. There should be enacted a *Law of Equal Opportunities in Political Careers*, whereby financial assistance will be warranted for female or male politicians with lack of resources, or representatives from disadvantaged minorities who intend to compete in political campaigns; by the same token, rich people and big companies must be audited by the Internal Revenue Service when entering such contest, paying taxes for their monetary involvement and expenses, and they can't receive any financial assistance from the state[167]; furthermore, the Law must establish the absolute gender equality whereby elective positions must keep the 50-50 proportion of females and males candidates taking turns in the electoral lists;

4. Either monopolies, cartels or trusts which stifle competition, as well as commercial and industrial indulgences, are to be regarded antisocial and have to be curbed or banned outright[168]; any working sector in the economy has to pay taxes, even judges, law-makers, trade union officers, churches, private universities and schools, and the like; under no circumstances retired people should pay taxes over their entitled pensions;

5. There ought to be enacted a *Law on Bank Malfeasance and Bad Practices*, by which financial institutions become accountable not only to their central banks but also to a bank for international settlements (like the Basel one, but with enforcement powers); investment banks are forbidden from engaging themselves in the tasks of commercial banks[169] or setting up social groupings that might include commercial sub-organizations; any material transaction might be tractable from the source through the application of the funds involved;

---

[167] As evidence increasingly exhibits, most of the time money fakes candidates who are sycophants of vested interests; in point of fact, political marketing also shapes candidates who in real life turn out to be dumbbells, clowns, corrupts, fascists, sociopaths, or populists. You name it.

[168] Tim Wu (2018) made a pithy remark in his book on antitrust regulation, underlining how concentration yields inequality and material suffering, while paving the way for fascism and dictatorship.

[169] Further analysis in chapter 4.

6. In social democracies, sheltering wealth in offshore locations should be forbidden and their citizens taking advantage of them will be prosecuted under the federal law disclosed in practice 22 above[170]; the only way to avoid being charged would imply declaring those foreign investments to their local Internal Revenue Service, with a compulsory statement of the source and application of funds, and paying highly demanding taxes over such transactions, inclusive of principal and interest;
7. Within the frame of the *Law on Bank Malfeasance and Bad Practices*, proven misconduct in banks and their managers, directors or stockholders, will be assessed as federal crimes; instead of bailing out corrupt financial institutions, they will be bankrupted and closed[171]; the central bank will weigh up whether or not healthy financial institutions could get access to the bankrupted bank customer-base;
8. Professionals behaving in connivance with organized crime, ecocide, and corruption will be prosecuted and punished outright[172]; professional bodies will compulsorily publish and update their statutes of governance and their workings[173] on behalf of crime fighting; otherwise they will be prosecuted on federal charges; lawyers and accountants must request from their clients a statement of origin of the funds paying their fees, with immediate linking to the Internal Revenue Service seeking auditing and due authorization for the transaction;
9. Accountability and transparency will be requested from public-office holders during their tenure in the government[174]; malfeasance will entail a federal crime;

---

[170] Further analysis in chapter 4.
[171] Further analysis in chapter 4.
[172] Professional bodies, more often than not, carry out the role of protective networks that connive with malpractice and malfeasance, on behalf of vested interests in corporations and criminal organizations alike. More on this in chapter 4.
[173] Further analysis in chapter 4.
[174] Further analysis in chapters 2 and 4.

On Ecocide

1. Ecocide will be qualified as a crime against mankind and human rights[175]; it should be enacted a *Law on Ecocide and Environment Protection*;
2. In social markets, externalities produced by private companies or state-owned firms, and harmful to stakeholders convey a behavior grounded on the contempt of law and human rights, whereby those organizations will be prosecuted on federal charges[176];

On Health Care

1. Health care and control of the pharmaceutical industry take priority in the government agenda, calling for the tightest standards of transparency and accountability[177];
2. Health care will be compulsory, universal, public, free and safeguarded because it is a human right; privately for-profit health care will be affordable for the wealthy brackets of society, without any support from the government[178], while their activities will be taxed;
3. Only pharmaceutical cooperatives will supply public hospitals and the whole public health-care and pension systems with medicines and related resources for their daily needs and operations; in contrast, the pharmaceutical for-profit industry must be privately owned and managed without support from the government, while their activities will be taxed[179];

---

[175] Ecocide was dealt with in chapter 5. For further details, see articles 1, 2, 3, 6, and 21, from the Universal Declaration of Human Rights, in section 7.2.c), this chapter.
[176] Further details can be found in section 7.2.c), this chapter.
[177] Further development in chapter 5. See articles 22 and 25 from the Universal Declaration of Human Rights in section 7.2. c), this chapter. Practices 30 and 31 are more demanding that article 26.
[178] Further development in chapter 5.
[179] Further development in chapter 5.

4. There cannot be distributed or sold any pharmaceutical product, neither instrumental devices for diagnosis and treatment, nor ancillary equipment for health care without audited authorization from the agency pertaining health and drug control in the government, including the signature and public report of officers working for the agency involved in the monitoring; similar procedures will be followed with food and beverages control[180];

On Education

1. Public education will be compulsory, universal, public, free, and safeguarded because it is a human right[181] at primary, secondary and university levels; as regards for-profit private education, it will be affordable to wealthy brackets of society, without any support from the government[182] and their activities will be taxable;
2. Public education, as well the for-profit private sector, will follow the highest standards of accountability, transparency and fiduciary duties; misdoings will be deemed federal crimes[183];

On Market Alternatives

1. Civil society and governments are to set up broad agreements and commitments to bolster market alternatives like the so-called popular economy and efficacious cooperatives, NGOs, and other communitarian arrangements[184] like small non-profits;
2. There ought to be enacted a *Law on Cooperatives*, by which consumers, producers and workers co-ops could be regarded as pivotal agents of social awareness on the path of development and

---

[180] See chapter 5.
[181] See article 26 in the Universal Declaration of Human Rights in section 7.2. c), this chapter. Principles 30 and 31 are more demanding than article 26.
[182] See section 7.1 and 7.2, this chapter.
[183] See section 7.1 and 7.2, this chapter.
[184] See section 7.1 and 7.2, this chapter.

growth; besides, co-ops are natural vehicles for federal devolution of entitlements on behalf of the native rights claimed by regional communities[185]; local consumers, producers and workers cooperatives have to be emboldened to own and manage utilities so as to fight global warming, pollution, waste and sludge[186]; cooperative misdoings will be regarded as federal crimes.

CONCLUSION

At the end of this book, it will be worth not only disclosing some concluding remarks but also to weigh up likely courses of action.

REMARKS

a) It goes without saying that the compact consisting of capitalism and the liberal market-system has neglected, more often than not, social concerns entailing opportunities for the have-nots; their supporters and zealots were only involved with their unrelenting pursuit of self-interest, greed, contempt of the law and institutions, fanatic adherence to economism[187]; complicit frames of denial; and the building of a sociopath's viewpoint of the world[188];

b) For this development to be brought into completion, leniency and connivance have been systematically nourished by neo liberals and their accomplishes:
- *leniency*, mainly when accountability, transparency and fiduciary duties became stumbling blocks along the neo liberal road;

---

[185] This relates to the Principle of Subsidiarity, a matter that was delved into the context of governance by Apreda (2007).
[186] Further details about this topic can be found in N. Klein (2015).
[187] Economism was put forward at the beginning of chapter 6.
[188] The sociopath character was reviewed in section 2, chapter 5.

- *connivance*, so as to enjoy freedom of punishment, and gain access to protection and blame avoidance.

An Agnostic Summing-Up of Foreseeable Courses of Action

It is at this juncture when we should wonder: which are the most likely pathways to overcome this appalling state of affairs? In search of an answer, let us consider three plausible candidates to stand for post capitalism: to wit, a new rendering of capitalism, state capitalism, or social democracy.

- *Capitalism can heal and fix their worst features; it did it in the past, it can try it again in the present.*

If this assumption held true, there would follow two broadly self-defeating options, namely:

- Let us take for granted that organized crime, corruption, and ecocide might be curbed to bearable levels; even that the more shameful social inequalities were lessened. Supporters of this scenery point to the powerful resources' capitalism could employ to redress its most blatant wrongs. But, with the wisdom of hindsight, critics reply that in due time a reversal would encourage once more the spreading of deviant behavior and criminal organizations on the same grounds as we dealt with in chapters 4 and 5.
- Alternatively, a long-ranged program of social reform, rebuilding institutions, and the sharpening up of the rule of law might be enacted and enforced. For this to be successful, and not replicate its own failing track record portrayed by the former scenery, capitalism ought to ensure sweeping changes in social issues. Sooner or later, such patchy endeavor would merge with social democracy, social

markets and a powerful welfare state[189], hence crossing the threshold that leads to post capitalism.

Be that as it may, technological and entrepreneurial activities through networking and globalization are making of capitalism a foreign remnant of the past.

- *Post capitalism will consist in authoritarian variants of state capitalism.*

If we look around, China, Russia and the host of middle-sized neighbors revolving around them, as well as several Arab and African countries, all of them are successfully practicing varieties of state capitalism with authoritarian governments. Belittling such block of countries would be ill advised, whereas expecting them to take the road this book advocates would be farfetched, to say the least[190]. Any imaginable coalition of state-capitalist countries might likely become adversarial, resilient, self-conscious, with a time-honored social capital rooted in their ancient history. Eventually, it may contest the Western leadership, and make a bid for power so as to rule the world or, at least, its own influential geopolitical area, which it does not seem a negligible course of action at the end of the day.

In spite of the fact that staunch supporters of authoritarian governments heap up praise after praise over their attainments and successes, we can't help thinking that they cling to self-denial mechanisms that patently resort to the Elephant in the Room metaphor and harbor many strands easily met in the sociopath's frame of mind, as we dealt with in chapter 5. They hold elections, yes, but entirely rigged, with the opposition parties pursued, ridiculed, debased or banned. We can agree that some of them grow economically and become influential, but utterly trumping human rights and

---

[189] Such would be the process envisioned by Joseph Schumpeter, as we noticed in section 2, this chapter.

[190] In my opinion, the following three basic books shed light on a kind of governance and politics that are in sheer contrast with the Western ones and, of course, deeply differing from what we have already predicated in the context of truly representative democracies. The chosen works are: a) *When China Rules the World*, by Martin Jacques (2012); b) *The Geography of Thought*, by Richard Nisbett (2003); c) *The Party*, by Richard McGregor (2012).

withering political activities (if in doubt, look China, Russia, Venezuela, Cuba and Middle Eastern oil-producing countries). We can't deny that several among them display powerful military-industrial complexes, but the social costs of such endeavors are outrageous when we witness their lack of social mobility, higher education access, gender rights empowerment, and affordable consumer conveniences, to say the least. The camp followers of authoritarian regimes will probably be hard-pressed to explain the sheer contempt of accountability, transparency and fiduciary duties found in their governances. There is no denying that in these political systems organized crime, corruption and ecocide are compounded to the extent that their counterparts in representative democracies certainly look pale in comparison.

- *Social democracy, social markets, and the welfare state will stand for post capitalism in representative democracies.*

It's time for us to steer clear of the crisp logic underlying the deterministic mind inherited from the nineteenth and twentieth centuries, based on blunt contrasts between black and white, bad and good, true and false, friend and foe. In our day and age, it seems healthier to keep an agnostic mind when we handle governance and politics, and to embrace a wholesome commitment with cooperative and decent human beings. Such is the proposal this book has set forth and enlarged at length, for the sake of social democracy, social markets, and the welfare state.

REFERENCES

Apreda, R. (2014) Accountability and Transparency as Learning Processes in Private, Public and Global Governance. *Working Paper Series, number 535, Ucema* (downloadable from www.cema.edu.ar and www.ssrn.org).

Apreda, R. (2013) Cooperatives: The Governance of Patronage Dividends (A Corporate Finance Approach). *Working Paper Series number 508, Ucema* (downloadable from www.ucema.edu.ar/publications).

Apreda, R. (2012) *Governance Risks in Organizations (A Clinical Approach with Tools for Decision-Making)*. Nova Science Publishers, Inc., New York.

Apreda, R. (2009) Governance Principles and Good Practices in Argentina: An Almost Disappointing Case in Point. In *"Codes of Good Practices Around the World"*, edited by Felix Lopez Iturriaga, Nova Science Publishers, Inc, New York, chapter 2, pp. 35-54.

Apreda, R. (2007a) Compliance risk and the compliance function could enhance Corporate Governance not only in banks but in other kind of organizations as well. *Corporate Ownership and Control*, volume 4, number 2, pp. 146-152.

Apreda, R. (2007b) *Public Governance: A Blueprint for Political Action and Better Government*. Nova Science Publishers, Inc., New York.

Apreda, R. (2006) The Semantics of Governance. *Corporate Ownership and Control*, volume 3, number 2, pp. 45-53.

Apreda, R. (2005) Corporate Rent-Seeking and the Managerial Soft-Budget Constraint. *Corporate Ownership and Control*, volume 2, number 2, pp. 20-27.

Apreda, R. (2001) Corporate Governance in Argentina: 1991-2000 (The Consequences of Economic Freedom). *Corporate Governance: An International Review*, volume 9, number 4, pp. 298-310.

Arvedlun, E. (2009) *Madoff: The Man Who Stole $35billion*. New York: Penguin Books.

Bank for International Settlements (BIS, Basel, 2009) *Report of Special Purpose Entities*. Basel Committee on Banking Supervision (downloadable from www.bis.org).

Bank for International Settlements (BIS, Basel, 2005) *Compliance and the Compliance Function in Banks* (downloadable from www.bis.org).

Bank for International Settlements (BIS, Basel, 2003) *The Compliance Function in Banks* (downloadable from www.bis.org).

Bank for International Settlements (BIS, Basel, 2002) *Internal Audit in Banks and the Supervisor's Relationship with Auditors: A Survey* (downloadable from www.bis.org).

Bank for International Settlements (BIS, Basel, 1998) *Enhancing Bank Transparency* (downloadable from www.bis.org).

Barber, B. (1984, 2003) *Strong Democracy: Participatory Politics for a New Age*. University of California Press, Berkeley and London.

Baumol, W. (1990). Entrepreneurship: Productive, Unproductive and Destructive. *The Journal of Political Economy,* volume 98, number 5, pp. 893-921.

Bentley, A. (1908) *The Process of Government (A Study of Social Pressures)*. Transaction Publishers, New Brunswick, 1995 edition, with an introduction by T. Lavine.

Black's Law Dictionary (1999), Brian Garner (Editor). West Group, St. Paul, Minnesota.

Bobbio, N. (1987) *The Future of Democracy*. Edited by Richard Bellamy. Polity Press, Cambridge, UK.

Braudel, F. (1981, 1992) *Civilization and Capitalism 15th – 18th Century* (volumes 1, 2, and 3). University of California Press, Berkeley.

Cabot, D. (2018) *Los Cuadernos.* Penguin Random House (Argentina, Sudamericana), Argentina. (At the time this book was published, there was no English edition available yet).

Carey, M.; Browse, S.; and Udell, G. (1993) The Economics of Private Placements: A New Look. *Financial Markets, Institutions and Instruments,* volume 2, number 3, Blackwell, Cambridge, Massachusetts.

Carson, R. (1962) *Silent Spring.* Mariner Books, Boston.

Coase, R. (1937, 1988) *The Firm, the Market, and the Law.* The University of Chicago Press. Chicago.

Coffee, J. (2002). Understanding Enron: It's About the Gatekeepers, Stupid. *Columbia Law and Economics Working Paper, number 207* (downloadable from www.ssrn.org).

Coleman, J. (1974) *Power and the Structure of Society.* New York: Norton.

Dahl, R. (1971) *Polyarchy.* Yale University Press. New Haven.

Dahl, R. (1963) *Modern Political Analysis* (5th edition, 1991). New Jersey: Prentice Hall.

Damgaard, M.R. (2018) *Media Leaks and Corruption in Brazil.* Taylor and Francis, New York.

De Bono, E. (2012) *Lateral thinking.* Penguin Books, London.

Diamond, J. (2011) *Collapse: How Societies Choose to Fail or Survive.* Penguin Books, London.

Diamond, J. (1997, 2017) *Guns, Germs and Steel: A short history of everybody for the last 13,000 years.* Vintage Books, London.

Frankopan, P. (2016) *The Silk Roads: A New History of the World.* Bloomsbury, London.

Ferguson, N. (2012) *The Great Degeneration: How Institutions Decay and Economies Die.* Penguin, London.

Finer, S. E. (1999) *The History of Government from the Earliest Times.*(volumes 1, 2, and 3). Oxford University Press, London.

Fitzgerald, R. (2007) *The Hundred-Year Lie: How to Protect Yourself from the Chemicals that are Destroying Your Health.* Plume, Penguin Group, New York.

Gabetta, D. (1996) *The Sicilian Maffia.* Harvard University Press, Boston.

Goleman, D. (1985, 2005) *Vital Lies, Simple Truths: the Psychology of Self-Deception.* Simon and Schuster Paperbacks, New York.

Gray, J. (1995, 2010) *Liberalism.* Second Edition, University of Minnesota Press, Minneapolis.

Haidt, J. (2013) *The Righteous Mind: Why good people are divided by politics and religion.* Vintage Books, New York.

Halpern, D. (2005, 2012) *Social Capital.* Polity Press, United Kingdom.

Hansmann, H. (2000) *The Ownership of Enterprise.* Harvard University Press, Cambridge, Massachusetts.

Hirschman, A. (1978) Exit, Voice and the State. *World Politics*, vol. 31, number 1, pp. 90-107.

Hirschman, A. (1977) *Exit, Voice and Loyalty.* Yale University Press. New Haven.

Hobsbawn, E. (1996) *The Age of Revolution: 1789-1848.* Vintage Books, New York.

Hobsbawn, E. (1996) *The Age of Capital: 1848-1875.* Vintage Books, New York.

Hobsbawn, E. (1989) *The Age of Empire: 1875-1914.* Vintage Books, New York.

Hobsbawn, E. (1996) *The Age of Extremes: 1914-1991.* Vintage Books, New York.

Hoffman, D. (2011) *The Oligarchs.* Public Affairs, New York.

Hood, C. (2011) *The Blame Game: Spin, Bureaucracy, and Self-Preservation in Government.* Princeton University Press, New Jersey.

Hume, D. (1777, 2007) *An Enquiry concerning Human Understanding.* Edited by Peter Millican, Oxford University Press, Oxford and New York, 2007.

Hume, D. (1751, 2004) *An Enquiry concerning the Principles of Morals.* Edited by Tom Beauchamp, Oxford Philosophical Texts, Oxford University Press, Oxford and New York, 2004.

Jacques, M. (2009,2012) *When China Rules the World: The End of the Western World and the Birth of a New Global Order*. Penguin, London.

Kahneman, D. (2011) *Thinking Fast and Slow*. Penguin Books, London and New York.

Kay, J. (2012) *Obliquity: Why Our Goals Are Best Achieved Indirectly*. Penguin Books, London.

Keen, S. (2001, 2011) *Debunking Economics: The Naked Emperor Dethroned?* Zed Books, London and New York.

Keynes, J. M. (1936, 1964) *The General Theory of Employment, Interest, and Money*. Harcourt, New York, 1964.

Klein, N. (2015) *This Changes Everything*. Penguin Books, London.

Klein, N. (2008) *The Shock Doctrine*. Penguin Books, London.

Klein, N. (2000, 2009) *No Logo*. Picador, 10th Anniversary Edition, New York.

Kornai, J.; Maskin, E.; Roland G. (2003). Understanding the Soft Budget Constraint. *Journal of Economic Literature*, volume 41, number 4, pp. 1095-1136 (downloadable from www.jstor.org).

Kornai, J. (1979). Resource-Constrained versus Demand-Constrained Systems. *Econometrica*, volume 47, number 4, pp. 801-820.

Krueger, A. (1974). The Political Economy of Rent-Seeking Society. *American Economic Review*, volume 64, number 3, pp. 291-303.

Kwak, J. (2017, 2018) *Economism: Bad Economics and the Rise of Inequality*. Vintage Books, New York.

Lakoff, G. (2009) *The Political Mind: A Cognitive Scientist's Guide to your Brain and its Politics*. Penguin Books, New York.

Lindblom, C. (2001) *The Market System: What It Is, how It Works, and What To Make of It*. Yale University Press, New Haven and London.

López Iturriaga, F. (editor) (2009) *Codes of Good Practices Around the World*, Nova Science Publishers, Inc, New York.

McGilchrist, I. (2010) *The Master and His Emissary: The Divided Brain and the Making of the Modern World*. Yale University Press, Yale and London.

McGregor, R. (2010, 2012) *The Party: The Secret World of China's Communist Rulers*. Harper Perennial, London.

Mair, P. (2013) *Ruling the Void: The Hollowing of Western Democracy.* Verso, London and New York.

Manin, B. (1997) *The Principles of Representative Government.* Cambridge University Press, London.

March, James (1962) The Business Firm as a Political Coalition, *The Journal of Politics*, volume 24, number 4, pp. 662-678 (downloadable from www.jstor.org).

Markovitz, D. (2019) *The Meritocracy Trap: How America's Foundational Myth Feeds Inequality, Dismantles the Middle Class, and Devours the Elite.* Penguin Books, New York.

Marx, K. (1992) *Capital: A Critique of Political Economy; volume 1 (1867), volume 2 (1885), volume 3 (1894).* In Penguin Classics, with an introduction by Ernest Mandel. Penguin Books, London.

Marx, K. (1858, 2011) *Grundriss: Foundations of the Critique of Political Economy.* Penguin Books, London.

Maskin, E. (1999). Recent Theoretical Work on the Soft Budget Constraint. *American Economic Review*, volume 89, pp. 421-425.

Mason, P. (2017) *Post Capitalism: A Guide to Our Future.* Farrar, Straus and Giroux. New York.

Meyer, R. (2007) *The Theory of Social Democracy.* Polity Press, London.

Mill, J. S. (2010) *On Liberty and other Essays.* Edited by Stephan Collini, Cambridge Texts in the History of Political Thought, Cambridge University Press, London.

Minsky, H. (1986) *Stabilizing an Unstable Economy.* Twentieth Century Fund Report Series, Yale University Press, New Haven, Connecticut. (2008 edition by McGraw Hill, New York)

Montesquieu, Charles Louis de Secondat. (1748, 1989) *The Spirit of the Laws.* Edited by A. Cohler, Basia Miller and Harold Stone, Cambridge Texts in the History of Political Thought, Cambridge University Press, London.

Moss, M. (2014) *Salt, Sugar, Fat: How the Food Giants Hooked Us.* Random House, New York.

Muller, J. W. (2016) *What is Populism.* University of Pennsylvania Press, Philadelphia.

Naim, M. (2005) *Illicit: How Smugglers, Traffickers, and Copycats are Hijacking the Global Economy.* Anchor Books, New York.
Naylor, R. T. (2004) *Wages of Crime: Black Markets, Illegal Finance, and the Underworld Economy.* Cornell University Press, Ithaca and London.
Nisbett, R. (2003, 2004) *The Geography of Thought: How Asians and Westerners Think Differently, and Why.* Free Press, New York.
Palan, R. (2003). *The Offshore World: Sovereign Markets, Virtual Places, and Nomad Millionaires.* Cornell University Press, Ithaca, New York.
Perkin, H. (2002) *The Origin of Modern English Society.* 2nd edition, Routledge, London.
Polanyi, K. (1944, 2001) *The Great Transformation: The Political and Economic Origins of Our Time.* Beacon Press, Boston.
Polanyi, M. (1966, 2009) *The Tacit Dimension.* The University of Chicago Press. Chicago and London.
Pollan, M. (2006, 2016) *The Omnivore's Dilemma: A Natural History of Four Meals.* Penguin Books, New York.
Ponting, C. (2007) *A New Green History of the World.* Penguin Books, London.
Ponting, C. (2001) *World History: A New Perspective.* Pimlico, Random House, London.
Pranger, R. (1965) The Clinical Approach to Organization Theory. *Midwest Journal of Political Science*, volume 9, number 3, pp. 215-234 (downloadable from www.jstor.org).
Przeworski, A.; Stokes, S. and Manin, B. (1999) *Democracy, Accountability and Representation.* Cambridge University Press, New York.
Reich, R. B. (2018) *The Common Good.* Vintage Books, New York.
Saul, J. R. (1995) *The Unconscious Civilization.* The Free Press. New York and London.
Schwartz, B. (2000) *The Costs of Living: How Market Freedom Erodes the Best Things in Life.* X-libris Corporation, New York.
Schumpeter, J. (1942, 2008) *Capitalism, Socialism and Democracy.* Harper Perennial, New York.
Shaxson, N. (2011) *Treasure Islands: Tax Havens and the Men Who Stole the World.* The Bodley Head, Random House, London.

Shin, H. (2009) Reflections on Northern Rock. *The Journal of Economic Perspectives*, volume 23, number 1, pp. 101-120 (downloadable from www.jstor.org).

Soto, H. de (2002) *The Other Path*. Basic Books, New York.

Sowell, T. (1980, 1996). *Knowledge and Decisions*. Basic Books, New York.

Stauber, J. and Rampton, S. (1995) *Toxic sludge is good for you: lies, damn lies, and the Public Relations Industry*. Center for Media and Democracy, Common Courage Press, Monroe, Maine.

Stout, M. (2005) *The Sociopath Next Door*. Harmony Books, New York.

Swedberg, R. (2003) *Principles of Economic Sociology*. Princeton University Press, Princeton and Oxford.

Tilly, C. (2005) *Trust and Rule*. Cambridge University Press.

Tullock, G. (1967) The Welfare Costs of Tariffs, Monopolies and Theft. *Western Economic Journal*, volume 5, pp. 224-232. Reprinted in D. Watson, ed., *Price Theory in Action: A Book of Readings*, Boston, Houghton Mifflin, 1969.

Varese, F (2005) *The Russian Maffia*. Oxford University Press, London.

Warren, M. (2004) What Does Corruption Mean in a Democracy? *American Journal of Political Science*, volume 48, number 2, pp. 328-343.

Watson, P. (2005) *Ideas: A History of Thought and Invention, from Fire to Freud*. Harper Perennial, New York.

Watson, P. (2001) *The Modern Mind*. HarperCollins, London.

Whincop, M. (2000). Another Side of Accountability: The Fiduciary Concept and Rent-Seeking in Government Corporations. *SSRN Working Paper, number 258668* (www.ssrn.or).

Williamson, O. (1996) *The Mechanisms of Governance*. Oxford University Press, New York.

Wollstonecraft, M. (1792, 2009) *The Vindication of the Rights of Men, and A Vindication of the Rights of Woman*. Edited by S. Tomaselli, Cambridge Texts in the History of Political Thought, Cambridge University Press, London.

Wu, T. (2018) *The Curse of Bigness: Antitrust in the New Gilded Age*. Columbia Global Reports, New York.

Zerubavel, E. (2006) *The Elephant in the Room: Silence and Denial in Everyday Life*. Oxford University Press, New York.

Zerubavel, E. (1997) *Social Mindscapes: An Invitation to Cognitive Sociology.* Harvard University Press, Cambridge, Massachusetts.

COPYRIGHT CREDITS

Grateful acknowledgment is made to the following publishers for permission to reprint previously published material:

Cambridge University Press
- Excerpts from *The Principles of Representative Government*, Bernard Manin (1997). Cambridge University Press, Cambridge and New York.
- Excerpt from *Trust and Rule*, Tilly, Charles (2005) Cambridge University Press, Cambridge and New York.

W.W. Norton
- Excerpt from *Power and the Structure of Democracy*, James Coleman (1974). W.W. Norton, New York.

ABOUT THE AUTHOR

Rodolfo Apreda, PhD
Independent Scholar

Professor Rodolfo Apreda holds a PhD in Administration (University of Buenos Aires), a Master in Government (Ucema, Buenos Aires) and bachelor diplomas in Economics and Mathematics. He was Visiting Fellow at New York University (Stern School of Business) and Visiting Scholar at the University of Delaware (Center for Corporate Governance Studies); besides, he taught over thirty years at high learning institutions in Argentina, among which we can name the National University of Buenos Aires, the Argentine Business University (UADE), and the National University of Comahue (Neuquen). After his retirement, he has become fulltime writer and political analyst. His field of interest comprises Governance and Politics, particularly representative and social democracies; cooperatives and state-owned firms; organized crime, corruption and ecocide.

This is his fourth book edited by Nova Science all of which he wrote in English, namely: *Differential Rates, Residual Information Sets and Transactional Algebras (New York, 2006); Public Governance: A Blueprint for Political Action and Better Government (New York, 2007); Governance Risks in Organizations: A Clinical Approach with Tools for Decision-Making (New York, 2012)*. The author also published nine books in Spanish.

In addition to his well-known books, several academic contributions by Professor Apreda appeared in international journals, most of which were previously presented at meetings held in the United States, Great Britain and Australia or were submitted to SSRN files; Nova Science also included five of his papers in separately edited books.

INDEX

A

abuse, 4, 25, 65, 95
accountability, vii, x, 6, 17, 21, 25, 27, 28, 29, 30, 32, 33, 35, 37, 39, 40, 42, 44, 46, 49, 50, 51, 52, 53, 54, 55, 56, 57, 58, 59, 90, 93, 95, 99, 100, 107, 108, 113, 122, 127, 131, 143, 144, 146, 149, 192, 213, 219, 220, 223, 226, 228, 229, 230, 231, 234, 235, 241,242
accounting, 95, 143, 205
acid, 158, 162
activism, 121, 159
actor, 9, 13, 16, 17, 18, 23, 30, 31, 38, 40, 41, 72, 125, 171
adversarial conflicts of interest, 61, 73, 74, 76, 79
agencies, 9, 22, 29, 33, 54, 56, 64, 69, 84, 86, 90, 102, 117, 119, 131, 141, 143, 151, 158, 159, 164, 184, 189, 190, 206
agency relationship, 2, 13, 16, 17, 18, 19, 20, 21, 23, 26, 72, 93, 97, 127
agenda building, 62, 72, 74, 75, 76, 102
assessment, 73, 80, 155, 172, 178, 195
assets, 67, 68, 91, 132, 136, 174, 187, 189, 200, 209
asymmetric information, 68, 69, 76
avoidance, 25, 29, 34, 37, 40, 41, 42, 43, 51, 58, 59, 64, 69, 95, 116, 132, 138, 146, 149, 158, 160, 163, 202, 232

B

bankers, 116, 151, 170, 174, 187, 189
banking, 25, 36, 44, 101, 112, 129
banks, x, 22, 35, 44, 67, 90, 93, 110, 111, 113, 114, 117, 203, 205, 228, 235
blame, 25, 29, 31, 34, 37, 40, 41, 42, 43, 51, 58, 59, 64, 69, 95, 104, 116, 132, 146, 149, 158, 160, 163, 202, 232
blueprint, 6, 90, 96, 108, 147, 218, 219
bondholders, 94
bonds, 84, 94, 107, 113, 114, 117
borrowers, 89, 114
bribes, 139, 147
building blocks, 28, 34, 71, 199, 224
businesses, 83, 84, 114, 119, 124, 150, 159, 191

C

campaigns, 23, 73, 111, 118, 120, 157, 164, 226, 227
candidates, 57, 91, 151, 227, 232
capital markets, 67, 114
capitalism, ix, xi, 29, 107, 121, 123, 124, 154, 156, 161, 165, 167, 168, 169, 170, 171, 172, 173, 174, 175, 176, 177, 178, 179, 180, 185, 186, 189, 190, 192, 195, 197, 198, 199, 203, 207, 208, 209, 210, 211, 213, 220, 221, 222, 231, 232, 233, 234
central bank, 37, 113, 114, 227, 228
checks and balances, 14, 15, 26, 172, 212
code of good practices, 40, 42, 83, 84
codes of conduct, 44
commerce, 123, 173, 203, 217
commercial bank, 89, 90, 91, 94, 95, 96, 97, 98, 99, 100, 101, 110, 227
competitors, 55, 113, 143, 150, 177, 179, 186
compliance, 15, 17, 27, 28, 30, 38, 44, 45, 46, 47, 48, 52, 56, 59, 89, 91, 96, 97, 100, 101, 106, 109, 115, 183, 211, 225, 226, 235
compliance function, 15, 28, 44, 45, 46, 47, 52, 59, 96, 101, 226, 235
conflict, x, 7, 12, 61, 62, 70, 71, 72, 73, 74, 77, 78, 79, 86, 88, 102, 149, 172, 219, 226
conflict of interest, 71, 72, 73, 74, 102, 149
Constitution, 64, 82, 171, 221, 222, 223
consumers, 40, 138, 163, 177, 181, 210, 230
cooperation, 13, 16, 23, 52, 76, 77, 181, 185, 186, 200, 209, 210, 213, 214, 215, 224
cooperative conflicts of interest, 73, 74
corporate governance, 87, 144
Corporate Social Responsibility, 43

corruption, 1, iii, vii, ix, x, xi, 15, 25, 29, 35, 36, 89, 90, 92, 95, 103, 104, 107, 116, 118, 123, 125, 126, 127, 131, 134, 139, 146, 165, 168, 177, 179, 184, 186, 189, 192, 194, 198, 202, 215, 220, 221, 222, 226, 228, 232, 234, 237, 242, 247
creditors, 36, 63, 84, 129, 130, 199, 206, 207
crime(s), 1, iii, vii, 59, 110, 134, 135, 138, 141, 142, 144, 150, 220, 226, 228, 229, 230, 231, 241
criminal behavior, 108
criminal gangs, 165, 220
criminals, 151
culture, 2, 12, 55, 81, 113, 129, 131, 169
customers, 35, 36, 40, 55, 63, 69, 89, 92, 97, 113, 143, 148, 149, 150, 205, 220

D

democracy, xi, 10, 11, 12, 141, 165, 167, 171, 186, 187, 195, 197, 199, 203, 206, 207, 212, 214, 215, 221, 223, 224, 232, 234
deposits, 93, 114, 162
destruction, 123, 152, 153, 156, 158
directors, 31, 58, 80, 85, 91, 93, 96, 98, 99, 101, 106, 110, 112, 113, 133, 161, 189, 204, 228
disaster, 107, 167, 190, 191, 193, 195
disclosure, 36, 49, 54, 99
discrimination, 142, 216
distribution, 143, 146, 149, 174, 182, 183, 189, 203
division of labor, 15, 69, 174
drugs, 143, 148, 192
dual governance, x, 61, 62, 87, 88, 91, 92, 93, 96, 101, 102

E

earnings, 29, 87, 97, 110, 152, 175, 203, 204, 206, 211, 221, 225
ecocidal organization, 159, 165
ecocide, 1, iii, vii, ix, x, xi, 15, 39, 108, 111, 123, 135, 137, 152, 157, 158, 159, 160, 165, 168, 177, 179, 184, 186, 189, 194, 198, 202, 206, 215, 220, 221, 222, 226, 228, 229, 232, 234, 247
education, 96, 142, 149, 161, 170, 172, 178, 205, 214, 216, 225, 226, 230
educational institutions, 119, 176
empowerment, 12, 118, 121, 234
endowments, 76, 122, 152
entrepreneurs, 109, 157, 161, 170, 174, 175, 183, 185, 187
equality, 124, 170, 215
equity, xi, 84, 91, 113, 188, 204
exploitation, 155, 202

F

faction, 77
factories, 174, 183
fairness, 2, 64, 96, 99, 114, 119, 131, 170, 181, 188, 189, 199, 210, 225
faith, 16, 17, 18, 19, 21, 58, 107, 145, 149, 170, 171, 179, 200
fiduciary duties, 1, 6, 13, 16, 17, 19, 20, 21, 23, 25, 26, 33, 58, 87, 99, 106, 108, 112, 117, 146, 149, 223, 230, 231, 234
financial, 19, 29, 35, 37, 42, 44, 45, 46, 47, 59, 63, 65, 67, 84, 89, 90, 91, 96, 100, 106, 108, 109, 110, 111, 113, 114, 115, 117, 118, 123, 126, 130, 132, 136, 145, 148, 174, 175, 177, 193, 203, 205, 208, 217, 220, 227, 228
financial crisis, 29, 65, 203
financial instability, 123, 193
financial institutions, 46, 84, 111, 113, 227, 228
foreign exchange, 89, 193
foreign investment, 228
forest fire, 161
formation, 70
foundations, 9, 19, 31, 36, 44, 80, 94, 116, 119, 122, 172, 181, 199, 223
freedom, xi, 30, 76, 113, 125, 142, 151, 170, 171, 172, 176, 177, 214, 215, 224, 232
freedom of choice, 125, 176, 177
funding, 91, 92, 94, 97, 141, 151, 226
funds, 35, 36, 67, 69, 84, 97, 111, 114, 115, 120, 127, 139, 197, 226, 227, 228

G

global village, 187, 192
goods and services, 21, 22, 68, 69, 174, 180, 181, 182, 184, 187
governance of organized crime, 39, 144
governments, x, 1, 2, 3, 10, 13, 31, 59, 61, 67, 70, 98, 103, 111, 115, 121, 123, 130, 136, 146, 152, 158, 168, 175, 176, 186, 191, 192, 194, 195, 208, 218, 221, 226, 230, 233
governor, 8, 90, 91
grants, 18, 151
greed, 145, 155, 164, 170, 175, 231

H

habitat(s), 32, 45, 62, 67, 68, 70, 76, 78, 80, 81, 153, 165, 169, 177, 182, 184, 188, 211, 221, 226
hard currency, 139
history, 4, 12, 21, 23, 64, 107, 140, 153, 156, 157, 170, 172, 175, 177, 195, 198, 233, 237
homeland security, 57, 192

human, xi, 7, 8, 10, 21, 22, 23, 24, 71, 74, 80, 86, 109, 132, 133, 136, 140, 142, 143, 144, 152, 153, 154, 155, 156, 158, 159, 160, 161, 164, 170, 172, 175, 177, 180, 184, 188, 189, 192, 200, 208, 209, 211, 212, 213, 214, 215, 216, 217, 218, 219, 220, 224, 226, 229, 230, 233, 234
human agency, 22, 153, 154, 156, 158, 161
human right(s), xi, 142, 144, 208, 211, 212, 213, 214, 215, 217, 218, 224, 226, 229, 230, 233

I

imprisonment, 192
income, 89, 110, 148, 154
independence, 11, 44, 46, 65, 94, 171, 202, 225
independence, 46, 48
individualism, 170, 212
individualistic values, 175
individuals, 31, 33, 35, 36, 66, 78, 124, 142, 209, 210, 213, 224
indoctrination, 177
industrial revolution, 161, 168
industrialization, 154, 156, 183
industries, 162, 164
industry, 40, 45, 183, 229
inequality, 65, 176, 189, 194, 208, 227
inflation, 123, 193
institutions, ix, 5, 6, 11, 41, 71, 99, 104, 113, 148, 168, 181, 186, 187, 202, 222, 228, 231, 232, 247
intelligence, 54, 56, 57, 141, 146, 179, 192
Internal Revenue Service, 9, 10, 25, 55, 63, 110, 226, 227, 228
international affairs, 79, 201
International Covenant on Civil and Political Rights, 217
international trade, 45, 89

investment bank, 35, 69, 80, 111, 117, 206, 220, 227
investment(s), 19, 29, 35, 42, 67, 69, 80, 84, 97, 110, 111, 113, 114, 117, 126, 197, 204, 206, 217, 220, 227
investors, 19, 36, 42, 89, 94, 114, 174, 210
issues, ix, 5, 10, 21, 26, 44, 46, 70, 72, 73, 75, 86, 88, 111, 117, 130, 149, 155, 161, 167, 169, 190, 209, 213, 232

J

journalism, 15, 25, 146, 147, 217
journalists, 15, 59, 80, 111, 138, 151, 160, 161, 168, 187, 218, 220
judiciary, 15, 66, 67, 90, 99, 132, 141, 151
jurisdiction, 214

L

lack of opportunities, 176, 198
learning, 4, 5, 6, 7, 26, 34, 50, 52, 53, 72, 128, 138, 148, 174, 190, 247
legislation, 106, 120, 149
liberalism, 115, 167, 168, 169, 170, 171, 172, 173, 182, 184, 185, 187, 188, 190, 192, 193, 194, 195, 197, 198, 199
liberty, 142, 215
limited liability, 9
loans, 35, 93, 94, 95, 114
lobbying, 159
local government, 22, 183
logistics, 29, 45, 136, 148, 149, 183, 189, 217

M

malfeasance, 24, 48, 51, 106, 113, 121, 130, 131, 134, 136, 159, 220, 228

Index

management, 3, 6, 15, 24, 25, 38, 44, 76, 78, 80, 89, 91, 93, 96, 100, 101, 105, 106, 112, 125, 143, 149, 152, 183, 207, 212, 225
manipulation, 139, 163, 175
manpower, 67
manufacturing, 174, 183
marginal costs, 182
market, 1, iii, vii, ix, xi, 39, 69, 79, 80, 87, 94, 106, 109, 114, 121, 123, 138, 144, 145, 149, 164, 165, 167, 168, 169, 171, 172, 177, 178, 179, 180, 181, 182, 184, 185, 186, 187, 188, 189, 191, 195, 198, 199, 203, 207, 208, 209, 210, 211, 212, 213, 220, 221,222, 226, 230, 231, 237, 239, 241
masterpieces, 156, 172
material resources, 8
media, 3, 31, 40, 63, 119, 141, 152, 224
metaphor, 80, 137, 138, 151, 163, 167, 171, 177, 188, 209, 233
military, xi, 20, 124, 141, 148, 161, 170, 191, 192, 193, 194, 198, 234
minorities, 16, 112, 122, 133, 142, 172, 211, 220, 227
mutuality, 16, 19, 30, 31, 32, 34, 52, 72, 102, 127, 200

N

network, 8, 21, 23, 109, 151, 181, 182, 190, 201, 210
networking, 149, 154, 180, 189, 233
non-price competition, 69

O

officials, 11, 33, 35, 99, 116, 118, 123, 128, 132, 138, 146, 151, 170, 220
offshore location, 22, 29, 34, 35, 110, 114, 143, 220, 221, 228
oil, 157, 162, 234
opaque governance, 29, 37, 55, 89, 107, 108, 115, 116, 132, 134, 144, 146, 220, 226
operations, 29, 42, 55, 89, 92, 141, 149, 181, 204, 220, 229
opposition parties, 16, 208, 212, 213, 233
organized crime, ix, x, xi, 15, 29, 35, 43, 51, 54, 69, 110, 113, 123, 135, 137, 138, 141, 142, 143, 150, 151, 152, 165, 168, 177, 179, 184, 186, 189, 194, 198, 202, 215, 220, 221, 222, 226, 228, 232, 234, 247
ownership, 9, 70, 76, 84, 89, 112, 152, 174, 212, 223, 224
ownership structure, 70, 76, 84, 112

P

participants, 21, 23, 25, 31, 53, 66, 72, 119, 131, 179, 182, 185, 209
perfect competition, 177, 185
perfectly competitive markets, 209
pharmaceutical, 144, 145, 149, 159, 183, 229, 230
political clientelism, 89, 90, 120
political conflict-system, 7, 61, 62, 79, 86, 88, 219, 226
political networks, x, 23, 31, 66, 119, 152
political opposition, 120
political parties, 9, 22, 31, 66, 67, 118, 121, 123, 132, 213, 224, 226
political party, 18, 65
political power, 133
political system, xi, 2, 5, 7, 11, 12, 64, 66, 114, 118, 150, 183, 199, 212, 213, 215, 217, 218, 222, 234
politics, vii, x, xi, 1, 2, 5, 6, 7, 9, 10, 12, 13, 14, 20, 23, 26, 31, 35, 41, 43, 61, 70, 78, 86, 87, 106, 125, 126, 127, 131, 135, 137, 150, 151, 160, 161, 165, 168, 172,

177, 182, 199, 202, 214, 218, 219, 220, 221, 222, 223, 224, 225, 226, 233, 234, 236, 238, 239, 240, 247
populism, 29, 65, 79, 103, 104, 118, 125, 126, 134, 194
portfolio, 19, 90, 91, 93, 98, 111, 189, 203
poverty, 65, 90, 155, 176, 182, 193, 194, 207, 210
predicate, 68, 74, 218, 220
primary cooperative, 204
principles, 5, 6, 11, 25, 47, 56, 81, 82, 83, 85, 86, 96, 144, 148, 170, 179, 203, 220, 221, 222
principles of governance, 81, 82, 220
private sector, 78, 96, 131, 230
privatization, 107, 193, 194
profit, 9, 44, 52, 70, 72, 84, 87, 89, 90, 129, 142, 143, 151, 154, 160, 170, 174, 188, 191, 202, 204, 206, 207, 225, 229, 230
property rights, 170, 171, 175, 223
protection, 36, 142, 151, 161, 209, 216, 232
public sector, 13, 112, 120, 129, 130
punishment, 57, 59, 104, 142, 145, 151, 200, 232

R

real estate, 19, 122, 152, 189
recognition, 31, 121, 200, 214, 215
regional economies, 89, 208, 225
regulations, 5, 29, 33, 34, 35, 38, 40, 44, 45, 46, 52, 55, 57, 64, 67, 84, 86, 94, 103, 104, 110, 111, 112, 113, 115, 116, 117, 118, 144, 148, 183, 226
regulatory agencies, 39, 70, 100
regulatory bodies, 31, 84, 116
regulatory framework, 68, 83, 89, 109, 111
rejection, 143, 144, 187, 200
reliability, 55, 108
remorse, 139, 140, 145

rent, 51, 90, 93, 94, 95, 103, 104, 108, 116, 118, 128, 129, 130, 131, 134
rent seeking, 103, 104, 128, 129, 130, 131, 134
reputation, 19, 41, 44, 49, 67, 68, 69, 118, 121, 200
resources, 5, 12, 19, 23, 24, 67, 71, 75, 76, 94, 97, 110, 118, 119, 120, 128, 132, 136, 143, 146, 150, 168, 182, 189, 199, 204, 210, 216, 225, 227, 229, 232
rights, iv, 2, 9, 19, 62, 64, 65, 70, 112, 118, 122, 128, 129, 142, 170, 172, 179, 202, 207, 213, 214, 215, 216, 223, 224, 225, 231, 234
risk(s), 24, 27, 28, 44, 45, 47, 56, 59, 90, 91, 94, 96, 97, 100, 101, 106, 115, 117, 139, 141, 183, 226, 235
root, 8, 74, 149, 152, 161, 188, 198
rule of law, xi, 16, 19, 32, 35, 115, 144, 146, 187, 223, 232
rules, 20, 34, 44, 45, 68, 73, 74, 75, 82, 118, 127, 148, 179, 181, 185, 200

S

sanctions, 44, 45, 47, 121, 191, 201
securities, 83, 84, 113, 114
security, 37, 114, 138, 141, 142, 170, 191, 192, 206, 215, 216, 220
shareholders, 55, 189, 207, 210
smuggling, 108, 143, 155, 160, 182, 183
social capital, ix, 2, 5, 12, 50, 52, 169, 172, 178, 197, 199, 200, 201, 202, 203, 220, 222, 223, 224, 233, 238
social democracy, 1, iii, vii, xi, 165, 195, 197, 203, 206, 207, 212, 214, 215, 218, 221, 223, 224, 232, 234, 240
social group, 3, 10, 16, 23, 25, 58, 84, 121, 122, 135, 142, 182, 201, 220, 227
social movements, 65, 182

Index

social network(s), 16, 21, 22, 23, 25, 178, 181, 201, 224
social peace, 182, 224
social responsibility, 211, 225
society, 9, 57, 89, 118, 119, 121, 128, 136, 138, 149, 170, 172, 176, 182, 187, 188, 199, 202, 208, 213, 214, 215, 216, 225, 229, 230
sociopath, 58, 137, 139, 141, 143, 144, 147, 150, 165, 231, 233
soft-budget constraint(s), 51, 90, 93, 94, 95, 103, 104, 108, 127, 128, 129, 130, 131, 134, 236
sovereignty, 36, 87
stakeholders, 16, 26, 29, 31, 34, 37, 38, 39, 45, 47, 51, 52, 53, 55, 57, 58, 59, 61, 62, 63, 67, 69, 70, 71, 75, 76, 79, 85, 99, 102, 111, 113, 118, 128, 129, 131, 202, 205, 211, 220, 225, 229
state-capture, 103, 104, 118, 121, 127
state-owned banks, 62, 81, 89, 92, 93, 96, 101, 102
state-owned enterprises, 9, 106
statute of governance, xi, 15, 40, 47, 56, 61, 62, 81, 82, 85, 86, 96, 102, 109, 207, 220, 221, 222
statutes, 97, 102, 226, 228
stock, 14, 107, 112, 123, 133, 140, 145, 151, 214, 221
stockholders, 161, 170, 207, 228
structure, 8, 22, 27, 28, 30, 31, 34, 57, 62, 69, 77, 79, 83, 87, 88, 89, 91, 101, 104, 108, 109, 112, 113, 143, 150, 151, 184, 185, 204, 205, 214, 225
survival, xi, 2, 29, 71, 104, 144, 149, 150, 152, 154, 179, 182, 198, 200

T

tax collection, 63, 90
tax evasion, 35, 36, 132, 143

taxes, 10, 56, 183, 189, 227, 228
terrorism, 36, 58, 108, 140, 141, 193, 194
terrorists, 140, 194
trade, 9, 16, 54, 55, 56, 65, 68, 75, 84, 94, 95, 96, 98, 118, 123, 124, 136, 139, 146, 151, 154, 173, 177, 181, 182, 183, 191, 204, 213, 216, 217, 224, 227
trade union, 9, 16, 94, 95, 96, 98, 118, 123, 146, 151, 177, 216, 224, 227
transactional environments, 45, 66, 78, 102
transactions, 23, 36, 62, 66, 68, 72, 89, 90, 92, 95, 97, 114, 115, 127, 180, 181, 182, 184, 187, 205, 228
transparency, vii, x, 6, 21, 24, 25, 27, 28, 29, 33, 34, 35, 37, 38, 39, 40, 44, 49, 50, 52, 53, 54, 55, 56, 57, 58, 59, 66, 90, 93, 95, 100, 107, 108, 113, 122, 127, 143, 144, 146, 149, 192, 219, 220, 223, 226, 228, 229, 230, 231, 234, 235, 236
treatment, x, 80, 86, 102, 116, 135, 137, 193, 219, 226, 230
trust fund, 89, 97
tunneling, 51, 94, 103, 104, 108, 110, 127, 128, 132, 133, 134, 143, 146, 182, 189

U

unions, 121, 123, 205, 213
Universal Declaration of Human Rights, 213, 214, 218, 223, 224, 225, 229, 230

V

varieties, 65, 79, 131, 159, 165, 182, 199, 233
vehicles, 4, 36, 65, 86, 103, 104, 114, 116, 128, 134, 162, 193, 231
venture capital, 84
vested interests, 175, 213, 227, 228
victims, 138, 145, 153
violence, 140, 208

W

war, 14, 80, 153, 193
warlords, 21, 135
waste, 131, 147, 150, 154, 155, 158, 161, 162, 231
wealth, ix, 122, 128, 136, 154, 161, 175, 176, 185, 189, 194, 197, 198, 210, 228
wealth distribution, ix, 176, 198
welfare, xi, 10, 165, 171, 176, 178, 182, 186, 188, 191, 193, 195, 197, 202, 203, 207, 208, 209, 210, 212, 215, 217, 221, 223, 224, 225, 233, 234
welfare state, 165, 171, 176, 178, 182, 186, 188, 191, 193, 197, 203, 207, 208, 209, 210, 212, 215, 217, 221, 223, 224, 225, 233, 234
workers, 52, 123, 124, 125, 149, 151, 155, 175, 176, 178, 203, 205, 207, 208, 225, 230
World Bank, 190, 195